CUMBERLAND AND WESTMORLAND ANTIQUARIAN AND
ARCHAEOLOGICAL SOCIETY

THE SOCIETY OF ANTIQUARIES OF NEWCASTLE UPON TYNE

HADRIAN'S WALL 1999-2009

A Summary of Excavation and Research

prepared for

The Thirteenth Pilgrimage of Hadrian's Wall, 8-14 August 2009

compiled by

N. Hodgson

Kendal, 2009

Cumberland and Westmorland
Antiquarian and Archaeological Society
and the
Society of Antiquaries of Newcastle upon Tyne

Hadrian's Wall 1999-2009: a summary of excavation and research
prepared for the Thirteenth Pilgrimage of Hadrian's Wall,
8-14 August 2009

British Library Cataloguing in-Publication Data
A CIP catalogue entry for this book is available from the British Library

ISBN 978-1-873124-48-2

Printed by
Titus Wilson & Son, Kendal
2009

CONTENTS

ORGANISING COMMITTEE FOR THE THIRTEENTH PILGRIMAGE OF HADRIAN'S WALL

Chairman: PROF. D.J.BREEZE, O.B.E., B.A., Ph.D., Hon.
D.Litt, F.R.S.E, F.S.A, F.S.A. (Scot.), Hon. M.I.f.A.

L. ALLASON-JONES, B.A., M.Litt, F.S.A., F.M.A., F.R.S.A., M.I.f.A.
P.S. AUSTEN, M.A., M.A, M.I.f.A.
I.D. CARUANA, M.A., F.S.A. (Scot.)
PROF. J.G. CROW, B.A., M.Litt, F.S.A.
W.B. GRIFFITHS, B.A.
R. HINGLEY, B.A., Ph.D., F.S.A.
N. HODGSON, M.A., Ph.D., F.S.A.
R. NEWMAN, B.A., F.S.A.
P.R. WILSON, B.A., Ph.D., F.S.A.

FOREWORD

An event with a history stretching over 150 years has, naturally, created its own traditions. One is that the direction of the Pilgrimage alternates each time; this year we start in the west and progress towards the east. However, new traditions can be created. In 1999, to mark the 150th anniversary of the first Pilgrimage, we laid a wreath at the memorial to John Collingwood Bruce in Newcastle Cathedral and this time we will repeat this action.

Certain walks have become traditional on the Pilgrimage. These include the sector from Housesteads west to Steel Rigg and from Cawfields to Carvoran. In 2009, we are not undertaking these walks but instead exploring quieter parts of Cumberland. One of the reasons for the change is to ensure that we do not contribute to the wear in the central sector. Another is to consider new research on the Wall.

In two specific areas, there have been significant contributions to knowledge. One is through the work of Humphrey Welfare in examining the surviving earthworks which have enabled him to draw out specific conclusions concerning the lack of causeways in front of milecastle north gates and the nature of the upcast mound to the north of the ditch. Elsewhere the geophysical surveys of TimeScape have revolutionised our knowledge of civil settlements outside forts, as well as providing significant evidence elsewhere relating to the location and nature of the various linear elements.

One of the most important new discoveries through excavation has been the pits on the berm, the space between the Wall and the ditch, by Tyne and Wear Museums. This has demonstrated that archaeological remains can survive well in urban contexts as well as providing Hadrian's Wall with an entirely new element. Furthermore, the apparent narrowing of the berm by T 11b allowed Paul Bidwell to make sense of the recording of the changing width of the berm in the sector west of Birdoswald in the 1930s. Recording and understanding the surviving remains is one thing, but interpreting them is another. Does the existence of the pits on the berm make it more or less likely that there was a wall-walk along the top of the Wall, as Lindsay Allason-Jones memorably asked?

The nature of the stone wall has been the subject of two books by Peter Hill. They challenge many of our preconceptions about the building of Hadrian's Wall, including the length of time it would have taken to construct. Acceptance of these points allows other theories to be developed about the building programme and its director.

All of this demonstrates that Hadrian's Wall studies are alive and well or, to put it another way, that Mortimer Wheeler was wrong when he said that all the problems of Hadrian's Wall were solved and all we had to do now was to dot the 'i's and cross the 't's. This companion for the 2009 Pilgrimage is a testimony to the vitality of Wall studies. At the time of the last Pilgrimage, it was decided to produce a different style of handbook and that proved so popular that we have repeated the formula this year. Here we have a statement of research on Hadrian's Wall over the last decade, ably brought together by one of the leading students of the Wall. It will have a life long beyond the Pilgrimage.

David Breeze
Chairman of the Organising Committee

PREFACE AND ACKNOWLEDGEMENTS

The Pilgrimage Book is traditionally not a guidebook to the Wall, but an account of new discovery and research, both on general themes and at individual sites. A scholarly, up-to-date and well-illustrated description of the sites is available in the form of David Breeze's fourteenth revised edition of the *Handbook to the Roman Wall* (2006) which readers are recommended to use in conjunction with the present work. The period covered here is the 10 years since the Pilgrimage of 1999, when Paul Bidwell compiled the most ambitious Pilgrimage publication to date in size and scope. The bibliography of research since 1999 is designed to form a supplement to the comprehensive bibliography of work 1989-99 provided in that volume.

At the request of the organising committee some passages are included (in italics) which describe the reasons for the 2009 Pilgrimage visiting some parts of the Wall that are off the usual beaten track. This is not just to avoid erosion in the well-trodden parts, but because neglected areas of the Wall often raise questions of real importance to which it is worthwhile drawing special attention. Some effort has been made to include plans and illustrations of sites to be visited by the Pilgrimage in 2009. However, even though the Pilgrimage in 2009 will travel from west to east, Chapter 4 of this book is organised in the traditional order of Wall sites from east to west, to make it easier for researchers to use in conjunction with the *Handbook to the Roman Wall* and other archaeological literature.

I am grateful to the organising committee for asking me to compile this volume and for their guidance, and particularly to David Breeze for his close interest and support throughout. I especially thank the contributors, who responded promptly to squeeze a vast amount of information into a short compass. I am grateful also to Brian Dobson and Paul Bidwell for reading and valuably commenting on the bulk of the text, and to David Breeze for similarly reading and most usefully commenting on Chapter 2. Typesetting and illustration work was carried out by Dave Whitworth and Roger Oram, and the text was expertly and rapidly proof read by Anne Killen.

I am extremely grateful to Alan Biggins and David Taylor of Timescape Surveys for kindly allowing me to make such extensive use of illustrations of their groundbreaking geophysical surveys, plans which at once illustrate the advance of archaeological technique and constitute one of the most striking achievements of the last 10 years (Figs 27, 29, 32, 33, 36, 41, 47, 50, 53, 54). The following are also gratefully acknowledged for supplying illustrations: the Portable Antiquities Scheme (3); Richard Annis, Archaeological Services University of Durham (16); John Zant, Oxford Archaeology North (17, 42-45); Tony Wilmott, English Heritage (18, 19, 34, 35, 48, 49); Brenda Heywood (28); Robin Birley, Vindolanda Trust (30, 31) and TWM Archaeology (4-15, 20-26).

The organising committee wishes to express its gratitude to the British Museum and Tullie House Museum, Carlisle for sponsoring a lecture by Dr Ernst Künzl on the Staffordshire Moorlands Pan and related vessels, which featured in a special exhibition at Tullie House to coincide with the Pilgrimage. The Organising committee is also most grateful to the Robert Kiln Charitable Trust for sponsoring two bursaries to allow students to attend the Pilgrimage.

N. Hodgson   *Arbeia*-South Shields, 2 June 2009

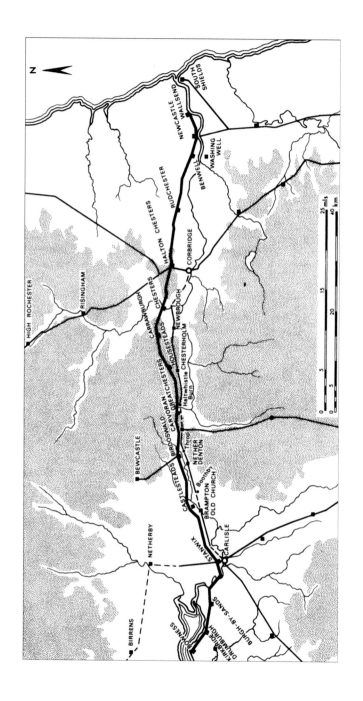

1. PREVIOUS PILGRIMAGES

N. Hodgson

The original Pilgrimage was led by John Collingwood Bruce in 1849. He had visited the Wall for the first time the previous year and had lectured enthusiastically during the winter on the wonders he had seen in the company of the artists Charles and Henry Richardson. The idea of the 1849 Pilgrimage was thus to show the reality on the ground, and to demonstrate that Bruce had not exaggerated the appeal of the Wall and its ruins. Bruce, now aged 81, led a second Pilgrimage in 1886, the first to be directly sponsored by the Newcastle and Cumberland and Westmorland Societies, which resolved henceforth to make it a decennial event. So the third Pilgrimage was in 1896, travelling this time from west to east, and the fourth in 1906 (east-west).

The fifth Pilgrimage was delayed by the First World War until 1920, visiting only the central part of the Wall from west to east, between Appletree and Chesters. The sixth pilgrimage of 1930 progressed east-west and was the first to use motor transport, and the first to have a Handbook, properly entitled *The Book of the Pilgrimage*, compiled by R.G. Collingwood. Preceding Collingwood's own modernisation of the *Handbook to the Roman Wall* (HB9, 1933) by three years, this was a detailed account of the remains on the ground to be visited by the Pilgrims which incidentally reported on the results of recent research.

The Second World War prevented a Pilgrimage in 1940, and the opportunity was taken in 1949 to have the seventh Pilgrimage on the centenary of the original (Fig. 1). This went east-west and included for the first time South Shields in the east and Maryport in the west. The accompanying book, compiled by Eric Birley, *The Centenary Pilgrimage of Hadrian's Wall*, developed the familiar format of a conspectus of research since the last pilgrimage followed by site-by-site accounts of recent work. The 1949 Pilgrimage was immediately followed by the very first International Congress of Roman Frontier Studies, organised by Birley at Newcastle upon Tyne. This began a tradition whereby the Limes Congress, as it is nicknamed, and which always meets on a frontier of the Roman empire, met in Britain in Pilgrimage years.

The eighth Pilgrimage of 1959 (west-east) had no handbook, because of a printers' strike, but Eric Birley compensated for this by producing the magnificent *Research on Hadrian's Wall* in 1961. This should be consulted for the history of the Pilgrimages up to 1959 (with Bidwell 1999a for additional detail on the early Pilgrimages). The 1959 Pilgrimage was followed by the fifth Limes Congress, held at Durham. The ninth Pilgrimage of 1969 went

Figure 1. The 1949 Pilgrimage at South Shields: L: I.A.Richmond, with the ranging pole; R: Rev. T. Romans, President of the Newcastle Society

east-west; the publication, *The Ninth Pilgrimage of Hadrian's Wall,* was compiled by Anthony Birley; the succeeding Limes Congress (the eighth) was at Cardiff. Brian Dobson compiled *The Tenth Pilgrimage of Hadrian's Wall* for the 1979 occasion, again east-west, and followed this time by Limes Congress XII at Stirling. The 1969 and 1979 publications were quite slim, but an increased amount of excavation on the Wall during the 1980s was reflected in the larger format adopted by Charles Daniels for *The Eleventh Pilgrimage of Hadrian's Wall* in 1989, when the Pilgrimage went from west to east. The subsequent Limes Congress XV was held at Canterbury.

The 1999 Pilgrimage, the twelfth, travelled from east to west. There was no Limes Congress in 1999. Paul Bidwell entitled the accompanying publication *Hadrian's Wall 1989-99,* emphasising its role as a summary of recent research in a work of reference intended for a wider audience than those joining the Pilgrimage. This was particularly necessary given the fact that no new edition of the *Handbook to the Roman Wall* had appeared since 1978. *Hadrian's Wall 1989-99* dropped the programme and instructions to pilgrims and became an entirely archaeological publication, though still recalling the history of past pilgrimages. This model has been followed by the present work.

In 2009 the thirteenth Pilgrimage will be followed by the XXI Limes Congress, once again in Newcastle, 60 years after the original. The Pilgrims of 2009 now have the benefit of David Breeze's 2006 revision of the *Handbook to the Roman Wall*, but given the occurrence since then of a major conference on the Wall, and the recent flaring up of certain long-running controversies, it has seemed valuable to continue the tradition of reviewing the progress of the subject since the last pilgrimage. The Pilgrimage, after all, should be an occasion where the many outstanding problems and controversies surrounding the Wall are discussed. As Collingwood wrote in the 1930 *Book of the Pilgrimage*: 'Even when the Wall became more widely known and more easy to visit, it was found that the pilgrimage offered an incomparable occasion for the discussion of new theories and new discoveries; and the practice has grown up of treating these excursions not simply as visits to a national monument, however important and interesting a monument, but as opportunities for expert archaeologists to discuss in public their latest thoughts about the complicated problems to which Hadrian's Wall has given rise'.

*

The last decade has brought with it the inevitable roll of losses of past pilgrims and other students of the Wall whom it is traditional to remember in this publication.

Professor J. C. Mann, who lectured at Durham in Romano-British history and archaeology from 1957 to 1981 and was involved in the organisation of the Pilgrimages of 1959, 1969 and 1979, died in 2002. His 1974 essay on *The Frontiers of the Principate* is one of the most elegant discussions of Hadrian's Wall and its analogues ever written, characteristically controversial.

Brian Hartley (1929-2005), who taught at Leeds, was an expert on samian pottery whose work established the basic chronological datum for the respective occupations of Hadrian's Wall and the Antonine Wall.

Professor Barri Jones (1936-1999) died just before the last pilgrimage. His archaeological interests extended far beyond the northern frontier, where he will be remembered for pioneering air-photographic work and his attempts to define the pre-Hadrianic frontier west of Carlisle.

Vivien Swan (1943-2009) was a disciple of John Gillam, a pottery specialist with extremely wide-ranging interests, instrumental in relaunching the Roman Northern Frontier Seminar in the late-1990s. Outspoken and vivacious, no archaeological conference seems complete without her.

John Dore (1951-2008), also a Gillam student, was an amiable pottery expert, excavator, and writer of important reports on many sites, including South Shields, Corbridge and Halton Chesters.

While not primarily engaged in research, the following should also be remembered:

Enid Hart (1926-2007) was the first woman to be President of the Society of Antiquaries of Newcastle (from 1985-7) and an enthusiastic Wall-pilgrim, one of the foremost organisers of the 1989 Pilgrimage.

Commander Brian Ashmore (1924-2004) deserves immense gratitude for rescuing the Senhouse Collection of Roman inscriptions at Maryport and establishing its new home in the Battery on Sea-Brows.

John Charlton (1909-2004) excavated on Hadrian's wall in the 1920s and 1930s before becoming an inspector of ancient monuments in the Ministry of Works. He was instrumental in saving part of the central sector of the Wall from destruction by quarrying in the 1940s.

Frank Graham (1913-2006) became one of the most effective advocates for the Wall, his local publishing firm issuing a stream of popular booklets, especially in the 1970s when public interest in the monument was at its unsurpassed height. He was a lifelong socialist who had been wounded in the Spanish Civil War. The Frank Graham booklets, many illustrated with the atmospheric and well-informed reconstruction paintings of Ronald Embleton (d. 1988), established the popular image of Hadrian's Wall and the Roman army for a generation.

2. A REVIEW OF RESEARCH ON HADRIAN'S WALL 1999-2009

N. Hodgson

Introduction

The last decade has seen some remarkable developments and discoveries on Hadrian's Wall, although there has been a noticeable downturn in the amount of large-scale excavation since the beginning of the new century. It might be that the period 1975-2000 will come to be seen as a golden age of excavation on the Wall. As throughout Britain, a pattern on the Wall is apparent where there are many more small interventions than in the past, but often carried out on a very limited scale and by a greater diversity of organisations than before. This is because of more rigorous curatorial policies and the developer funding that pays for most of the work. This has led to important breakthroughs in the last few years, as we shall see. The actual line of the Wall has been fixed at a number of places in urban Tyneside where it had been lost over the centuries. Most notably there is the addition of a whole new component to the anatomy of the Wall, a regular series of obstacles or defensive installations on the berm. Here is something that a research design in 1999 would have been unlikely to discover or predict. This discovery alone, the first addition to the repertoire of regular Wall-works in modern times, has vast implications for our understanding of the Wall and demonstrates the power and potential of developer-funded archaeology carried out under the aegis of Planning Policy Guideline 16 (the government guidance, instituted in 1990, that says such archaeology must happen and that it is the developer who pays).

A second outstanding discovery has been (not on the Wall, but in Staffordshire), the discovery of a vessel of the Rudge Cup-Amiens Patera type, which gives the names (again) of the forts at the western end of the Wall but, astonishingly, most probably tells us what the Wall was called by contemporaries: *Vallum Aelium*, 'the Wall of Hadrian'. Like the developer-funding that has revealed the berm-obstacles, this discovery is very much a product of our times, for the Staffordshire Moorlands Pan was found by metal detectorists, and it is thanks to them and the Portable Antiquities Scheme that it has come to the notice of students of the Wall.

This does not mean that there has been no role for research for its own sake, and a third development illustrates this: the superb and striking geophysical surveys of sites on the Wall, particularly the extra-mural settlements, carried out and published by Alan Biggins, David Taylor and their colleagues, which have advanced our knowledge of the form and extent of these settlements far beyond the minimal level at which it stood in 1999.

Over the last 10 years there have still been large-scale excavations at South Shields, Vindolanda and Carlisle, but excavation on the line of the Wall itself has been very small scale, either for the purposes of management, or development-mitigation, as described above. An evaluation excavation of the cemetery at the fort of Beckfoot, on the Cumberland Coast, represents an important step forward in the poorly understood area of cemetery archaeology on the Wall.

The last decade has seen a significant amount of pre-1999 or even older excavation work brought to full publication, and Chapter 4 tries to take account of this, as such publications add to the body of evidence with which to address the problems of the Wall just as decisively as new fieldwork. These include reports on the forts at Wallsend (1997-8 work only), Newcastle, Halton Chesters, Housesteads (imminent at time of writing) and Birdoswald (post 1997 work).

General publications

A fourth, revised, edition of Breeze and Dobson's *Hadrian's Wall* (first published in 1976) was issued in 2000. This remains the standard work on the Wall. But it is an interpretative history, not a site by site catalogue. A major event in Hadrian's Wall studies was the publication in 2006 of a new, fourteenth edition of the *Handbook to the Roman Wall*, fully rewritten by David Breeze. The *Handbook*, originally the *Wallet-Book*, of the Wall was first published by John Collingwood Bruce in 1863. It started life as a guide-book to the line of the Wall, the full length treatment being given in Bruce's own *The Roman Wall* (1851, 1853, 1867). But the Handbook, as edited in the ninth edition by R.G. Collingwood (1933) and later by I.A. Richmond (1947; 1957; 1966), while maintaining its compact format, became the standard specialist description of the Wall and its problems, giving a descriptive catalogue of sites, visible and invisible, reporting new discoveries and changes of interpretation, and containing, as it still does, the only bibliography of Wall sites. This should not be confused with the present work, the so-called Pilgrimage Handbook (never the official title), which restricts itself to summarising work in the 10 years since the preceding Pilgrimage. The last edition of the *Handbook to the Roman Wall* had been the thirteenth, by Charles Daniels, in 1978. So after 28 years a new *Handbook* was badly needed and eagerly anticipated. It has also meant a disproportionately large task for the editor, David Breeze, having to take a generation of new research into account. Breeze has stuck very much to the traditional format, but has not allowed a single page to go by without complete re-writing or some revision. New illustrations are provided throughout, including, particularly usefully, plans of Wall-sites to a common and comparable scale. The trusty bibliography is still there, in updated form, and this is likely to become the most thumbed set of pages to be found on the shelves of any Wall-archaeologist. The interpretation of the Wall that emerges from the pages of the new *Handbook* embodies many more uncertainties and contingent views than its predecessors, which tended sometimes to be characterised by bold statements delivered from on high. The particular views of the editor shine through, but they will already be well-known from his many other writings on the Wall.

In November 2006 a conference was organised by the Arbeia Society at South Shields to mark the publication of the fourteenth edition of the *Handbook*, with David Breeze inviting a series of speakers to give their own view of various of the topics tackled in the new edition. This, amazingly, was the first conference devoted solely to the subject of Hadrian's Wall since 1974. Fourteen papers have been published in the conference proceedings (Bidwell (ed.) 2008a). Several of these raise important problems and the whole is an inestimable resource for students of the Wall. Apart from the papers mentioned in their appropriate places in what follows, note also: David Breeze's introduction (2008b), on the study of the Wall 1848-2006; Brian Dobson's (2008) eye-witness account of how the Wall-period scheme was dismantled between 1966 and 1978; Andreas Thiel (2008) on the German equivalent to Hadrian's Wall; David Woolliscroft (2008) on signalling on Roman frontiers; and David Shotter (2008) on the conquest of the north-west. The final paper in the collection, by Paul Bidwell (2008b), goes back to basics, detailing arguments for Hadrian's Wall having a wall-walk and parapet and forcefully reasserting the practical capability of the Wall as a fighting platform. This introduces a level of controversy into Wall-studies that has been lacking in recent times, and we will return to the debate that this opens up towards the end of this review.

Originally inscribed a World Heritage Site in 1987, Hadrian's Wall is now (since 2005) part of the *Frontiers of the Roman Empire* multi-national World Heritage Site, which includes the Antonine Wall in Scotland and the Roman frontier in Germany. As Chris Young explained in the last Pilgrimage Handbook, World Heritage Site status has facilitated the funding by bodies such as the Heritage Lottery Fund, of important conservation projects, some involving excavation. This is one way in which the management of the Wall can promote research. It is stated in the management plan for the Hadrian's Wall part of the World Heritage site that there should be a *Research Framework* to promote understanding of the WHS and hence assist in its preservation and management. Hadrian's Wall now has that Research Framework, a document sponsored by English Heritage and written by members of and in consultation with the archaeological community engaged with the Wall. The document is intended to:

1. Assess what is known
2. Define priorities in research and set a research agenda
3. Set out a strategy to pursue the agenda

The printed version of the Research Framework was published just as this book was going to press: Symonds and Mason 2009. As with all such documents the *Hadrian's Wall Research Framework* has something of the air of having been written by a committee. Clearly not all who have contributed think along the same lines, but that is a reflection of real life and it is always difficult to produce such an all-encompassing document that will please everyone. Fears of the Framework as a bureaucratic interference in the freedom of research are alarmist: if the document arrives at proposals for a series of pieces of work that are practicable and which would at the same time advance our knowledge in problem areas, it will have served its purpose. Most fieldwork on the Wall over the last 20 years has been disproportionally weighted to the forts and although immensely valuable has largely been funded because of management and tourism agendas. While not seeking to diminish that activity, the Research Framework does try to suggest practical approaches, for which funding might just be obtainable, to some of the neglected elements – including the Wall itself. The document also contains a vast amount of information not easily consulted elsewhere and, in an age where increasing numbers of organisations and agencies are involved in fieldwork on the Wall, some inexperienced in the intricacies of the subject, it should be a really useful compendium of the most up-to-date knowledge and interpretation. The framework will be an important piece of Wall-literature for some time. It will be interesting to see how many of the actions proposed in the strategy section are translated into reality in the coming years.

A.R. Birley has revised his 1981 *Fasti of Roman Britain* as *The Roman Government of Britain* (Birley, A.R. 2005). This has detailed entries on all known governors and senior officials and officers throughout the history of the Wall, and in passing contains significant narratives of the history of the northern frontier written from the point of view of the historical and epigraphical evidence, an increasingly neglected perspective now that archaeologists are less likely to be as conversant with inscriptions and Latin and Greek sources than they were a generation ago. In this area a further notable event has been the publication of a third volume of Vindolanda writing tablet texts (Bowman and Thomas 2003).

Other general surveys of importance include Crow 2004a, which takes quite a different view from the version of the Wall familiar from Breeze and Dobson; Breeze 2002b, a concise account of the Wall in its wider setting; Bidwell 2007, an extensively revised edition of a general work on forts, which contains much material on Hadrian's Wall; Shotter 2004b (north-western perspective); Wilmott 2004. Note also: Bidwell 1999b, a review of Wall research 1989-97 which appeared too late to be cited in the last Pilgrimage book, as did Woodside and Crow 1999, an overview of archaeological work on the National Trust estate in the central sector.

Popular books, guides and maps
No attempt is made here to list or review the popular works and guidebooks that have proliferated in recent years, especially since the opening of the Hadrian's Wall National Trail. To turn straight to the quality, the English Heritage souvenir guide to the Wall (Breeze 2006b) is a clear and reliable guide, well kept up to date. This editor would also strongly recommend the relevant chapter of R.J.A. Wilson's *Guide to the Roman remains in Britain* (last revised 2002) as well-informed, critically intelligent and engaged with modern research. A non-specialist touring the Wall with this and David Breeze's new edition of the *Handbook to the Roman Wall* will be as well equipped as he or she could reasonably be expected to be, and will in fact be carrying handbooks that are at once superbly accessible to all and used by professional archaeologists.

Sadly the only good map of the whole Wall which clearly depicts the sites, visible or invisible, against a modern map background is still the long out-of-print older version of the Ordnance Survey Map of Hadrian's Wall (first and second editions, 1964 and 1972), though this is easy to find second-hand.

It seems that the writers of marvellous classics of popularising Wall-literature, such as David Harrison (*Along Hadrian's Wall*, 1956) and Hunter Davies (*A Walk along the Wall*, 1974) leave no heirs in the twenty-first century. A bookshop browser is likely now to pick up Alistair Moffat's *The Wall, Rome's Greatest Frontier* (2008), but this is riddled with errors and unevenly informed about the serious archaeological background. Rather more up to date in its sources is Geraint Osborn's *Hadrian's Wall and its people* (2006), but this is not a balanced introduction to the subject, rather a manifesto which urges a non-military perspective on the Wall.

Mapping and survey
On historic maps, note Shannon 2008, on depictions and descriptions before Camden; this is particularly important in showing that there were earlier descriptions of the Wall than those cited in Birley's *Research on Hadrian's Wall*. For the first (1577) printed account of the Wall, see Edwards and Shannon 2001. Note also, on Robert Cotton and the early development of Roman Wall studies: Hepple 1999. Whitworth (2000) has examined the fate of the Wall structures and their mark in the landscape in post-Roman centuries: it is a vital handbook for the archaeologist who wants to understand

why the archaeology on the ground survives as it does at a particular Wall-site.

Important aerial survey evidence is collected and discussed in Jones and Woolliscroft 2001. For English Heritage Hadrian's Wall Mapping project see p. 57, and for the English Heritage programme to record the fabric of the Wall, see p. 56.

For a first-hand account of the saving of much of the central sector from destruction by quarrying in the 1940s, see Charlton 2004.

Iron Age settlement in northern Britain and the impact of the Wall

The main outlines of a revised understanding of the late pre-Roman Iron Age were in place before the last Pilgrimage. These involved an appreciation of the extent to which the landscape was cleared and cultivated before the Roman period, particularly on the east side of the country, and a realisation of the sheer number of settlements of probable Iron Age date in the Wall area. Tim Gates, whose programmes of aerial reconnaissance did much to bring about this new perception, has written more recently on the subject (Gates 2004). Another aspect well-established before 1999 was the frequency with which pre-Roman agricultural regimes were found beneath Roman forts and indeed under the Wall itself. For the more general impact of the Roman conquest of the region and the construction of the Wall on native society, there was still the problem that the number of excavated and dated settlements had hardly advanced from the time of the pioneering work by George Jobey in the 1950s and 60s.

The last 10 years has at last yielded new information about native settlement in the Wall-zone, thanks largely to the opportunities afforded by large-scale developer-funded archaeology. The resources made available through developer-funding mean that it is now possible to date sites which are poor in artefacts, by means of programmes of radiocarbon dating. The excavation of Iron Age settlements at East and West Brunton, Newcastle Great Park (5km north of the Wall), at Delhi Opencast, Blagdon Hall (12km north of the Wall) and at Pegswood (near Morpeth, 22km north of the Wall) has revealed much of great interest. In all cases the rectilinear enclosure form was part of a more extensive enclosure complex. The enclosures were a development of the later pre-Roman Iron Age, in fact the latest phase on sites that had been occupied continuously for many centuries. Taken in conjunction with the air-photographic evidence this group of sites shows that later-Iron Age Northumberland was densely settled and had much greater affinities with contemporary landscapes further south in eastern England and the Midlands than previously thought. Environmental samples from these sites also show that spelt wheat was the predominant cereal crop, as it was further south: there was no shift at the Tyne to a more primitive agrarian regime based on emmer wheat (*contra* van der Veen 1992). None of these enclosure complexes continued in use for long into the Roman period, a point whose significance will be discussed later in this chapter. But the essential point is that on the eastern side of the country we now have extensively excavated sites that are known without doubt to have been in use when the Roman military moved into the area. Given the direct evidence from Wallsend and Denton that native agriculture there was active on the eve of the building of the Wall, it would be reasonable to suppose that the newly revealed settlements were still in occupation when the site of the Wall was chosen in the 120s.

For a recent general essay on rural settlement in the north, see Hingley 2004.

A pre-Hadrianic frontier? (Fig. 2)

A series of sites along the Stanegate, the Roman road between Corbridge and Carlisle that takes its name from its medieval successor, have been seen by various commentators as forming a linear frontier, earlier than the Wall, since the idea was proposed by Forster in 1913. These comprise forts, fortlets and towers, arranged by Eric Birley in 1961 into a schedule of alternating larger and smaller sites, some known, many predicted. It is easy to forget that in the 1950s Birley followed Richmond and Gillam in abandoning the Trajanic frontier interpretation of the Stanegate, concluding that the latest forts and the fortlets were Hadrianic, intended to function with the Wall before the fort decision. The Trajanic view was only reasserted by Hartley in 1966, with the additional suggestion that the pre-Hadrianic frontier will have extended from sea to sea, as far as South Shields in the east. The changes in thought on the Stanegate through the twentieth century are now reviewed in the Hadrian's Wall Research Framework.

With the forts, Carvoran and Old Church, Brampton are usually seen as additions of Trajanic or Hadrianic date to the earlier series of Corbridge, Vindolanda, Nether Denton and Carlisle. Although there is a late-Roman fort at Newbrough, the early site predicted there by the Birley spacing has never been found. Now Burgh by Sands I and Kirkbride are thrown into the equation. The best established Stanegate fortlets are Throp and Haltwhistle Burn (0.31-0.36ha), although only the latter has yielded a plan, recovered in 1907-8, and this is not well understood in detail. Most significant is the extensive use of stone construction — something not seen in the reconstructions of *c.* 105 in the forts. Alongside work at Old Church, Brampton this apparently represents an innovation on the isthmus. Castle Hill, Boothby is vindicated as

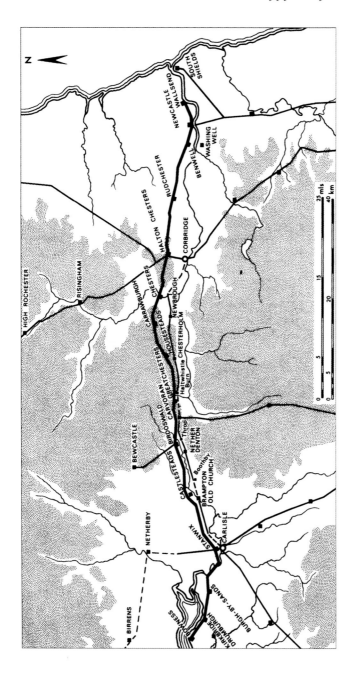

Figure 2. Map of Hadrian's Wall and Stanegate forts

a fortlet by a convincing air photograph by J.K. St Joseph recently published by Jones and Woolliscroft (2001, 58). Other fortlets predicted by the scheme of regular spacing, as at Grindon and Wall, have never been found. Finally, a number of towers are thought to have pre-dated the Wall – Pike Hill, Mains Rigg, Birdoswald, Turret 45A, and Barcombe, and were fitted by Birley into his schedule, although no regular series of towers is known.

Paul Bidwell showed in the last pilgrimage handbook (1999a, 111-13) how the closely dated structural sequences at Corbridge, Vindolanda and Carlisle coincide in having a phase of rebuilding c. 105, and this suggests that it was indeed at that time that more of Lowland Scotland was abandoned and the Tyne-Solway isthmus saw a more intensive military occupation. From c. 105, the Tyne-Solway was evidently the northernmost zone of military dispositions in Britain, but was it taking on the character of a preclusive frontier? The most sceptical view of a 'frontier system' on the Stanegate line had been voiced by Dobson in 1986: 'There is no firm evidence that a frontier system was created on the Tyne-Solway isthmus between the abandonment of the Lowlands and the building of Hadrian's Wall' (Dobson 1986, 2).

A return had been made to the question, this time from the perspective of exactly contemporary arrangements of military sites on the frontiers of Germania Superior and Raetia (Hodgson 2000). Two main points were made. Arrangements of large and small forts, and fortlets, occurred along lines where there was no road or route, and where the formation of a screen or cordon controlling access to the province can have been their only raison d'être. Secondly, these combinations of sites do not form regularly spaced 'systems' like the milecastles and turrets of Hadrian's Wall. On the German frontiers sites were irregularly sized and spaced to suit local topographic circumstances. Thus the failure of the regular system of alternating large and small sites to appear on the Stanegate (as Birley in 1961 had predicted it should) does not give grounds for disposing of a frontier-control function for the installations on the pre-Hadrianic Tyne-Solway line. Meanwhile, in the light of the Continental parallels, fortlets such as Haltwhistle Burn or Throp are as likely to have exercised a frontier control function as to have guarded points where the Stanegate road crossed rivers. Taken together with the observation that the metalled road may post-date the fortlet sites themselves (Poulter 1998), this means that we should re-open the question of whether the greater dispersal of forces along the isthmus was intended to prevent hostile movement into the province.

In addition Hill (2002b) has advanced the suggestion that that there is a greater concentration of Stanegate installations between Brampton and Haltwhistle Burn because of a particular threat of infiltration in that area, and has linked this to the occurrence of larger milecastles on Hadrian's Wall within the same sector.

There is, then, mileage left in the debate about whether the Stanegate was a frontier before Hadrian. However, any attempt to rehabilitate the Stanegate as a pre-Hadrianic frontier does rely on the acceptance of the view that sites like Haltwhistle Burn and Throp are Trajanic, and date to the period around 105 or shortly after. But this is not certain: the big outstanding question is whether the known fortlets and isolated watchtowers really originated in the Trajanic period or whether they formed part of a first scheme for the Wall. All debate on the date of the fortlets has been hamstrung by a lack of evidence from excavations carried out using modern techniques. Even with further excavation and the recovery of datable finds from the sites, such a fine distinction in date might be impossible to establish for certain. One site might now strengthen the case for attribution of the fortlets on the Isthmus to the period 105-22, and therefore to a 'Stanegate frontier': Castle Hill, Boothby, for which a Stanegate post between Nether Denton and Brampton seems the only likely context. But the fortlet is south of the Irthing and quite cut off from the Wall and milecastle system, and therefore unlikely to belong to any early scheme for the Wall.

There are no new discoveries to shed light on the postulated 'Western Stanegate', the pre-Hadrianic road and associated watchtowers, ditch, and fence or palisade lines between Carlisle and Kirkbride, described over 20 years ago by the late Barri Jones, but further reports have been published which allow some of the evidence to be examined in more detail than before (Jones and Woolliscroft 2001, 62-71; Woolliscroft and Jones 2004). Unfortunately none of the sites in question has produced unequivocal evidence of Roman military origin and in some cases there must be a suspicion that the recorded features are part of the pre-Roman Iron Age agricultural landscape. Nevertheless, the existence of Burgh by Sands I, 1km south of the later line of Hadrian's Wall, does show that a route between Carlisle and Kirkbride via this site is a reasonable expectation. More extensive fieldwork is required. It remains as utterly uncertain as it was 10 years ago whether there was ever an extension of the Stanegate east of Corbridge (the road running east out of the Roman town may have been associated with Hadrian's Wall).

Haterius Nepos

A Vindolanda tablet published in 2003 (*Tab. Vindol. III*, 611) resolves one problem with accepting that there may have been a pre-Hadrianic 'Stanegate frontier'. This is written to the prefect Flavius Genialis – therefore probably in the 90s of the first century – by Haterius Nepos, apparently based at Corbridge, where he perhaps commanded the *Ala Petriana*. This is apparently the same man as the T. Haterius Nepos thought to be honoured on a career inscription in Italy (ILS 1338) which also describes him as having served as *censitor Brittonum Anavion[ensium]*. Because Haterius Nepos was procurator of Greater Armenia within the period 114-117, it has been supposed that his earlier posting in Britain must have been not too long before this, *c.* 112. The Anavionenses were most likely the people of Annandale in south-west Scotland. This has been difficult to reconcile with an abandonment around *c.* 105 of territory north of the Tyne-Solway isthmus, and is even cited as an objection to the notion of a Stanegate frontier by Crow (2004a, 118). The importance of the Vindolanda text is that it suggests that Haterius' operations as *censitor* were conducted in the 90s, when Annandale was still within the Roman military orbit, the *censitor* then having a long career break before his Armenian appointment. Annandale could, therefore, have been abandoned by *c.* 105. A.R. Birley (2001) has argued that the Anavionenses were probably paying tax in the form of recruits, destined to form the *numeri Brittonum* on the German frontier. But the apparent date of this activity would perhaps be too early for it to have caused a revolt early in Hadrian's reign, as Birley suggested in the last Pilgrimage Handbook (Bidwell 1999a, 47).

The relationship between the Stanegate and Hadrian's Wall

The commonly stated idea that the Stanegate forts were all simply given up and their units transferred to the new Wall forts when the 'fort decision' occurred can no longer be accepted. There is no evidence to support the old assumption that Corbridge was evacuated in the Hadrianic period. At Carlisle there were changes of function in the Hadrianic fort, including a possible growth in industrial activity, but the *principia* still functioned and there is no doubt that the site was still occupied. Some Trajanic forts in the area were given up, but a number were retained in the Hadrianic period alongside the new Wall forts. This meant that significant pairings of sites occurred at Corbridge / Haltonchesters, Vindolanda / Housesteads and Carlisle / Stanwix, and this may be seen as a deliberate policy. Bidwell (1999a, 20) has written that: 'The fort decision ...can now be seen much more as an augmentation of the number of units in the Wall zone rather than a transfer of units from the Stanegate to new forts on the line of the Wall'. In fact, we can only identify for certain three full-size Stanegate forts that might have been abandoned to transfer units to the Wall, Kirkbride, Old Church and Nether Denton, and at the first and last of these there have been suggestions of occupation continuing into the Hadrianic period. The detached fort at Burgh by Sands I, probably part of the pre-Wall arrangement, was certainly occupied in the Hadrianic period, as recent study of its pottery has shown (p. 152).

War and frontier building under Hadrian

A war in Britain in 124-6?
Scholars have recognised since Ritterling in the 1920s that the *expeditio Britannica* mentioned in the career inscriptions of two participants, Maenius Agrippa and Pontius Sabinus, cannot have been the war in Britain attested on Hadrian's accession in 117-9 and must be placed later in the reign. Sabinus' career shows him holding centurionates in two legions between the Parthian war of 114-17 and achieving the primipilate and being sent on the *expeditio Britannica*. This is too long an interval for him to have been in Britain in 117-9. The traditional solution proposes a second war in *c.*128-30. Jarrett (1976) dismissed this as 'an unnecessary war', suggesting that Sabinus may well have reached the primipilate rapidly enough to have come to Britain with Hadrian in 122 and that as there was absolutely no other evidence for a war after 117-9, 122 must be the date of the *expeditio*.

This view has been challenged by Frere (2000) on the grounds that 'expeditio' always means active campaigning against the enemy, which Hadrian's visit to Britain in 122 was not, and because Maenius Agrippa is described as being sent by, not accompanying the emperor. Frere seeks to revive the idea of an *expeditio Britannica* in the period 128-30, with the formidable general Julius Severus arriving in c.130 to complete the task. Breeze (2003a) has argued for an intermediate possibility: that warfare broke out (possibly in 123) and an *expeditio Britannica* was raised and conducted in the period 124-6, during the construction of Hadrian's Wall, with the building of the forts of the recently implemented 'fort decision' being interrupted by this warfare. Breeze cites Alexandrian coin issues identified by John Casey as referring to victory in Britain (no warfare being known anywhere else at that time) in 124/5 and 125/6, and various structural indications of interruption in the building of Hadrian's Wall. This revives a forgotten argument of C.E. Stevens (1966), who placed the *expeditio Britannica* in 125 and used it to explain disruption in the building of the Wall and the Narrow Wall decision. Breeze's paper actually changes the proposed date for the 'fort decision', pushing it back to 123 from the date of 124 suggested in Breeze and Dobson 2000 and all preceding editions. Presumably this is done because an *expeditio* starting later than 124 would be too late for the Nike coin issues to be relevant. An alternative possibility, not considered by Breeze, is that warfare beginning in 123 *led to* the fort decision and an *expeditio* in 124.

Wilmott (2006a) has responded to Breeze with the observation that a perceived dislocation in the building of the stone fort at Birdoswald could not possibly have occurred as early as 123 given the long pre-stone fort Hadrianic sequence at that site. It seems possible that the structural dislocation, observed by Peter Hill at various places and cited by Breeze in support of warfare starting *c*. 123, may have other causes – and not all necessarily the same cause. Nevertheless, a second Hadrianic war in Britain (following that of 117-9), starting soon after the inception of the Wall, and possibly contributing to changes in its plan, is now on the agenda in a way that it was not ten years ago.

On the question of why a withdrawal had to be made to the Tyne-Solway Isthmus, and why the Wall was sited exactly where it was, see Hodgson 2005c (arguing that military difficulty and overstretch rather than inertia played a part) and Breeze 2005a (suggesting that the northern boundary of the Brigantes was the deciding factor in the site of the Wall).

Building and the order of the works (Fig. 2)
The fourth edition of Breeze and Dobson's *Hadrian's Wall* (2000) still divides the wall into 5-mile legionary building lengths, but the legions in question are now no longer named. Instead they are referred to as legions A, B and C, a sign of ebbing confidence in the evidence used in the past to attribute building styles to particular legions. There has been no new overall study of the building of the Wall on the scale of the studies of C.E. Stevens (1966) and Breeze and Dobson (1976 and successive editions), but Bennett (2002) has published a summary of his PhD thesis in which he challenges the notion of the 5-mile legionary lengths and suggests much longer building-allotments and a revised chronology (which includes a start before 122, under Pompeius Falco). Hill (2004; 2006) has examined aspects of the building programme, techniques and logistics from the perspective of practical experience in masonry building. One of Hill's recurrent and interesting themes is the basically poor standard and artless solidity of much of the stonemasonry on the Wall.

Hill's work contains a number of suggestions that have a bearing on the order and chronology of the building work. He argues, for example, that none of the original Broad Wall or Broad Wall structures were completed, suggesting therefore that the change to Narrow Wall, and the fort decision, could have occurred after a much shorter time than hitherto envisaged, perhaps while Hadrian was still in the province in 122. It is difficult to reconcile this proposition with the absence of reliably recorded Narrow Wall in the 18 miles west of Newcastle, where there is every indication that excavated lengths of curtain at Denton and Heddon were built to full height at the 10 foot gauge.

The view that the Broad Wall west of Newcastle was nowhere completed relates to two other ideas that have been advanced in recent years: that the Wall was originally planned to terminate at Wallsend, not Newcastle (Hill

2001); and that the building of the Wall started at Portgate (near MC 22) and ran east to Wallsend (Breeze and Hill 2001). If accepted these would be radical deviations indeed from the long-understood sequence of Wall-building, in which building of the Broad Wall commences at Newcastle and progresses westward (with a later extension east to Wallsend). Hill based his belief on the spacing of milecastles between Wallsend and Milecastle 9, but given how few of the sites are actually known this is rather to work from the unknown, and it is also possible that the spacing he deduces may have been used even if the Wall east of Newcastle was an extension. Hill's other basic argument was that the Broad Wall has not been found in central Newcastle, and he predicts that Narrow Wall should be found east of Milecastle 7, as Broad Wall, progressing from the west, was not used, or intermittently used, after this point. This has been decisively rebutted by Bidwell (2003) who reminds us that the difference between Broad and Narrow is one of constructional technique as well as width, and of the fundamental observations on which the theory of a Newcastle-Wallsend extension was originally based. Critical is a supposed sighting of Broad Wall at 'Turret ob'. Here subsidence fissures had visibly widened the foundation which, crucially, was of clay and cobble construction, characteristic of Narrow Wall but not Broad Wall. Bidwell stressed the simple fact that west of the assumed original terminus at Newcastle only Broad foundation, and to the east only Narrow foundation, have been seen. The prediction is also refuted by a more recent discovery: a fragment of Broad Wall found in central Newcastle in 2004, just 130m west of the Castle Keep (p. 90).

The argument that building started at Portgate on Dere Street is based on the belief that construction was divided into five-mile legionary lengths, and that complete examples of these run from Portgate (Wall Miles 7-22), but not from Newcastle or Wallsend. Leaving aside the question of whether the five-mile lengths are proven (cf. Bennett 2002), the idea of linear progress towards Newcastle again sits uneasily with the evidence for Broad-gauge building in the Newcastle area with a sharp switch to Narrow gauge at the Lort Burn. It would be an immense coincidence for the decision to reduce the width of the Wall to have occurred at exactly the point in time when the broad foundation reached central Newcastle. If (as conventionally) the section east of Newcastle is seen as an extension, it would remove some of the difficulty of having building taking place from Portgate eastwards, but that the Broad Wall (foundation or superstructure) had a terminus relating to the bridging point at Newcastle, does suggest that it would be premature to abandon outright the long-held model of building beginning at Newcastle in favour of one which suggests that it advanced towards Newcastle from a point 18 miles west. Bennett (2002) offers a variation: that building commenced simultaneously at Newcastle and at the North Tyne, working inwards to a central point. This receives some support from the work by Symonds on the construction order of milecastles (see below). Building starting simultaneously from various points, including the North Tyne, Portgate and Newcastle seems entirely conceivable.

The Wall between Newcastle and the North Tyne was almost certainly surveyed from east to west, as a series of studies by John Poulter (based on observation of how changes of alignment are made on hilltops) reveals (Poulter 2005; 2008; 2009). As he concedes, this does not necessarily give us the direction of actual building, which could have been started at any point or number of points after the line had been surveyed.

A further contribution on the order of building is offered by Symonds (2005), who attempts to reconstruct the building order of the milecastles by isolating those with walls of Broad Wall gauge, which he sees as clustering at points of strategic importance, such as the rivers Irthing and North Tyne. He shows that there was a move towards use of an intermediate gauge in otherwise 'Broad Wall' milecastles, which would appear to pre-date the decision to build the Wall itself to a narrower gauge (compare the discussion by Bidwell 2003, 20-21). Symonds contends that the large size of Milecastles 47 and 48 is explained by their early construction, before the fort decision, but that does not explain why apparently completed Broad Wall milecastles elsewhere (e.g., 10, 11) were not as large. Could the larger size of milecastles 47 and 48 have something to do with local circumstances, as Peter Hill has suggested (2002b), commenting on the number of Stanegate installations in this area?

'The fort decision'
It is still generally accepted that the addition of full-size auxiliary forts to the line of the Wall had not been planned from the outset, but represented a change of plan. Symonds (2005), for example, explains the unusual size and layout of earliest milecastles to be built in terms of their completion before the fort decision. Poulter (2008; 2009) has proposed that the siting of the Wall was determined by a concern to maintain a view of rearward installations, thus concurring with Woolliscroft's earlier explanations for the exact siting of particular milecastles. Problems for such a view are raised by Crow (2004a, 126-9) who has restated his reservations about the reality of a 'fort decision', pointing to the lack of rearward units that could have supported the completed Broad Wall east of the North Tyne and asserting that forts must therefore have been intended there from the first. Austen, in a very stimulating paper (2008), tackles the problem of why only certain forts were built to project from the Wall, questioning the statement that 'the Wall-

forts, wherever local topography allowed, were positioned astride the Wall' (Breeze and Dobson 2000, 47): in the Turf Wall sector, with the exception of Birdoswald, it is possible that the familiar model of projecting forts does not apply at all.

After the dislocation caused by the fort decision and introduction of Narrow gauge, Hill's studies (2004; 2006) have detected a 'second dislocation' at forts and milecastles signalled by a drop in the quality of the work and the use of unfinished blocks. We have noted how Breeze has taken this as evidence for warfare interrupting the building programme. A counter argument would be that it is dangerous to fit a small number of isolated phenomena into one common event horizon: this was the way archaeological evidence was used to support the general 'Wall-periods', now abandoned.

Note also: Edwards 2003 on sources of lime for Wall-building, doubting that this had any influence on the decision to build the western sector in turf.

Vallum Aelium – the contemporary name of the Wall?

In 2003 metal-detectorists found a copper-alloy pan near Ilam in Staffordshire, now known as the Staffordshire Moorlands Pan (sometimes 'The Ilam pan') (Fig. 3). Only 89.5mm in diameter at the rim, this skillet or *trulla* once had a handle and is clearly part of a group of related vessels of which the Rudge Cup and the Amiens Skillet are the best known. Like those vessels, the new discovery has an inscription listing forts at the western end of Hadrian's Wall. Rather than a stylized representation of the Wall, however, the external decoration of coloured enamel is of an abstract form, apparently influenced by pre-Roman Iron Age traditions. A preliminary reading and discussion of the text has been published by R.S.O. Tomlin (*Britannia* 35 (2004), 344-5).

The text is as follows:

RIGOREVALIAELIDRACONIS MAIS COGGABATA VXELODVNVM CAMMOGIANNA

rigore val(l)i Aeli Draconis Mais Co(n)gabata Uxelodunum Cam(b)og(l)anna

There are two possible translations of the Latin: 'On the line of the Wall, [the product *or* property] of Aelius Draco...' or, 'On the line of the Aelian Wall, [the product *or* property] of Draco...'. Tomlin concludes that 'The absence of a *praenomen* [to go with 'Aelius Draco']... 'is far from decisive, but it lends support to the idea of taking AELI with VAL(L)I. It would then follow that Hadrian's Wall was literally so-called: *vallum Aelium* (not *vallum Aeli*)'. There is a real possibility, then, that this object reveals the contemporary

Figure 3. The Staffordshire Moorlands Pan (courtesy of the Portable Antiquities Scheme)

name of Hadrian's Wall. There are good parallels: most obviously *pons Aelius*, both in Newcastle and Rome, and Jerusalem, refounded by Hadrian as *Aelia Capitolina*.

The Draco of the inscription must have been the manufacturer, or much more likely a retired soldier from the Wall for whom the vessel was made.

There is much of interest in the series of fort-names, which compares with the other vessels of this type, and two written sources, as follows:

Staffordshire Pan	MAIS	COGGABATA		VXELODUNUM	CAMBOGIANNA		
Rudge Cup	MAIS		ABALLAVA	VXELODUM	CAMBOGLANS	BANNA	
Amiens Skillet	MAIS		ABALLAVA	VXELODUNUM	CAMBOGLAS	BANNA	ESICA
Ravenna	MAIS		AVALANA	VXELLVDAMO	GABAGLANDA	BANNA	ESICA
Notitia Dignitatum	?	CONGAVATA	ABALLABA	PETRIANIS	AMBOGLANNA		

Previously the Notitia Dignitatum was the only source for the name *Congavata*, presumably Drumburgh. Because of its absence from other sources it has sometimes been suggested that the fort was a later addition to the Wall, but here we find it in a second-century, possibly Hadrianic context. That raises questions about what sort of fort was at Drumburgh under Hadrian, and why it does not appear on the other vessels. Possibly the site was abandoned for a time in the later-second century. Conversely, Burgh by Sands, *Aballava* on the other vessels and documents, is missing from the Staffordshire Moorlands Pan. This could mean that the Rudge Cup and Amiens Skillet date to after *c*. 160, possibly when the Wall-fort at Burgh was added (see p. 152), while the Staffordshire Moorlands Pan depicts the Hadrianic situation. That would tally with the move away from its abstract pre-Roman Iron Age motifs that we see on the later vessels, which depict the Wall itself. Tomlin indeed argues that the very use of the term *vallum Aelium* indicates that the Staffordshire Pan is likely to be of Hadrian's reign, for later sources do not use this appellation, speaking simply of 'the Wall' – *vallum*, or *murus*.

See also: Künzl 1995.

The Anatomy of the Wall

Forts
It was reported to the last Pilgrimage that the primary, Hadrianic barracks in the fort at Wallsend were of timber, and that this was possibly true of all the

stone Wall-forts. Since then it has been established that the primary phase of barracks in the known stone fort at South Shields, built around 160, was also of timber, only being replaced in stone at some point in the second half of the second century. At South Shields the four barracks in the *retentura* of the second century fort were found on excavation in 1999-2001 to have been cavalry barracks of the same sort as found at Wallsend and described to the last Pilgrimage. At both these forts the primary plan consists of combined stable-barracks for four *turmae* of cavalry in one half of the fort, and barracks for six centuries of infantry in the other. This shows that these forts were designed for a single and complete unit, a *cohors quingenaria equitata*. This could have been true of almost all the other forts on the Wall, both under Hadrian and following the reoccupation of the 160s. This presents a contrast with the Antonine Wall, where part-units must have garrisoned some of the very small forts there, and also presents a clear exception to the often made statement that we should not expect forts to have accommodated single complete units.

On the dimensions, construction methods and possible reconstructions of the buildings of the Hadrianic Wall forts, there is a detailed study by Taylor (2000).

Milecastles

In 1999 and 2000 English Heritage conducted a programme of field evaluations on milecastle sites under potential threat from ploughing, in order to inform the future management strategies for these sites (Wilmott 2009b). As well as establishing the state of preservation and level of threat to these sites, the work added new information on all of those examined. This is reported site-by-site in the relevant places in Chapter 4.

In the last Pilgrimage Handbook Paul Bidwell (1999a, 34-5) laid down a gauntlet: where are the routes that must have crossed the Wall-ditch at milecastles, if the Wall was intended to control but not prevent movement? He pointed to this as a question that could be addressed through modest programmes of survey and excavation of observable remains on the ground. At the time the situation seemed to be that causeways across the Wall ditch in front of milecastle gateways were only known at Turf Wall milecastle 50 and possibly at Turf Wall milecastle 54.

In 2000 Humphrey Welfare rose to the challenge, examining the evidence on the ground for the remains of primary causeways over the Wall ditch in front of milecastles. The evidence on the ground from 31 milecastles is presented in detail. This is a permanently valuable corpus of field observations, one of those papers that will always be turned back to by researchers on the Wall. In most cases, however, there are elements of ambiguity and uncertainty in what the field archaeology means. Of the 31 sites examined there seem to be ten or less where there are indications of a causeway that would have belonged to the Roman period, as for example at Milecastle 25 where a visible causeway has apparently been blocked in an attempt to impede access to it – unlikely in a post-Roman context. The evidence for cut away or blocked original causeways is most persuasive at MCs 23, 25, 26, 29, 32, 33, 34 and 47. Welfare concluded from this that milecastles were originally provided with causeways across the ditch. Most were disabled or cut way within the Roman period: Welfare attributes this to a modification of the Hadrianic scheme for the Wall, 'probably in the later second century, to create a more rigid barrier in which milecastles and the gates through them played a much more minor role'. If there was widespread provision of original causeways, what does that mean? We are still left with basic uncertainly about whether such provision was for the convenience of the military or whether it indicates an intention to allow civilians to cross the Wall at milecastles. Excavation or geophysics might reveal the presence or absence of roads or tracks leading north that would surely have formed had there been a regular pattern of civilian passage at milecastles, and relatively small scale excavation could decisively prove or disprove some of the hypotheses advanced by Welfare on the basis of the visible remains.

Breeze (2002a; 2003b) has usefully collected the meagre epigraphic evidence that might shed light on the source of the soldiers who manned milecastles.

Turrets
There has been no new fieldwork on turrets since 1999 – but note below (p. 26) a suggestion about the relationship between turrets, the width of the berm and the berm-obstacles in the primary design of the Wall.

The Ditch
Two contributions have stressed that the Wall ditch rarely conformed to the well-known ideal section published by Parker Brewis in 1927. Wilmott (2006b) has shown that there is little evidence for the square sectioned 'ankle-breaker' slot in the base of the ditch, which is such a familiar feature of the text-book sections. Welfare (2004) has noted a number of variant types of ditch profile, used, pragmatically, in various circumstances. These include the use of a pronounced counterscarp bank when the ditch faces a downward slope, as just west of Milecastle 33; the continuation of a 'minimal ditch' and scarp and/or a counterscarp bank in isolation for when the ditch and glacis (levelled out counterscarp bank) are discontinued on arrival at the crags (e.g. approaching Milecastle 40 from the east); the 'minimal ditch',

i.e. where only the overburden is removed over dolerite on slopes in the central sector, leaving a terrace, sometimes accompanied by a slight outer counterscarp bank, in place of a ditch (e.g. Milecastle 40 again, and west of Caw gap, approaching T41a) ; and the use of river cliffs and elevated scarps rather than a dug ditch where the Wall fronts the river Eden and the Solway marshes.

Welfare's survey reveals that extraordinary care was taken by the engineers of the ditch to adapt it to circumstances so that the security of the Wall was not endangered at risky points where a steep downward slope might have neutralized the delaying power of the ditch unless its northern lip was enhanced, or where the cessation of the ditch on arrival at the crags might have provided an opportunity for ingress. The scarps used to make the transition from ditch butt-end to crags 'were, in a sense, small enhancements of the crags themselves', recalling Horsley's statement that 'the precipices... in some places seem to have been made steeper by art, in order to make them more inaccessible' (1732, 146). The most dramatic revision of our view of the ditch, however, is to do with its behaviour in relation to an entirely new element of the anatomy of the Wall, the obstacles on the berm.

Obstacles on the berm (Fig. 4)
The last pilgrimage handbook described the discovery of a defended *vicus* attached to the west side of Wallsend fort, south of the Wall. North of the Wall, on the berm, were three rows of large post holes, extending eastwards from the point where the annexe defences met the Wall. These were interpreted as emplacements for branches with sharpened ends (*cippi*), set in staggered rows to form an impenetrable entanglement. This was seen as a strengthening of the Wall 'where it formed the northern side of a defensive circuit attached to the east side of the fort. An irregular series of post-holes showed that at some stage the system had been extended westwards...'. These features were cast in a wholly new light by the unexpected discovery, in 2001, of a similar system of emplacements for obstacles on the berm at Shields Road, Byker (Wall Mile 2), and later the same year over a 1km length between Throckley and Heddon (Wall Miles 10-11).

It has been shown (Bidwell 2005a) that rather than being man-traps (*lilia*) these rectangular and vertical sided features were most probably emplacements for an impenetrable entanglement of forked branches, closer in appearance and function to what Caesar described as *cippi*. The frequent description of the emplacements in archaeological literature as 'pits' or *lilia* are therefore misleading, for although they survive archaeologically as pits they denote the presence of a substantial above-ground structure. Observations at Byker and at Walbottle indicate that a small mound, around 1.75m wide and 0.60m high, was raised on the south lip of the Wall-ditch. The probable purpose of this was to restrict access to the lowest parts of the upright obstacles (where there may have been gaps) and to place those approaching the Wall in what, if the height of the forked branches was increased from front to back, would have been an exposed position in full view of the wall-top.

The berm obstacles were also almost certainly a regular feature of the Antonine Wall in Scotland: observations of the distinctive arrangements of pits at five sites along the easternmost third of the Antonine Wall are collected by Bidwell (2005a, 56). This, with their occurrence at several different locations, including the continuous 1km stretch at Throckley, makes it very unlikely that they were localised peculiarities. In all probability they extended along the whole length of both Walls. That they were originally intended everywhere is shown by the width of the berm in both cases. At some 6m, this, unusually great by the standards of Roman military design, is governed by the width of the strip of emplacements and indicates that they were envisaged from the first. If this reasoning about the width of the berm is correct, they were either intended or built in the Hadrianic period. At Byker and Walbottle the emplacements had been reconstructed in a second phase; at Buddle Street, Wallsend, finds in the pits suggested that the obstacles were current in the third century.

Bidwell has gone further and collected what records there are of the width of the berm in the area to the west of the Irthing. These appear to indicate a pattern whereby the wide berm to accommodate obstacles was the norm, but a narrow berm is recorded in front of turrets. Working from this sample he has proposed the hypothesis that the ditch and obstacles converged with the Wall in front of turrets, allowing the turret complete command over the ditch and an unimpeded view along its length to either side of the turret. Obstacles converging with the Wall and a fragment of the in-turning ditch have actually been seen at Turret 11b. The in-turning ditch will not always be apparent where the ditch survives as an earthwork because in later times, probably when many of the turrets were demolished, the ditch was recut on a straight alignment. At milecastles there is no evidence for a narrow berm. A further point that Bidwell makes is that obstacles should be expected on the north side of the ditch, particularly in front of turrets where they are omitted on the berm, but possibly elsewhere; these might take the form of man-traps (*lilia*), whose purpose was to break up a charge before it reached the defences; and indeed it is *lilia* in the true man-trap sense that are found north of the Antonine Wall ditch at Rough Castle. There is obviously much more to be learned about these previously unsuspected elements of the Wall. What has emerged so far is evidence for a primary design that binds together the functions of Wall, berm, ditch and turrets in a unitary whole.

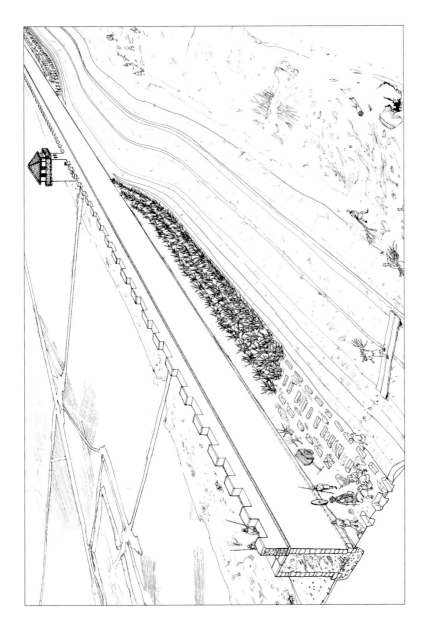

Figure 4. Conjectural reconstruction of berm-obstacles, showing behaviour at a turret (drawn by Graham Hodgson.)

The Vallum
There have been major publications of research on this element of the Wall. These include the excavations carried out by Brenda Heywood in the 1950s on the Vallum at Milecastles 23, 30 and 42 (Heywood and Breeze 2008). The report demonstrates that there was certainly no primary causeway across the Vallum opposite Milecastle 42, and almost certainly none at 23 or 30. This discovery torpedoed an old idea of Richmond and Birley's that all milecastles had causeways to allow travellers wishing to cross the Wall onto a route along the south berm (this on the model of Milecastle TW50, where there was an original causeway but an uninterrupted south mound). Breeze and Dobson (1976 and subsequent editions), and Heywood and Breeze (2008), prefer the idea of a route along the north berm, but it has been observed that the infrequent occurrence of metalling 'hardly suggests that there was regular traffic along the Vallum berms' (Bidwell 1999a, 22; cf. Wilmott 2008, 122).

In all three cases a causeway was eventually supplied, perhaps at the time when the Vallum was systematically breached in the Antonine period. However in each case the causeway was later retained, probably because it was opposite a re-occupied milecastle. At Milecastle 23 the Vallum was carefully redefined as an obstacle by restoring the north and south mounds, which might imply that the secondary causeway was simply to allow the milecastle garrison to cross the Vallum ditch if necessary. Similarly at Milecastle 42 the retained causeway was accompanied by no gap in the south mound, only a slight depression. Here some metalling coming off the causeway and petering out on the south berm was the only significant berm metalling to be found in all 3 excavations.

West of the Milecastle 42 causeway the marginal mound consisted of clean material like ditch upcast, not silt, and was laid over a stony layer on the same ground surface as the primary Vallum mounds. Samian from a secondary dump of silt over the marginal mound showed that here the Vallum ditch was being cleaned or re-defined as late as the late-second or early third century. The report states that the marginal mound had never been continued across, i.e. that it respected, the secondary causeway (the same statement is made for Milecastle 23).

Recent excavations on the Vallum at Black Carts and Appletree are now fully published (Wilmott 2009a). Wilmott has reconsidered the problems of the Vallum here and in a valuable discussion paper (Wilmott 2008). At Black Carts and Appletree, Wilmott found the marginal mound to be of clean material, not ditch silt, and lying at the same stratigraphical level – directly overlying subsoil – as the main Vallum mounds. Taken with the observation of clean marginal mound material at Milecastle 42, this has convinced Wilmott that the marginal mound is in fact a primary, or 'near-primary' component of the Vallum, giving it two mounds on the south facing side, which is the appearance that instantly meets the eye in the Cawfields sector. This interpretation contradicts that of Simpson and Shaw (1922) which has always held the field: that the marginal mound was part of the reconditioning of the Vallum after the crossings were removed. Their basic evidence was the appearance of the marginal mound where causeways had been removed, its absence where causeways were never removed, and the fact that unlike the Vallum mounds, it was never cut through at the crossing points. In many places these archaeological observations remain unassailable, although there are exceptions to these rules, as at Black Carts, where there are extant crossings in conjunction with the marginal mound. On the crucial point that the marginal mound is not cut at the crossings, Wilmott has responded by suggesting that the surface of the crossings may only have been inserted to half of the depth of the Vallum mounds, which would be level with the top of the marginal mound, while the space between the marginal and south mounds may have been filled with solid material. But it seems inconceivable that such a process would not have left a visible archaeological trace, and that there would not be some areas where a primary marginal mound was slighted. Such fundamental uncertainty thrives on the limited amount of excavation that has been carried out on the Vallum. For example, there seem to be only six observations of the kind of material composing the marginal mound (four excavated over half a century ago), all from narrow sections across the works, and of these, three were of clean redeposited subsoil (taken to support the theory of primacy for the marginal mound) and three were of mixed material (suiting the idea of a reconstitution of the Vallum). As Wilmott says (2008, 127), echoing Brenda Heywood before him, it is clear that much more fieldwork-based evidence is needed before we can improve our understanding of the Vallum. Until then it would be premature to dismiss the conclusions of Simpson and Shaw out of hand.

See also: Woolliscroft 1999 (on possible functions of the Vallum); Poulter 2009 (on the surveying of the Vallum, concluding that it was surveyed outward from the forts).

Lateral Communications
As will be seen throughout Chapter 4, there have been several records made of the Military Way in recent years, and a similar road is now well attested on the Cumberland Coast as well as along the Wall itself. At Benwell the Military Way has been found to be accompanied by no less than two lesser tracks. Presumably not are all are the same date. This is the first observation in recent

times of the phenomenon of the 'Lesser Military Way'. One possibility must be that one of the lesser tracks at Benwell represents an arrangement for communication along the Wall in the Hadrianic period, before the Military Way was instituted.

*

The following sections on the later history of the Wall are necessarily selective, concentrating on developments since 1999. Note Hodgson 2008b, an attempt to provide an archaeological and historical framework for understanding changes on the Wall over the period 160-400. This paper suggests that we need to make more use of archaeological evidence (as opposed to written sources) to characterise changes from period to period on the Wall, and that there are indeed major periods of distinctive character, although these are separated by broad horizons of military crisis and social change rather than by episodes of destruction and rebuilding as were the old 'Wall-periods'. David Breeze (2005b; 2005c) has reviewed the way evidence for episodes of destruction on the Wall has been interpreted at different times in the past, arguing that the belief in destruction by enemies was very much a product of its time, and reaffirming his own preference for other explanations.

The Antonine Wall and reoccupation after the Antonine Period
There has been little new information over the last decade about how sites on Hadrian's Wall were used during the Antonine occupation of Scotland, which is now generally agreed to have lasted for only a short single period, c. 140-c.160. Hadrian's Wall was certainly being rebuilt in 158. A paper in preparation by the present writer will seek to show that manuscript evidence exists which proves that an inscription of that date (RIB 1322) came from the Wall (probably the curtain itself, certainly not from a fort), and furthermore that it was one of a group, indicating an extensive building operation. The stones were found in the Throckley area, not Heddon, as is usually stated. Rather than prefacing a second occupation of Scotland, the building in 158 was the beginning of the permanent reoccupation of Hadrian's Wall. The Antonine Wall was probably held until the rebuilding of the southern Wall was quite complete – perhaps in the early 160s – in order to protect the province from invasion while the work was in progress (Hodgson 2009).

In the mid-Antonine period (the 160s), then, the Wall was reoccupied, but not the minor structures on the Cumberland coast. Most would date the rebuilding of the Turf Wall sector in stone to this time. The Vallum was re-commissioned in a modified form and the Military Way added to the Wall. As well as new forts at South Shields and in the hinterland of the Wall, it was possibly at this time that Burgh by Sands II, the fort actually attached to the Wall curtain, was built to replace the detached fort at Burgh I (p. 153). We still know of very few actual units stationed in Wall forts in this period: part of *cohors I Vangionum* and some legionaries at Benwell, *cohors I Hamiorum* at Carvoran on the basis of an inscription re-used in the granaries there (Crow 1999, 125) and that unit's dedication to all the gods and goddesses on the advice of the oracle of Apollo at Claros (RIB 1579), which, paralleled by nine inscriptions from outside Britain, possibly dates to the time of the great Antonine plague of *c.* 165 (Jones 2005). One possibility is that the Tungrians and the Hamian archers at Carvoran had been transferred from the Antonine Wall to their posts on Hadrian's Wall as early as *c.* 158, for there is evidence at each of their previous bases on the Antonine Wall that a different unit may have taken over at this time. The Tungrians at Housesteads, if in garrison this early, went on to be associated with the fort until the end of the Roman period. Following the discovery of the diploma of 158 reported to the last Pilgrimage, it also seems very likely that *cohors I Aelia classica* was stationed at Ravenglass from then until the end of the Roman period. The other 'permanent' Wall garrisons – the ones that we know in the third century through inscriptions, and later through the Notitia Dignitatum – were perhaps shuffled into place in the late 170s or early 180s: *ala II Asturum* was at Chesters by then, if not earlier. Again, as far as we can see, the policy in this period was for forts to accommodate single complete units: the barracks at Wallsend were rebuilt to exactly the same plan as in the Hadrianic period, evidently for a *cohors quingenaria equitata*, only now in stone. The fort of the 160s at South Shields had an identical barrack layout to Wallsend.

The 160s also saw a transformation overtake the fort at Corbridge. See Hodgson 2008a for a study of the structural evidence for the transition of the fort into what was probably a base for detachments of legions VI and XX. This concludes that Site XI, the courtyard building (probably, to judge from the best parallels, a storage and marketing centre, a great *macellum* or *emporium*) was probably commenced somewhere in the period 165-180. It was also in the 160s that a religious enclave was built somewhere at Corbridge to house the cults favoured by the legionaries. This is graphically attested by a large collection of architectural fragments from classical temples recovered at Corbridge before the first world war, along with the better known fragments of religious sculpture studied to such striking effect by Richmond in 1943. The buildings represented by the architectural fragments are presently unlocated and are not to be identified with the so-called temples on the site which are probably buildings of a later date and much more mundane purpose.

The Site XI project at Corbridge was never fully completed, and much of the site was affected by a destructive fire, very possibly the result of enemy action. It is concluded in Hodgson 2008a that, despite deficiencies in the records and doubts that have been expressed, the famous 'Corbridge destruction deposit' really did exist and, as its excavator, John Gillam, argued, represents a destructive event that could well coincide in date with the attested crossing of the Wall by barbarian invaders in the early 180s, although of course such a connection cannot be directly proven. A broadly similar conclusion was reached by the late John Dore in his posthumous publication (Dore 2009) of the 1960-61 excavations at Halton Chesters, where again the character of the destruction deposit is cautiously reaffirmed and the possibility of its dating to *c.* 180 confirmed, although once more this is only one of many possible explanations.

The Severan period and the earlier-third century
One breakthrough here is the demonstration (from the discovery in 2000 of lead sealings of Severus and his sons in construction levels) that the supply-base at South Shields indeed originated under Septimius Severus, and not earlier, as has sometimes been supposed. See Hodgson 2001 for an interim report on the discovery of the latest sealings and discussion of the possible historical contexts of the supply-base.

Corbridge remained a legionary detachment base in the third century, for vexillations of legions II and either VI or XX. The legionaries were accommodated in the well-known walled compounds at the centre of the civil town, and no doubt continued to maintain their religious sanctuary (see Hodgson 2008a). There were also legionary detachments (of II and XX) in the third century at Carlisle, apparently accommodated in a fort rather than compounds.

In the 1999 Pilgrimage book Paul Bidwell made an explicit link between the circular buildings that replaced Stone Fort 1 at Vindolanda with Severan work on the Wall, suggesting that they may have housed levees of civilian labour from the southern *civitates*, mentioned, possibly with the Brigantes, on some well-known building stones from the Wall which have usually been assigned a much later date (RIB 1672-3, 1843-4, 1962, 2022). These stones have now been reconsidered by Fulford (2006) who assigns them an even earlier date, associating them with the reconstruction of the Turf Wall in stone in the 160s. The general principle of an earlier date than that conventionally given now seems unassailable – there is nothing very late-Roman about these inscriptions – but none of Fulford's arguments preclude a Severan date. If they are of this period the inscriptions sit alongside the supply-base at South Shields in indicating large scale requisition from the civil part of Britain – both supplies and labour – for the maintenance of the northern frontier and the conduct of war in the north.

Note also: Hornshaw 2000, for a suggestion of how the Severan restoration of the frontier might have changed the appearance and operation of the Wall.

Changes in forts from the third century

The third century is conventionally seen as a time of peace and stasis on the northern frontier. It is certainly true that the forts and the military *vici* on the Wall were at the peak of their expansion and material prosperity for the first few decades of the century, but our perception of a 'third-century peace' probably owes something to the almost complete absence of historical records for the period. Archaeological evidence attests some striking changes and trends during the course of the third century.

Foremost among these is a change in the appearance of barracks, discussed at some length in the last Pilgrimage book. Barrack reconstruction in a new style is recognised at some Wall-forts to occur in the period 225-50. These barracks have a reduced number of *contubernia*, usually five or six. They display a diversity of plans and building techniques. Examples have been excavated at Vindolanda, South Shields and Wallsend, and others may be recognised in older plans that have been subsumed under the term 'chalets' and generally thought, incorrectly, to have originated in the late-third or early-fourth century. In the case of infantry barracks – and it is now possible to tell the difference, following the recognition of the standard form of cavalry accommodation – the new plans imply that centuries in northern Britain had been halved in size before the middle of the third century. There is no independent historical evidence for this, but that is no reason to ignore the suggestion of the archaeological evidence. Cavalry barracks also changed. The principle of accommodating men and horses under the same roof was apparently maintained, but with fewer and larger *contubernia*, suggesting the possibility of six horsemen in each of five *contubernia* maintaining a *turma* strength of 30. In the light of discoveries at Wallsend it is possible to reconstruct from Richmond's records the likely original plan of a third-century cavalry barrack at Halton Chesters. Newly obtained barrack plans are collected, with full discussion and references, in Hodgson and Bidwell 2004.

A second major trend of these times was the import to the northern frontier of Britain of a considerable number of irregular units of Germanic origin, known primarily from inscriptions. It is possible that the datable inscriptions, many of which are of the reign of Severus Alexander (222-235), are misleading and that this practice was established in the later-second century. The phenomenon is discussed in general terms in Hodgson 2003, 148-52 in the context of the discovery of an irregular cavalry barrack of third-century date at Wallsend, inserted into the regular fort plan, probably one of a pair. It is hypothesised that this was to house irregular cavalry of the kind so common in this period. These Germanic irregulars have also been extensively treated by Carol van Driel-Murray in the Ninth Horsley Memorial Lecture, delivered to the Newcastle Society in 2005. This study (publication in preparation) sought to demonstrate how modern archaeological techniques shed light on the recruitment of trans-frontier populations into Roman military service, revealing the family groups that accompanied Germanic irregulars as they were moved from beyond the Lower Rhine frontier to Hadrian's Wall.

A classic archaeological tracer for these populations on the Wall has been a characteristic form of hand-made pottery, the so-called Housesteads ware, which occurs at a number of sites along Hadrian's Wall. José Peeters has undertaken a study of this ware (2003), with important results. On the basis of a detailed analysis of both published and unpublished material from both sides of the North Sea, Peeters has suggested that the best parallels for both individual forms lies in the western coastal region of present-day Noord-Holland (around Schagen) and the island of Texel. This accords well with the epigraphic evidence for Frisian irregulars at Housesteads. Mineralogical analysis concluded that Housesteads ware was made on Hadrian's Wall but using Frisian forms and technology (Peeters 2003, 16-18). Developments in the British repertoire closely follow those in the Frisian homeland, suggesting regular contact between the two areas throughout the late second and much of the third century. Most Housesteads ware has been found outside the forts, and at Birdoswald in what seems to be a separate settlement of wooden buildings, though at Housesteads it occurs in two of the barrack blocks, as well as in the *vicus* (Peeters 2003, 23-9).

A.R. Birley (2008b) has reconsidered the deities worshipped by these German soldiers and suggested a link between these immigrant communities and the variously spelt 'Veteribus' dedications found on so many, probably third-century, portable altars, exploring a suggestion that the name might refer to the Germanic god Loki. Rushworth (forthcoming) has reconsidered the Germanic units attested at Housesteads, concluding that more groups are attested than usually recognised, and distinguishing the *cives Tuihanti* (from Twenthe in the Netherlands) from the more northerly *Frisii*.

Bidwell (2005d) has explored the possibilities of enduring links between regular auxiliary units and their homelands, concentrating on the example of the Spanish units, and casting doubt on the long-held model of predominantly local recruitment by the later-second and third centuries.

The Military *vici*
As will be evident throughout this handbook, the civilian extra-mural settlements – referred to here as military *vici* – have been graphically revealed at a new level of detail by the survey work of Alan Biggins, David Taylor and their colleagues. This work can truly be said to be nothing short of revolutionary in what it has revealed about the extent and complexity of the plans of these settlements. In this handbook it is only possible to give a selection of the plots and interpretations that Biggins and his colleagues have produced. Although the majority of these surveys have been promptly published, it is very much to be hoped that all of them will be brought together into a single volume which would immediately become one of the classic books of Wall-archaeology.

Enclosures or defences are now known at two Wall-*vici*, Wallsend and, as the geophysical survey shows, Housesteads, and a possible boundary ditch can be traced at Maryport. However, the geophysical surveys suggest no defences at Halton Chesters, Chesters, Carvoran, Birdoswald, Castlesteads, or Maryport. Defended *vici* do not seem to be such a feature of the Wall as they are of the hinterland, where many examples may be recognised. The enclosures at Wallsend and Housesteads were perhaps connected with particular local circumstances. In addition a new geophysical survey has shown that there was a heavily defended, compact annexe attached to the west side of the outpost fort at High Rochester (this was not a pre-Roman Iron Age enclosure as suggested in the last Pilgrimage handbook). This is presumably a military annexe rather than a defended *vicus*, on the basis of its small size, partly open interior, and regular, geometrical planning in relation to the fort.

The scale and implied prosperity and trading links of the military *vici* of the Wall as revealed by geophysical survey makes all the more striking and significant the contraction or disappearance of the *vici* that occurs in the second half of the third century. This was evident at the time of the last Pilgrimage, but the general trend is supported by observations and publications since then. An excavation in the *vicus* at South Shields in 2002 showed that occupation did not outlast the third century and that the buildings of the vicus were replaced by a system of fields. The defences surrounding the area south and west of the fort at Wallsend were abandoned in the later third century. The continuing excavations at Vindolanda have confirmed a general lack of fourth-century material from the *vicus*. The publication of the *vicus* excavation at the Vicarage Garden, immediately outside the eastern wall of Burgh by Sands, confirms that occupation there ceased in the later-third century. This pattern of *vicus*-abandonment is not peculiar to the Wall, but holds good for the majority of forts in the hinterland. For example, the recently published report on Piercebridge (Cool and Mason 2008) confirms that occupation in the *vicus* there, well-known from aerial photography, had ceased by the late-third century.

For a recent and wide-ranging consideration of the plans, function and individual buildings of military *vici*, including those of the Wall-zone, see Sommer 2006.

Later-third century abandonment in forts
In 1999 Paul Bidwell pointed out that the widely accepted idea, based on small-scale excavations at Rudchester (1972) and Halton Chesters (1960-1), that these forts and others may have been derelict between *c*. 270 and *c*. 370, did not find support in more recent excavations of Wall forts. Now the facts have once again been reconsidered in John Dore's posthumous publication (2009) of the Halton Chesters work. His conclusion is that the excavated evidence does not bear the weight that was put on it; phases likely to be of late-third or early-fourth century date and later-fourth century date were conflated, and the layer of earth supposedly denoting abandonment was probably a levelling up for major phase of late-third or early-fourth century rebuilding. This certainly seems a more convincing interpretation of the evidence, and the idea of Rudchester and Halton Chesters being allowed to fall into decay in the fourth century is probably best dispensed with.

The Fourth century
Much had changed by the end of the third century. With the demise of the *vici* there came an end to long-established economic links with the Mediterranean via the Rhone and Rhine trade routes: the ubiquitous olive oil amphorae cease to be imported, and samian ware is no more. The end-date of the military *vici* also coincides in broad terms with the near-cessation of the practice of monumental epigraphy and sculpture on the Wall. From this point on we are forced to navigate the history of the Wall without the aid of inscriptions, or with very few. Inscriptions of the period 276-82 from Birdoswald (*J. Roman Studies* 51(1961), 194), and probably Vindolanda (RIB 1710), are the latest certain epigraphic attestations of the long-standing Wall units. Although the unit-name is not known, an inscription found at Chesters in 2004 is important in being one of the very latest in the high-empire style known; it dates to 286. It is now generally accepted that by 314 the outpost forts north of the Wall had been abandoned.

The army of the Wall in the fourth century is much poorer in terms of artefacts. Coins are more common in this period (from about 320 onwards), because they had a lower intrinsic value than before the third-century inflation. But military equipment, brooches and other personal ornamentation, objects of bone and glass, and pottery, are all much scarcer in excavated fourth-century levels than earlier. With an absence of inscriptions and sculptural representations, there is not such a strong visual impression of the fourth century Wall-soldiers, who have a much more shadowy identity than their high-imperial predecessors. This situation will be partly rectified by the forthcoming publication of the *Finds from the Frontier* conference, held at Newcastle University in 2008, where a series of stimulating papers explored aspects of the material evidence for the inhabitants of the Wall in the fourth century (Collins and Allason-Jones forthcoming). The impression is of effective but essentially static frontier soldiers lacking the wealth and spending power and Mediterranean-inspired epigraphic and religious culture of their second- and third-century ancestors. But there is no need to return to the model of a peasant militia. There is no reason to disbelieve the evidence of the *Notitia Dignitatum*, which has the same units (mostly) in the Wall-forts in the fourth century as in the third. At least some commanding officers maintained their social status and had Mediterranean origins, to judge from the excavated *praetoria* of this period at South Shields and Vindolanda. Barracks, where they have been excavated, were still organised on the basis of the traditional *contubernium*. The complete late-Roman plan of South Shields, designed for a new unit with an apparent strength of 300-400 around *c.* AD 300, also proves that frontier units of the Tetrarchic period were not universally reduced to the tiny sizes that some commentators have suggested were standard (see discussion in Hodgson 1999 and Hodgson and Bidwell 2004). It is clear that for the first half of the fourth century at least, most of the Wall forts could have accommodated units of 300-400 in number.

Markets at forts
At four separate sites on the Wall the last decade has offered a vivid insight into the changed mechanism for supplying the soldiers – and whatever communities may have shared the forts with the military units – following the disappearance of the *vici*. These sites have revealed evidence of markets *inside* the forts, indicated by concentrations of low value fourth-century coins in one particular area. This occurs at Wallsend, inside the *porta quintana sinistra* (minor west gate) (some 30 coins: Hodgson 2003, 166–7), Newcastle, on the street in front of the *principia* (105) (Snape and Bidwell 2002, 275), at Vindolanda, in and along the street just inside the west gate (perhaps 800) (see p. 120) and at Carlisle, again in front of the headquarters building (250) (see p. 148). At Newcastle the peak of activity was in the period 330-350, but went on until the 370s, the same fall off in the 370s occurring

at Wallsend and Carlisle. The patterns of coin loss can best be explained by cash-based markets held within these forts during the fourth century, the practice fading out by 380. At Vindolanda the excavator notes that the market was held on a wide street in front of the granaries. The Newcastle report notes the occurrence of sherds of native 'local traditional ware' in the levels associated with the postulated market, and linked the presence of a market with a possible north-south route across the Wall at Newcastle, something that would also apply to Carlisle. But the Wallsend and Vindolanda evidence suggests that the phenomenon occurred at other forts. Perhaps the markets were periodic and peopled by traders travelling to the forts: at Wallsend and Vindolanda there is a clear link with gates. It is interesting and puzzling that at Carlisle a market should be held within the fort when the town in which the fort was situated was presumably itself an active marketing centre.

The Towns, late-Roman communications, and milestones
It is clear that the urban centres at Corbridge and Carlisle flourished in the fourth century in contrast to the military *vici*. The later-Roman vitality of these two towns mirrors that of many of the 'small towns' of lowland Britain. There has been no recent work on the problems of late-Roman Corbridge, but Paul Bidwell has drawn attention to neglected evidence (Wright 1941) for ambitious refurbishment of the main Stanegate road running west out of Corbridge during the second half of the fourth century. The new road was of elaborate and heavily built character, presumably an imperial or civic initiative, and the work is closely and confidently dated to the period after 364 by sealed Valentinianic coins and Crambeck pottery. The main road surface in the centre of the town was very probably resurfaced at the same time, using sculptures, architectural fragments and inscriptions from demolished temples (Hodgson 2008a, 81).

A new milestone from Langwathby records a distance of 19 miles from Carlisle ('Lug[uvalium])' and gives the earliest firm date yet for time by which the tribal capital of the Carvetii ('civitas Carvetiorum', almost certainly at Carlisle) was established: AD 223 (Edwards and Shotter 2005). As at Corbridge, there is no firm evidence for a walled circuit at Carlisle, although possibly unfinished early-third century defences have been found at one point. McCarthy (2002) suggests that the wall famously shown to St Cuthbert in AD 685 was that of the Roman fort within the town. The many archaeological observations of Carlisle since 1978 cry out for a synthetic study with location and distribution maps.

On the apparatus of civic government in the Wall-zone: Breeze 2008a. On milestones in general: Edwards 2008.

The later-Fourth century and beyond

An abandonment of regular arrangements inside barracks is documented at South Shields and Vindolanda (Hodgson and Bidwell 2004, 153-4) as occurring around or after *c.* 370. The limited sample of modern excavations we have suggests that in barracks in general the sort of rupture with the traditional *contubernium* arrangements, once associated with 'chalets' and dated to the early-fourth century, actually occurred in the years after *c.* 370. This occurs alongside other changed patterns of occupation from this time. For example, the late-Roman *praetorium* at South Shields lost its Mediterranean-inspired character and ceased to function as accommodation for an aristocratic household by about this time, undergoing alteration and partial demolition. Wilmott (1997, 203-20) has documented changes in the use of the granaries at Birdoswald occurring in this period. The coin lists at certain extensively excavated sites, such as Wallsend and Housesteads, dry up in the 380s, suggesting (but far from proving) that some Wall-forts were abandoned, or ceased to have coin-using occupation, this early. At other forts, including South Shields, Newcastle, Vindolanda, and Birdoswald, the latest types of Roman coins (of the House of Theodosius) usually to be expected in Britain are present.

Paul Bidwell (2005c) has taken issue with a redating of Crambeck parchment ware proposed in the report on the Birdoswald excavations (Wilmott 1997). In this report the date of the introduction on this ware was advanced to *c.* 350 on the basis of numismatic evidence from Birdoswald, but Bidwell shows that in all other cases without exception, Crambeck parchment ware only appears in contexts securely dated to after *c.* 370, and is absent from those securely dated *c.* 350-70. Almost certainly the crucial context at Birdoswald was of later date than the latest coins within it. Along with grooved 'Huntcliff-type' pottery, Crambeck parchment ware remains a secure signal for the very latest phase in Roman Britain, post *c.* 370.

A number of important sequences which take us through this period, and into the fifth century, have been excavated or published in detail since 1999. At South Shields further work has taken place on some of the very latest deposits to have accumulated before the collapse of Roman buildings, specifically gullies and pits filled with dark earth and discards from deer-antler working. Some of this antler has returned a radiocarbon date suggesting the activity was going on after 450. At Vindolanda very late Roman sequences have been excavated, particularly in the area of the southern rampart and south-west angle of Stone Fort 2, on the west rampart south of the west gate, and in the area of the granaries and the adjacent stretch of the *via principalis*. Here, continued occupation into the sixth and seventh centuries is claimed on the basis of artefacts, although the argument has yet to be published in detail.

The two published sequences are at Newcastle and Carlisle. At Newcastle (Bidwell and Snape 2002) late-fourth century occupation was intensive, and there was a rare occurrence of building work – a new floor in the *principia* – post dating a slightly worn Theodosian coin, therefore after *c.* 390. But there was no certain indication of how long occupation continued after 400. At Carlisle (Zant 2009) a very-late fourth century sequence in the area of the *principia* almost certainly continues into the fifth century, but again there is no way of gauging for how long.

It seems clearer than it did in 1999 that there was activity, perhaps for a considerable part of the fifth century, at a number of Wall forts. One way in which very-late Roman and post-Roman sequences on the Wall could be better dated and understood in future is by increased use of radiocarbon dating. The later-Roman deposits tend to preserve animal and human bone well and if enough dates are obtained, particularly from objects that can clearly be associated with the stratum in which they lie (as for example the bones making up a buried skeleton or animal, or like the antler at South Shields, associated with some craft activity or butchery being practised at an identifiable horizon in the sequence), then there is every prospect that sub-Roman sequences could be very closely dated and compared with one another. Such scientific dates come of course in the form of a bracket rather than an exact date, but with modern AMS dating these can be quite tight and multiple dates can be statistically combined to produce a very narrow result indeed. Radiocarbon analysis should become routine in the investigation of sequences like this where the traditional methods of Roman archaeological dating are no longer available.

However, even exact dating of fifth-century structures and deposits will rarely tell us whether the community involved was directly descended from the late-Roman inhabitants, or whether the site was simply being utilised, after an interval or dislocation, by newcomers. Since 1999 there has been no further advance in the debate between those favouring the former idea – warlord descendants of the last Roman garrison (Casey, Wilmott) – and others (Dark) who see a later re-use of the Wall by British kingdoms following a decisive break in the early-fifth century. The identity of those inhabiting the ruins of forts in the fifth century may long remain impenetrable. It is also worth remembering that all of the above refers to forts: the last days of the Wall itself, and installations such as the milecastles (which in some cases were occupied until at least *c.* 370) are, in Charles Daniels' phrase, 'as yet seen through the very darkest of glasses'.

A Theodosian coin of 406-8 closing a hoard reported from Great Whittington (near the Devil's Causeway, a short distance north of the Wall), published in Collins 2008 and discussed by Rob Collins on p. 58 below, would appear to be one of the latest numismatic attestations of activity in the Wall area.

For the problems of the Wall in the fourth and fifth centuries, note the papers in Wilmott and Wilson 2000, particularly: Wilmott 2000 (recapping the late-Roman sequence at Birdoswald); Brickstock 2000 (discusses fourth-century coinage) and Esmonde Cleary 2000 (a perceptive and thought-provoking summing up). Here and elsewhere, Dark (2000) recapitulates his views on the post-400 life of Hadrian's Wall.

Anglo-Saxon re-use of Roman sites and monuments
Whatever the truth of continuity of occupation or community at particular sites, there can be no doubt that the Wall and its forts and towns were of great material importance and had immense cultural resonance for Anglian kings and churchmen. This can be seen in the quite deliberate use of Roman monumental masonry and inscriptions in the seventh-century church and crypt at Hexham, which a survey described below has shown to derive largely from the Roman bridge and the mausoleum at Shorden Brae. Artefacts from South Shields recognised since the time of the last Pilgrimage indicate seventh to ninth century occupation on the fort site, and the possibility has been proposed that this was a secular power centre at the time when the monastic sites at Jarrow and Monkwearmouth were founded (Wood 2008). At Newcastle the emerging publication of the Roman and post-Roman levels offers structural details, unparalleled at a Wall fort, of a horizon of Anglo-Saxon construction over the Roman levels. Towards the other end of the Wall, McCarthy (2002) has explored the transition from the *civitas* of the Carvetii to the kingdom of Rheged, describing a horizon of seventh- to ninth-century building over the Roman levels at Carlisle, and examining the historical context in which the place went on to become a secular and ecclesiastical centre in post-Roman centuries.

Finds research
There is insufficient space to summarise all aspects of find research in this review. Note the overview of the state of research on the 'material culture' of the Wall by Allason-Jones (2002) and, also by Allason-Jones, (2008) a study of the objects that must once have existed but which no longer survive in the archaeological record, thus shedding light on little-considered aspects of life on the Wall.

Over the last decade the late Vivien Swan was indefatigable in her quest to recognise legionary and ethnic signatures in Roman military pottery assemblages. Much of her thought bearing on Hadrian's Wall was brought together in a massive paper (Swan 2008). This is particularly valuable in characterising the sort of local pottery production carried out by the army in the Wall area in the early-second century (e.g. The Brampton kilns), before a sophisticated network of importation from pottery industries further afield was fully in place. The often anonymous looking and unrecognised wares produced in this period remain a poorly understood and untapped resource, but work on them is progressing on other fronts, such as the North East Regional Museums Hub Hadrian's Wall Ceramic Database.

For coin circulation on the Wall, see Brickstock 2005.

For finds reported to the Portable Antiquities Scheme, see p. 57.

Contributions since 1999 on life, death and religion on the Wall

On health care: Allason-Jones 1999.

For the gods worshipped by the army see Irby-Massie 1999 (cf. the comments by Brian Dobson in AA^5, 29 (2001), 301-2).

On Mithras: Allason-Jones 2004; on Belatucadrus and the Carvetii: Edwards 2006.

Social and cultural history

The study of Hadrian's Wall now encompasses more than the traditionally archaeological: the study of the subject has become a subject of study in its own right. There is a notable growing interest in the history of the Wall as a social and cultural artefact, its varied meaning to different times and audiences. This is evident in Ewin 2000, and is the preoccupation of the current 'Tales of the Frontier' research project, based at Durham University, which seeks to explore academic and popular ideas about the significance of Hadrian's Wall and its landscape: see dur.ac.uk/roman.centre/hadrianswall/. In addition, Hingley (2008a) has discussed the antiquarian investigators of the Wall from an unusual perspective, examining the extent to which they were influenced by changing notions of civility, nationhood and empire between the sixteenth and nineteenth centuries. Note also the treatment of the Wall as one episode in a longer landscape history evident in Woodside and Crow 1999.

The wall-walk question and the function of Hadrian's Wall

According to Breeze and Dobson (2000), the forts on one hand, and the Wall curtain and minor installations on the other, possessed quite distinct functions. The units in the forts were for the defence of the frontier and the province. The Wall itself was concerned only with the supervision or control of movements by individuals across a border, specifically by monitoring passage through the milecastle gates. In the last Pilgrimage Handbook, Paul Bidwell raised what he saw as certain difficulties with the function of the Wall as set out by Breeze and Dobson. One was that Hadrian's Wall eventually became 'virtually a closed frontier, with civilian access confined only to the very few Wall gates'. A second difficulty was 'the strengthening of the likelihood that it [the Wall] had a walkway along its top, presumably with a parapet' (Bidwell 1999a, 33-5). Since then, the long-running debate on the existence of a wall-walk, and the wider question of the function of the Wall that this leads on to, has flared up again.

The last ten years has yielded a remarkable addition to the archaeological evidence available: the recognition of the obstacles on the berm, planned from the outset as part of the Wall-anatomy (above, p. 25). The impenetrable entanglement of forked branches most probably accommodated in the berm-emplacements is close in appearance and function to what Caesar described as *cippi*. The purpose of the *cippi* or obstacles closest to the defences at Alesia was, on Caesar's explicit authority, to render attackers vulnerable to projectiles directed from a small number of troops on a defensive rampart, and thus impede their progress for long enough for reinforcements to arrive. It follows from this reading of the function of the obstacles that they would only have been effective if the ditch and berm of Hadrian's Wall could be commanded from the Wall-top. The discovery of the obstacles can be seen to lend support to the view that there was a wall-walk and parapet along the top of the Wall from which defenders could engage attackers.

In his new edition of the *Handbook* (2006) David Breeze re-examined the arguments for a wall-walk and concluded that none of them was decisive. The most telling argument for Bidwell in 1999, the discovery that the Wall had been carried across the rivers Tyne and Irthing by footbridges in the Hadrianic period, was dismissed by Breeze: 'The bridges... may have taken a path across the river, but this in itself does not confirm the existence of a wall-walk'. In 2008 Breeze restated his preference for envisaging 'the Wall without a walkway along the top', and suggested that the obstacles on the berm 'are but another element of control, created in order to ensure that people wishing to enter the empire did so through the specified gates' (Breeze 2008b, 1-3). Bidwell (2008b) has responded with a detailed article which while not proving the existence of a wall-walk, demonstrates that this is the most reasonable interpretation of the evidence. There is not room here to recapitulate all the points, but tmost dramatic and telling is the comparative illustration which shows that the scale of Hadrian's Wall is out of all proportion to the Continental barriers lacking walkways and parapets, so it is both unreasonable to use these as a basis for arguing that Hadrian's Wall did not have a wall-walk and impossible to explain the width of the Wall in any other way. This point – that the thickness of Hadrian's Wall in all its versions is not adequately explained by any other means than the existence of a wall-walk – was emphasised because the discussion in HB14 did not tackle this unique characteristic among Roman frontiers. The comparative scale of the Wall, taken in conjunction with the berm-obstacles, the string-course stones known from the north side of the Wall – an architectural convention always employed when the top of a defensive wall was crenellated – and plenty of parallels for walls with functioning fighting platforms no wider than Hadrian's Wall, makes for a compelling case. In the same article Bidwell dealt point by point with the arguments employed by Collingwood in his famous article of 1921, showing that none decisively establishes that the wall-top was not defensible and sometimes defended.

There has been no refutation of this battery of arguments in favour of a wall-walk, and Breeze has stated that he accepts them. Although that particular debate seems to have been decisively resolved, another is set to take its place. Breeze accepts the existence of the wall-walk but sees this as an aspect of the personal design of an ideal frontier Wall by the emperor Hadrian (Breeze 2009). In seeing the Wall as an architectural caprice by the emperor, Breeze's message is that we are not entitled to draw general conclusions about the function of Roman frontier works from Hadrian's Wall. Against this view Bidwell and others maintain that as well as being provided with a wall-walk and capable of defence, the Wall was actually used in this way, as its continual reconstitution and maintenance under later emperors suggests. In particular, Crow (2004a, 130-132) restates his earlier arguments for a military function, pointing out that barrier walls in the Balkans were used to resist barbarian attack in the better documented late-Roman period, and stressing the Greek tradition of defensive long-walls that would have been familiar both to Hadrian and to Platorius Nepos, who had governed Thrace, where one of the long-walls was still to be seen.

The suggestion that soldiers actually fought from the Wall-top is still guaranteed to provoke outraged disbelief. This is because in most minds an image is instantly conjured of the might of the Roman army lining the top of the barrier to repel the assault of an organised barbarian army or horde. But the Wall would allow quite limited numbers of troops to delay an invading force – whether a large raiding band of a more substantial invasion – for long enough for an appropriate military response to be organised. The rapid movement which attackers of the province relied upon would be prevented. Rather than reinforcing an attempted crossing point, the alerted forces would tackle the enemy north of the Wall, or to the south if the attackers had been let through or succeeded in penetrating the province. Such a hypothetical model of how the Wall curtain and turrets might have functioned has the virtue of not having to abandon the belief that a large Roman force would have preferred to operate against its enemies in the open, nor are we driven back to the implausible view of a great army facing a barbarian horde face-to-face over an eight foot wide wall-top. The actual defenders on the Wall-top would have played a small but critical role in the whole process. Theirs was a role of initial observation, communication and delay. Hand-to-hand fighting with attackers trying to climb over the Wall was a means of delaying them but might also be a matter of personal survival. As far as petty raiders were concerned, the moment that larger Roman forces were alerted to their presence, the operation had gone wrong; before that happened, every second of delay counted against them, and so the actions of men on the Wall-top could be decisive. In larger invasions, if attempts were made in concert to organise simultaneous attempts to cross the Wall in a number of places, or if the units in nearby forts were depleted in numbers because of operations elsewhere, then the ability of the small numbers immediately available to hold off the intruders from the Wall-top for as long as possible would become even more critical. There is indeed some evidence that on occasions there might be formidable invasions aimed, *inter alia*, at destroying Wall installations, such as the attested crossing of the Wall shortly after 180, which has been linked to destruction deposits at Corbridge, Rudchester and Halton Chesters. The numbers of invaders were enough for a Roman general to be killed in battle. Here the Wall evidently failed, but it was only in the event of such a catastrophic breakdown of the system of protection for the province that the Wall became irrelevant to defence.

A view of the Wall as defensible presupposes that there were groups of invaders or raiders of varying size who attempted to cross the Wall. There has never been a serious attempt to analyse the origins, motives and nature of the likely attackers of the Wall, partly because of the lack of direct evidence from the earlier-Imperial period. However, no-one has ever produced detailed models or arguments to justify the usual assumption – that there were regular movements of goods and people that the Wall was intended to tax or control. Note however the comments by Breeze (2002b) on these cross-frontier matters.

One of the challenges for the next ten years is to use archaeological and historical evidence to construct a theoretical model of how groups within Iron Age societies far north of Hadrian's Wall might have developed a practice of seizing wealth from Roman province and used it to enhance their position and prestige in their homelands distant from the empire. That such raiding – or outright attacking – occurred is hardly in doubt, as sources for Britain from Hadrian onwards and the generality of later-Roman sources on the Continent show, but no serious attempt has been made to model the development of the practice as a consequence of the permanence of the imperial frontier and the reaction of external Iron Age societies to the settled prosperity of Roman provincial society. All of this also raises the question of why the diplomatic arrangements with peoples beyond the frontiers that presumably allowed the second-century German frontier to be such a modest affair proved impossible in Britain. These questions take us into the next area where there has recently been much discovery and thought, the question of Hadrian's Wall in its wider setting.

The Wall in its wider setting
Breeze and Dobson (2000, 215) have acknowledged that the story of Hadrian's Wall 'will never be complete until it can be set in the context of the peoples it controlled and divided', while lamenting that 'the story of the native population is unwritten, only to be found on sites poor in material remains and especially artefacts, sites which it is impossible to date closely'.

Our knowledge of contemporary native settlement in the area of the Wall has continued to be strongly influenced by the almost single-handed programme of research conducted a generation ago by George Jobey. The predominant settlement form in the north-east is seen as the small rectilinear enclosure containing roundhouses, typically producing very few Roman sherds of pottery or objects. Jobey tended to see the rectilinear enclosures as flourishing in the Roman period – perhaps a reflection of the *pax Romana*. There was apparently no discernible difference in the zone to the south, between the Wall and the Tees, with native settlement forms continuing unchanged and no real signs of Roman-style settlement or architecture emerging. A recent essay on Iron Age settlement in the north-east (Frodsham 2004b) paints a picture of generally peaceful co-existence, with an Iron Age way of life continuing with little change despite the presence of Hadrian's Wall. One development since Jobey's time has been the discovery from the air of many more sites of later-Iron Age type situated very close to the Wall, and assumed to be contemporary with it.

Iron Age society north of the Wall
The excavation of a group of Iron Age settlements north of the Wall (East and West Brunton, Newcastle Great Park; Pegswood, near Morpeth; Delhi Opencast, at Blagdon Hall) has shown that enclosure complexes (of which the rectilinear element recognisable from the Jobey sites was but one component) that had developed in the last two centuries BC on sites where

there had been unenclosed occupation for centuries. All these sites came to some sort of abrupt end relatively early in the Roman period. Radiocarbon dates demonstrate that the West Brunton settlement was abandoned at some date between AD 66 and AD 140. No more than a scrap of Roman pottery reached East Brunton. At Pegswood the settlement that had evolved over centuries was abandoned and replaced by a much smaller non-settlement enclosure, possibly a stock-corral, by the second century AD. The Delhi site was in use at the end of the Iron Age but has produced no later radiocarbon dates and no Roman material.

This new evidence calls for a re-assessment of the question of whether the generality of Iron Age settlements in the region north of the Wall lasted for very long into the Roman period. It has long been recognised that Roman material occurring on the sites investigated by Jobey was, with very few exceptions, not later than second-century in date. Jobey himself was reluctant to concede that these sites were not occupied in the later-Roman period, and argued that later-Roman material was available to the settlements in smaller quantities. But it is the near absence of earlier-third century pottery, of the period when the Wall-forts and *vici* were at the peak of their material prosperity, that is most telling. The Northumberland settlement at Huckhoe, which stands out from all the others in having abundant later-Roman material, suggests that its absence from the generality of Iron Age sites in the north-east is significant. There are also native sites outside the northeast, south of the Wall in Cumbria, that produce fourth-century Roman material. Note also the Longhorsley hoard, found in 2002, which shows that 45km north of Hadrian's Wall shortly after 160 bronze coins were being melted down for re-use rather than being used for any marketing transaction (Abdy 2003).

At present we can only speculate on what kind of social upheaval might have led to the widespread abandonment of a centuries-old landscape of densely spaced settlements. It is hard to escape the conclusion that the imposition of the Roman frontier on the Tyne-Solway Isthmus played some part, either following the 120s or the permanent consolidation of the 160s. Some form of social disruption has also been detected among northern Iron Age societies much more remote from the Wall. It has recently been argued that in northern Scotland there is a horizon of change occurring around AD 200 (Hunter 2007). The traditional Iron Age sites of the region do not yield radiocarbon dates later than the mid-third century AD. Corresponding to this is the emergence of a smaller, distinctively later-Roman Iron Age repertoire of artefacts that identify the northern peoples of the third and fourth centuries. Fraser Hunter has suggested that the cutting off of Roman subsidies in the earlier-third century undermined a traditional social elite and allowed new social groupings to emerge. It must be a possibility that it is in these areas, 150-250km north of Hadrian's Wall that we should be seeking the social explanation for the raids on the Roman province that the Wall was intended to prevent. It is possible that the very existence of the empire with its internal wealth and permanent frontiers led to transformations within the societies beyond those frontiers. This has recently been argued for northern Europe in general (Heather 2005). In some ways it would be surprising if similar changes did not occur in the regions north of Hadrian's Wall, and in the material on the late-Roman Iron Age in Scotland gathered by Fraser Hunter (2007) we may be seeing such a process at work.

The hinterland of the Wall
On the eastern side of Britain the picture south of the Wall has also changed, and civil life outside the fort-*vici* is no longer represented solely by sites in the Iron Age tradition. Over the last 10 years a number of Roman villas have been excavated in or near the Tees Valley (at Quarry Farm, Ingleby Barwick; Dalton-on-Tees; probably at Faverdale, Darlington (although here the main house has not been discovered). Again, the new developer-funded archaeology is crucial here, although the Dalton villa has been revealed by the efforts of local researchers. These are the northernmost villas known in Britain. The discovery of these sites strongly suggests that the Roman remains long known at Old Durham, just outside Durham City, should be rehabilitated as a probable villa site, bringing the development of villa estates to within 22km of the Wall. In developed Roman provincial landscapes villas always go hand-in-hand with marketing centres – towns. In this connection a most striking discovery (a product of research, by Time Team, Durham University and Durham County Council, not developer archaeology) has been the Roman settlement at Hardwick Park, Sedgefield. The spectacular geophysical survey of this site reveals a plan that if found in southern or midland England would be regarded as that of a small town, and small-scale excavations have revealed traces of the industrial activity and a pottery industry typical of such centres. None of these important new sites is yet published, but to judge from preliminary reports (and the published material from Old Durham) these typical forms of Roman provincial settlement emerged relatively early, during the second century. Of the fate of the traditional Iron Age sites of County Durham we have as yet no consistent picture. A series of new radiocarbon dates from Thorpe Thewles suggests that the final, open roundhouse settlement (superseding the late pre-Roman Iron Age enclosure) may be of the Roman period.

On the west side of the country the picture is less clear. There is a conspicuous lack of evidence for villa development south of the Wall, although that would have appeared to be true of the north-east until very recently. There are some settlements of native type south of the Wall that produce late-Roman finds, which contrast with those to the north, where, as in Northumberland, the Roman objects found tend to be first or second century.

Implications for the function of the Wall and understanding other frontiers
These discoveries suggest that Hadrian's Wall was no mere backcloth against which rural life went on much as before. They reveal the possibility of a major social dislocation occurring north of the Wall, and the creation of a rudimentary Roman provincial society to its south. The Wall perhaps represents a sharp line of distinction between the two different kinds of development. In this Hadrian's Wall would not be alone among Roman frontiers: it has long been known that on parts of the Upper German and Raetian frontier, *civitas* territories surrounding Roman towns, and large numbers of small villa estates, ran right up to the running frontier barriers, so that a colonised landscape was enclosed and protected by the frontier.

The current trend in historical writing on Roman frontiers is not to see frontiers as sharp lines of separation: rather frontiers are currently interpreted as zones of gradual transition into economic marginality. According to such theorising, the actual frontier line (in the case of Hadrian's wall, the Wall itself) is an arbitrary line for the purposes of border control, and the populations on either side of the line will have more in common with each other than with the imperial power maintaining the border. One of the most influential exponents of this view has been C.R. Whittaker (1994). This belief found some support when the archaeological evidence from the Wall zone seemed to point to the existence of a (to quote Breeze and Dobson (2000, 249-50) 'real people of the land, who lived with the Wall in their midst, who seemed little affected by Rome materially, but nevertheless enjoyed or endured the *pax Romana*, with peace, communications and markets as never before'. That the Wall had a destructive effect on traditional Iron Age society to the north, and protected a nascent provincial society (whether created through indigenous initiative or Roman policy) is a starkly different model, but one that must be seriously considered in the light of emerging archaeological evidence. It is a gratifying thought that over the next ten years developer-funded archaeology is bound to bring to light more previously unknown sites north and south of the Wall which will improve our understanding of the wider context in which the frontier operated. There is also a challenge here for researchers: the question of whether the numerous undated Iron Age sites in the immediate vicinity of the Wall survived for any significant length of time after the building of the Wall could be pursued through relatively modest programmes of excavation.

The simple presence or absence of Roman objects in conjunction with key radiocarbon dates would soon indicate whether these sites represent a population contemporary with the Wall.

As well as suiting the 'frontier-zone' model of Whittaker, the belief in a native society existing in peaceful and parallel co-existence with the Roman army fits with the view of Hadrian's Wall as primarily a facility for the control of individual movement, by 'civilians, whether merchants, local farmers moving their cattle and sheep or simply local people visiting relatives on the other side of the Wall' (Breeze and Dobson 2000, 40). The possible dislocation or disappearance of traditional society to the north of the Wall must cast some doubt on such movement being the *raison d'etre* of the Wall. Conversely, rapid creation of villa estates not far south of the Wall compels reconsideration of the Wall as a practical defensible barrier against raiders from the north. Such raiders need not have come from the area close to the Wall, but from areas far out of reach of immediate Roman retaliation, in Scotland.

The future of Hadrian's Wall research
A malaise in the subject, or at least its image, has been sensed by Breeze, who points out (2003c, 15) that Wall studies have been seen by some as the work of an introspective elite. This, he suggests, may have had the effect of putting off those from outside with original or refreshing views. That such an image-problem still exists can be seen from a paper such as James 2002, which portrays the subject as dominated by a prosopographic and epigraphic tradition and wary of modern approaches. Similarly, Hingley (2008b), proposes the introduction of overtly theoretical archaeology into the subject as a remedy for declining interest. See also the acute comments of Esmonde Cleary in Wilmott and Wilson 2000. Much of the criticism is misdirected, as I hope the present volume shows: there is some excellent and very modern archaeology going on the Wall, which involves ideas as well as facts. Yet the fact that the Wall, as an area of research interest, has such a low reputation among historians and archaeologists in other areas, should be a matter of grave concern. It may be that because there has been such apparent consensus about the basic purpose and function of the Wall (non-military) for so long, that non-specialists assume that all problems are now solved and there is nothing further to debate, while in the current model of 'frontier zones' the Wall structures are seen as having no historical, only bureaucratic, significance. Those not directly involved with archaeology on the ground tend neither to appreciate the true scale of the Wall nor to consider the achievements of this imperial project in the fields of architectural art and military science. It could be said that the literature

currently available on the Wall fails to get this across. Something is very wrong when a distinguished ancient historian can write: 'For one-third of its 70 miles the 'wall' was just a turf bank, which would hardly have kept out a party of determined children' (Beard 2008). Even before the discovery of the berm-obstacles, this betrays unawareness of the basic archaeological facts. Crow (2004a, 130), questioning the non-military view of the Wall, puts it well: 'Most of those who maintain the military significance of the Wall have been involved in excavations of the Wall itself'. There is archaeology taking place on the Wall that tells a dramatic and interesting story: this needs to be better disseminated, and if new discoveries re-open the debate about the military role of the Wall, that can only help dispel the notion that the subject is worked-out and fundamentally unimportant.

Teno

3. A ROUND-UP OF OTHER DEVELOPMENTS SINCE 1999

The following sections describe developments in a number of areas that were not discussed in detail in Chapter 2. Two of these are brief updates on much longer sections in the 1999 Pilgrimage publication: statements on environmental and scientific archaeology, and of recent changes in the geography of the institutions charged with the management of the Wall. In addition there are sections on two completed English Heritage initiatives, the recording of the fabric of the Wall, and the Hadrian's Wall Mapping project, while an account is given of finds from the Wall reported to the Portable Antiquities Scheme.

Environmental Archaeology and Science along Hadrian's Wall: ten year update

Environmental sampling, as well as collection of animal bones or shells during excavation ˙ become routine in order to investigate aspects of diet, economy and landscape ˙ ˙ll as examining other aspects of archaeological science. Small, predominan planning-led, interventions along Hadrian's Wall over the last 10 years ha\ tended to extend and consolidate our understanding of these aspects rathe ˙an make large leaps forward. Clearly it will always be the larger excavatic ˙hat enable us to make some of these leaps – both in archaeology and environmental archaeology – although group value of the many small sites can focus ideas and lead to research questions being formulated. They have, for example, been important in helping to develop several sections of the forthcoming Hadrian's Wall Research Framework. Of the "leaps", samples from the large area excavations undertaken by TWM Archaeology north of Newcastle upon Tyne have determined that spelt wheat was, indeed, grown north of the River Tyne during the late pre-Roman Iron Age – making that area little different from lowland County Durham in this respect (ASDU 2008). It has become clear that the emmer/spelt divide proposed by van der Veen (1992) is not the River Tyne but more likely an upland/lowland divide after all.

In the central section of the Wall a programme of intense sampling was undertaken at Vindolanda when the granaries were excavated in 2008. This was to investigate whether there were divisions within the granaries allowing separate storage of commodities rather than a bulk storage of grain, and as had been suggested for the granaries at Birdoswald where wheat, barley and hay seems to have been stored at various times (Huntley 1997). Although the Vindolanda analyses are ongoing it is clear that there were at least physical divisions across the granary with concentrations of burnt wood, mainly hazel roundwood, across some areas. A detail of interest is the abundance of small holes of what look like woodworm galleries – giving an impression of somewhat old and rotting partitions! As with most other granary contexts, spelt-type wheat is common but some bread wheat also is present. The spelt-type grains are all cleaned and hence not being stored in their spikelets. This again is the norm for northern England despite the received wisdom suggesting that this glume wheat was typically stored as spikelets. The added benefit of such extensive sampling is that the residues from the floatation samples are starting to provide fascinating information about the small mammal fauna as well – an aspect not otherwise well studied along the Wall at all. Material from earlier excavations at Vindolanda explored the nature of fuel in hearths and ovens. The charcoal analysed suggested that some features may have been used for industrial high temperature processes with fuel comprising more or less pure oak, whilst others could have had a more domestic function where heather wood/twigs formed the bulk of the fuel. This would have produced a very hot, but rapidly burning, fire useful for cooking flat breads for example (Huntley 2003; Huntley 2007).

Further west, major excavations at the Millennium site in Carlisle (by Oxford Archaeology North) are detailed elsewhere in this volume. Suffice to say that their samples have provided a wealth of evidence for landscape and economy – unparalleled in the *published* record for the city.

On the southern side of the city, along Botchergate, excavations by the former Carlisle Archaeology Unit and subsequently by the Lancaster University Archaeology Unit (now Oxford Archaeology North) uncovered remains of a Roman cemetery and major industrial complex. This part of the city seems to have been the focus for Roman burials – both inhumations and cremations – with early records being summarised by Charlesworth (1978). The industrial complex was clearly smelting lead and smithing iron during the second to early third centuries with considerable remains of slag, furnace fragments, lead and lead ore (galena) fragments. Detailed chemical analyses of the ore lead demonstrated a high silver content leading to the conclusion that the ore was being mined probably in the Tynehead area although the Caldbeck Fells, on the edge of the Lake District some distance to the south of Carlisle, were another possibility. Low levels of tin and copper were found in several of the lead objects pointing to re-melting of scrap items that had been soldered. This might well therefore indicate that workshop activities were also taking place on the site with ill-formed or damaged articles being re-cycled (Zant *et al.*, forthcoming).

The Roman cemetery at Beckfoot in Cumbria is well-known and has been eroding into the Solway for centuries. In 2005/6 English Heritage funded an assessment excavation, by Oxford Archaeology north, to investigate the nature and extent of the cemetery since long-term *in situ* preservation is not a viable option. The unpublished assessment report confirmed the high potential of this site to answer questions related to cremation burials and funeral pyres in particular through analysis of human bone and charcoal.

Pollen work at West Brunton (ASDU 2008), East Bog and Spadeadam (both Oxford Archaeology North) has taken us away from the direct influence that the Romans had upon local vegetation – for a long time the almost sole question asked of pollen sites along the Wall. West Brunton provided evidence for the local vegetation around the site from investigation of pollen in ditch deposits. Patches of alder, hazel and birch woodland/scrub were nearby but there was little evidence for taller woodland. Most of the assemblage consisted of grass pollen grains with a selection of herbs suggesting pastureland close by. Pollen grains as well as macrofossils of aquatic taxa indicated the presence of water in the ditches at times although the generally poor state of pollen preservation strongly suggests that this was not a permanent feature. The East Bog site (NY 7486 6687) was a section through the Vallum ditch and thus is similar to that at Black Carts. However the pollen results differ in that those from Black Carts demonstrate a more or less open sedge and grass-rich vegetation from before the arrival of the Romans whilst East Bog indicated only partial clearance of woodland at this time, with the existing woodland also secondary in character. Woodland clearance continued throughout the Roman period with no immediate regeneration afterwards. The radiocarbon dates from East Bog suggested that the ditch started to infill immediately after the initial construction of the Vallum. The assessment of the palaeoenvironmental potential at three mires on RAF Spadeadam, whose southern edge abuts the Wall WHS, does not relate specifically to the Wall or the Romans but has demonstrated that two of the mires are unusually intact with deposits spanning from early prehistory until the present day (most mires/bogs in the region have lost the last 1000-2000 years through peat cutting or drying out). Pollen is exceptionally well preserved and therefore the deposits have high potential to address quite detailed questions relating to vegetation and, by implication, climatic change through the millennia.

This brief overview only touches on a few of the more exciting aspects of environmental archaeology/science over the last 10 years but certainly demonstrates that Wall zone retains high potential for further and important discoveries. The more detailed resource assessment of work undertaken and what could be done is provided in the forthcoming Hadrian's Wall Research Framework. Whilst planning-led interventions may be the norm, and certainly provide a constraint in terms of what is done where, they have nonetheless provided opportunities to study in areas otherwise perhaps not

likely to have been studied as they were not directly associated with the Wall itself, always a focus of investigation.
Jacqui Huntley, English Heritage

Recording the Roman Wall
The decision to record the visible sections of the Roman Wall was made in the early 1980s by the Department of Environment, now known as English Heritage. It was realised that no drawn records existed of the Monument and that this policy of consolidating the Wall without prior recording could no longer continue and therefore was considered vitally important to produce a full and detailed record of what was in the care of the State.

The Wall was being nominated for inclusion as a World Heritage Site and the recording of the fabric was part of the application process for this status and was included in the role of the initial Management Plan.

The recording programme, funded by English Heritage, began in 1985 and continued until 2000 by which time all of the upstanding visible fabric of the Wall and most of its associated structures had been recorded on a stone-by-stone basis to a scale of either 1:50 or 1:20. The completed drawings are held in the English Heritage Plans Room in Swindon and copies at the English Heritage office in Bessie Surtees House, Newcastle.

The drawings are used as the primary base record of the monument and as a permanent management tool for recording areas of stone replacement, new areas of re-pointing and consolidation. The base record can also be used to assist in any potential research programme.

The initial phase of the recording was the production of a series of rectified 1:50 photographs by specialist contractors. The rectified photographs were then traced on to waterproof draughting film to enable the work to be carried on throughout the year. In areas where such photography was not possible the Wall fabric was drawn by hand measurement. Every facing stone on both sides of the Wall was checked to ensure that all of the visible fabric was recorded. This on-site enhancement meant that any small anomalies could be added to the drawings such as sections and widths of horizontal offset courses as well as vertical offset or inset courses. A number of these vertical offsets were noted both in the consolidated and the so-called 'Clayton' sections of Wall. Also recorded were any areas of surviving Roman mortar within the Wall fabric, the location of the drains through the Wall, areas of course changes and probable re-building as indicated by different coursing levels. The location of all in situ phallic symbols and various inscribed building stones are noted (together with the relevant publication references relating to their description and translation) as well as all incised building blocks with 'diamond broaching', together with possible Roman numerals in the shape of x or v, sometimes inverted, which may be related to the process of quarrying. Also noted were blocks with a blank panel surrounded by an incised line.

It is interesting that from Harrow's Scar mile castle 49 westwards for 800 metres to turret 49 is the largest concentration of blocks having some form of inscribed symbol: 3 phallic symbols, 7 inscriptions, 8 inscribed blocks and 3 blank panels.

Two relevant articles by the author describing the 20th century uncovering and consolidation of the Wall by Mr Charles Anderson of the Ministry of Works and a previously unknown set of 19th century drawings of the Wall by James Irwin Coates have just been published (Wilmott 2009a).
Alan Whitworth

National Mapping Programme survey of Hadrian's Wall
The Hadrian's wall mapping project is part of English Heritage's National Mapping Programme (NMP), which aims to provide a comprehensive synthesis of the archaeological information available on aerial photographs. A new survey of the Hadrian's Wall World Heritage Site was completed in 2008. The survey, based on aerial photographs taken over the last 66 years, has mapped the entire World Heritage Site, placing the Roman frontier within a historic landscape with remains ranging in period from the Neolithic through to the Cold War. The project began in 2002 and encompassed an area of 1725 square kilometres, covering the entire length of the Wall and the Cumbrian coastal defences. The surveyed area is a broad band, up to 15km wide, with Hadrian's Wall running along its centre. Work was carried out by investigators from English Heritage's Aerial Survey & Investigation Team, who identified, interpreted and recorded all archaeological features visible on 30,500 aerial photographs taken between 1930 and 2006. The mapping project has revealed little in the way of previously unknown Roman military sites or installations connected with Hadrian's Wall, but provides an invaluable new resource for the study of pre-Roman and Roman Iron Age landscape and settlement. In addition the evolution of the landscape in post-Roman centuries is graphically illustrated. Records and reports from the Hadrian's Wall Survey are available to the public through the National Monuments Record.

Finds reported through the Portable Antiquities scheme

Finds from Great Whittington
A number of artefacts have been recovered by metal detectorists in 2007 and 2008 from the village of Great Whittington, Northumberland, the

interpretation of which suggests a rural site north of Hadrian's Wall with late Iron Age–early Roman occupation, and possible late Roman–early post-Roman occupation.

In June 2008, 12 objects were found by a local metal detecting club, 9 of which were Iron Age to Roman in date. The two largest were the remains of two *paterae* of first- to second-century date (acquired by the Society of Antiquaries of Newcastle on Tyne).

In May 2007, a group of eight copper-alloy *nummi* were found. The eight coins range in date from an issue of Constantine I of AD 318 to a House of Theodosius *Gloria Romanorum* issue of AD 406–408. The small number of coins, combination of mints, and broad range of dates suggests that the coins were the contents of a purse that was lost accidentally rather than intentionally deposited. Based on a *terminus post quem* provided by the latest coin, the group can be dated to the early fifth century at the earliest. The group is significant because it has provided the latest dated *nummus* to have been found in the Hadrian's Wall corridor (see Collins 2008 for full details of each coin).

Without the *Gloria Romanorum* coin, the issues and mix of mints would be unexceptional in Britain, containing 5 coins of the House of Constantine and two of the House of Valentinian. A comparable group may be the hoard from Heddon on the Wall that consisted of 31 copper-alloy coins (Bates 1886, 242, n.6). The latest coin from the Great Whittington group suggests that at least one person journeyed from the Eastern Mediterranean in the fifth century, or the coin was passed on by several people in several stages. Significantly, this provides evidence for direct or indirect contact with people from the Mediterranean in the fifth century that probably post-dates the traditional end date for Roman Britain, c. AD 409 or 410. This is reinforced by a second early 5th century coin, the *Urbs Roma Felix* issue from the Heddon hoard.

The importance of many of these objects found at Great Whittington must be stressed. Not only do they indicate a site that is otherwise unknown, but some of the artefacts are particularly rare, at both the regional and national scales. Full details for each object found at Great Whittington can be viewed on the Portable Antiquities Scheme database (www.findsdatabase.org.uk).

Finds from Corbridge
Over 160 artefacts were retrieved by divers in the River Tyne downstream from the Roman bridge at Corbridge in the 1990s. These objects have been recorded with the Portable Antiquities Scheme. In total, the artefacts represent at least one erosion event of the riverbank, which saw the redeposition of stratified Roman archaeology on the riverbed. The objects were mixed in date, from the first century to the fourth, and there were also a number of early-

medieval and medieval artefacts. A few of the Roman objects were made of gold and were fragmentary remains of jewellery, but most were made from a copper alloy. The largest functional group of objects was military fittings, which included individual scales from a set of scale armour, a scabbard slide, a belt plate, and a buckle plate. There were 86 Roman coins found, mostly of fourth-century date, with the latest coin possibly an issue of the House of Theodosius (AD 378–402).
Rob Collins, Portable Antiquities Liaison Officer

The Management of Hadrian's Wall

Hadrian's Wall became a World Heritage Site in 1987. When the German *Limes* was similarly inscribed in 2005, the two Sites amalgamated to become the Frontiers of the Roman Empire World Heritage Site. These two elements were joined by the Antonine Wall in Scotland in 2008. Other countries, so far only in Europe, have expressed an interest in nominating their sections of the Roman frontier for inclusion within this trans-national WHS (for a discussion of Hadrian's Wall within this wider context see Breeze and Jilek 2008).

Every WHS requires a Management Plan. Preparations for the creation of a new Management Plan for Hadrian's Wall began in 2006. The Plan was completed in 2009 and is now available on the internet: http://www.hadrian's-wall.org/page.aspx//About-the-World-Heritage-Site/Management-Plan. The preparation of the Plan was overseen by a working group chaired by Professor Peter Stone of the University of Newcastle: our two societies have a joint representative on the working group. The work of preparing the Plan ran in tandem with the formation of a new body to manage Hadrian's Wall, Hadrian's Wall Heritage Ltd, which was formally incorporated in 2006. With core funding from the two northern development agencies, English Heritage, and Natural England, the primary focus of the new body is to realise the contribution the WHS can make to economic and social benefit of local and regional communities, primarily through sustainable tourism development. To that end it is undertaking a number of initiatives, including an ambitious capital programme to up-grade interpretation of the WHS and of associated visitor facilities, refinement and re-launching of the Hadrian's Wall Country brand including 'locally produced' and sustainable access opportunities and the up-grading of all tourist literature about the Wall.

While Hadrian's Wall Heritage Ltd relies on its sponsors for its core funding, finance for all other activities has to be raised separately. The new company has been successful in obtaining funds to purchase Camp Farm at Maryport on which sits the Roman fort and civil settlement and it has now moved on to the next steps of seeking money to establish a new museum in the farm buildings and start a research project at the site, working closely with the Senhouse Museum Trust.

The final major structural change on Hadrian's Wall has been the establishment of the National Trail, opened in 2003, and now managed by Hadrian's Wall Heritage Ltd. As a preparation for the National Trail, a base line survey had been undertaken, marking the current state of all sections of the path, and a rigorous monitoring regime of fixed-point photography and annual walk-over surveys has continued. It was therefore possible two years later to re-assess the National Trail, when a significant level of deterioration was recorded. The statutory bodies acted with commendable speed and provided resources for the better management of the Trail. Nevertheless, the pressure of visitors, including those undertaking the walk along the Wall for charity or as part of a training project, is still causing damage to the grass cover along the Wall and more hard-surface paths are being created as a result. One difficulty here is that the National Trail is designated as a highway and therefore it is not possible to prevent access by anyone wanting to walk the path. Large groups who contact the Trail authorities are warned that they may cause damage to the Wall if they walk or run along it in wet conditions as this is likely to damage the grass sward, though such warnings are not always heeded, and winter use of the Trail is discouraged. Nevertheless, the present regime of proactive surface management is generally holding up. A new guide-book to the National Trail was published to coincide with its opening (Burton 2003) and other guides have followed which, of course, encourage 'doing' the Trail.

David Breeze

4. SURVEY AND EXCAVATION ON HADRIAN'S WALL, 1999-2009

Introduction

Although the 2009 Pilgrimage will travel from west to east, these summaries are arranged in the traditional east-west order to allow ease of cross-reference to standard works such as the *Handbook to the Roman Wall*. The summaries attempt to give as much prominence to major publications that have appeared over the last decade as to fieldwork. This section is not intended to list every piece of fieldwork that has taken place on the Wall but rather to summarise significant results where obtained. For work before 1999 the fourteenth edition of the *Handbook to the Roman Wall* (2006), which contains the only detailed bibliography of Wall sites, should be consulted. Additional references will be found in the last Pilgrimage Handbook, Paul Bidwell's *Hadrian's Wall 1989-1999: a summary of recent excavations and research*. Annual entries for sites in the 'Roman Britain in 19xx' section in the journal *Britannia* are not cited unless they constitute the only publication available or a source of significant further detail.

The abbreviation HB refers to the *Handbook to the Roman Wall*, specifying the edition: the full list with editors and dates can be found in the new HB14 (Breeze 2006a).

SOUTH SHIELDS – *Arbeia*

Excavations have taken place at South Shields every year since the 1999 Pilgrimage. The work has been financed principally by the Earthwatch Institute, the Heritage Lottery Fund and South Tyneside Council. The following summarises the principal discoveries and developments in interpretation and site presentation since 1999. Work since 1999 has been directed by Paul Bidwell, Nick Hodgson, and in individual areas by Graeme Stobbs and Margaret Snape.

Pre-Roman
The multi-period prehistoric site discovered beneath the E quadrant of the Roman fort has been fully published (Hodgson *et al.* 2001). Unfortunately the area in question was no longer occupied by structures and was under cultivation by the beginning of the Roman period, so the whereabouts of the immediately pre-Roman settlement nucleus is unknown and we have as yet no knowledge of how it was affected by the arrival of the army.

The earliest Roman occupation and the pre-Antonine fort(s)
The date of the earliest Roman occupation remains unclear. Buildings, roads, and a possible parade ground found beneath the stone fort of *c.* 160 are not

of a character likely to belong to a fort interior. They are interpreted as extra-mural activity associated with a yet to be discovered early fort away from the known site. There are finds from the site indicating the possibility of a Flavian presence, including South Gaulish samian, but the earliest material that can be associated with Roman structural remains is Hadrianic. A road, timber buildings and a possible unfinished timber granary of this date were found in 2002 beneath the later *vicus*, WSW of the known fort, in advance of the building of an extension to Hadrian School. The whereabouts of the earlier fort – or forts – is unknown; the higher ground SE of the known site is a possibility.

The first stone fort (Fig. 5)
The first known fort (1.67ha) was built of stone from the outset in the mid-Antonine period (around 160). Its plan is similar to that of Wallsend, built around 35 years earlier. Two of the *retentura* barracks (B6, B8) were completely excavated in 1999-2001 as part of an HLF funded programme of reconsolidation of remains in the central part of the fort. The barracks were timber to begin with and replaced in stone after an interval. These were of the stable-barrack type first proven at Wallsend, where each barrack houses a turma of 30 cavalrymen and their horses, three men and mounts per *contubernium* (horses in the front room, signified by an underfloor urine-soakaway; men in the rear room, signified by a hearth). As at Wallsend, these barracks had only nine *contubernia*, the difference between the 27 troopers thus accommodated and the theoretical strength of 30 being made up by the junior officers and decurion, whose shared accommodation was revealed in detail at the rampart-end of each block. The W ends of the two barracks in the other side of the *retentura* have also been excavated and these were also cavalry barracks. The overall arrangement of the accommodation thus has the four *turmae* of a *cohors quingenaria equitata* in the *retentura,* and the six centuries of infantry in the *praetentura.*

N of barracks B6 and B8, a building first planned by Richmond (A6) was completely re-excavated in 1999. A6 is believed to have been demolished before the barracks came into commission; it occupied what was intended as a wide street between the barracks and the central range. It contained a series of rooms with hearths and much evidence of occupation and is interpreted as a temporary building to house soldiers overseeing the construction of the fort, being removed when the fort buildings had been completed around it.

A length of the fort-wall foundation, rampart and *intervallum* road of the first stone fort has been excavated NE of the SE gate (*porta decumana*) between 2005 and 2008. This revealed that the rampart had been cleared

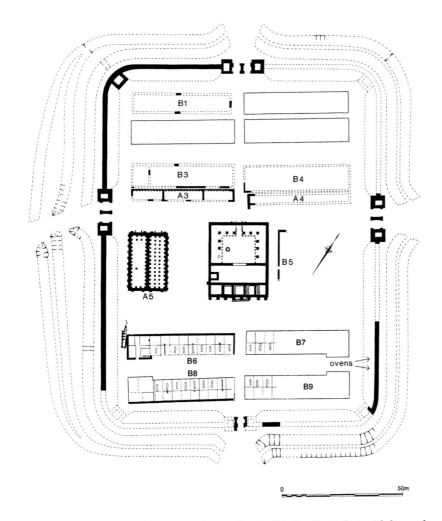

Figure 5. The later second-century fort at South Shields (Period 4) with barracks
rebuilt in stone

away and a timber building of uncertain purpose inserted during the life of
this fort (c. 160-208).

The fort was given an extension towards the S, increasing its size to 2.1ha
in order to create the well-known supply base. This happened in two stages:

Period 5A (Fig. 6): a dividing wall separated a supply-base of 11 granaries
from a proposed accommodation area, whose planned arrangement of

63

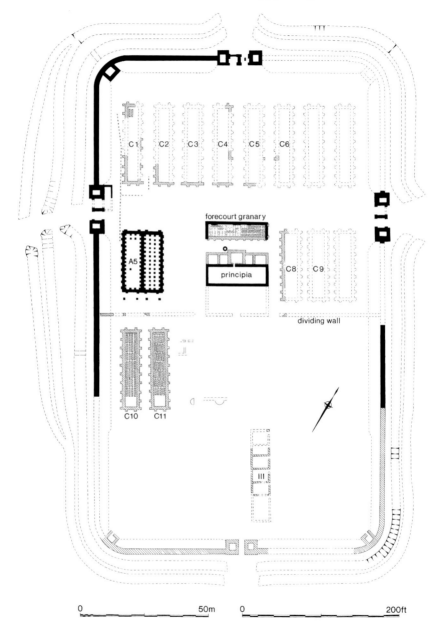

Figure 6. The Period 5A supply-base at South Shields – Severan, unfinished layout

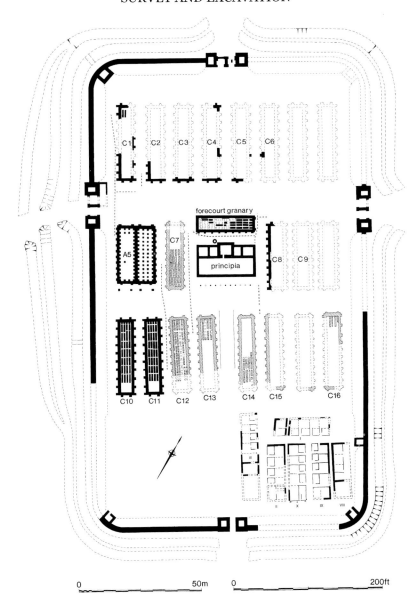

Figure 7. The Period 5B supply-base at South Shields – Severan

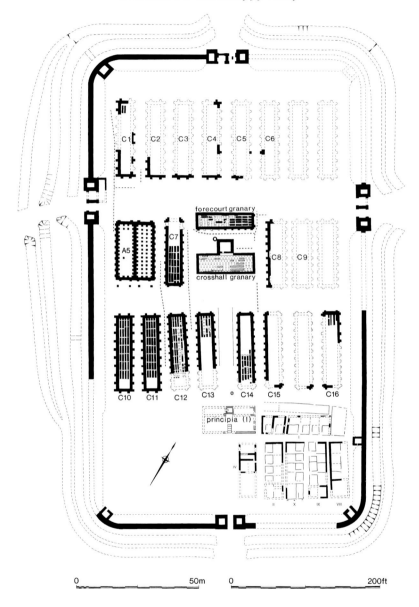

Figure 8. The Period 6A supply-base at South Shields - early-third century

buildings was never finished. Two granaries and an isolated barrack-like building (III) were completed, and work begun on a possible *praetorium*.

Period 5B (Fig. 7): six more granaries were built to the S of the dividing wall and the wall itself now removed. Thus the supply-base had expanded to 21 granaries and spilled over into the intended accommodation area. At the same time three bipartite barracks were built in the E corner of the fort – six buildings in total, making up three barracks each divided into two. One of these was inserted into Building III of Period 5A.

In 1999 it was still believed that the enlargement of Period 5B occurred at some remove from Period 5A, in the 220s. However, from the primary make-up of the street between granaries C12 and C13, immediately above the demolished Period 4 barracks and aborted Period 5A foundations, there came in 2000 a group of six lead-sealings of the type bearing busts of Severus, Caracalla and Geta, datable to the time of the British expedition of 208-11. The Period 5A plan was never completed, so that cannot significantly predate Period 5B. Pottery evidence makes it clear that the two-stage conversion occurred no later than the early-third century. The two-stage conversion to supply-base can therefore be dated firmly to the time of the Severan campaigns of 208-11. A later-second century date (under Commodus, say) can now be decisively ruled out.

A few years later, Period 6A (Fig. 8) saw the construction of a new *principia* towards the S end of the fort, while the site of the central *principia* was now occupied by an extra granary. The transfer of the *principia* coincided with a rebuilding of the barracks in the E corner, to the same plan. Their demolition levels contained a lead-sealing of *cohors V Gallorum*. This suggests that this unit had been present since at least the beginning of Period 5B, when the barrack plan originated.

Period 6B (Fig. 9), commencing no later than *c.* 225 on pottery evidence, saw the replacement of the bipartite barracks in the E corner by a series of new barracks for five or six centuries of infantry. Each century comprised only five *contubernia*. One of these barracks is the subject of a full-size reconstruction completed *in situ* in 2001. This arrangement of a 24 granary supply-base with unit accommodation in the SE end of the fort was retained for the remainder of the third century. The supply-base had presumably become a permanent facility for the supply of the units on Hadrian's Wall.

This period was closed when a fire, probably the result of an enemy attack, destroyed parts of the fort. The fire was followed by a general replanning (Period 7: Fig. 10) of at least the S half, the N perhaps being retained as a reduced supply-base or used for some other special purpose. The new *principia*, ten barracks and a courtyard house formed a plan of recognisable late-Roman type (paralleled for example at Diocletian's place at Split) based

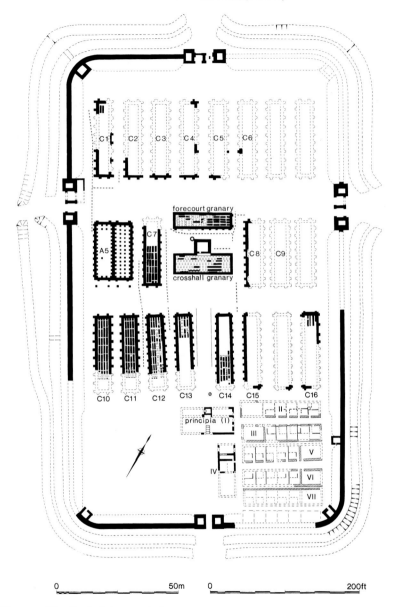

Figure 9. The Period 6B supply base at South Shields – c. 222-35 – late-third century

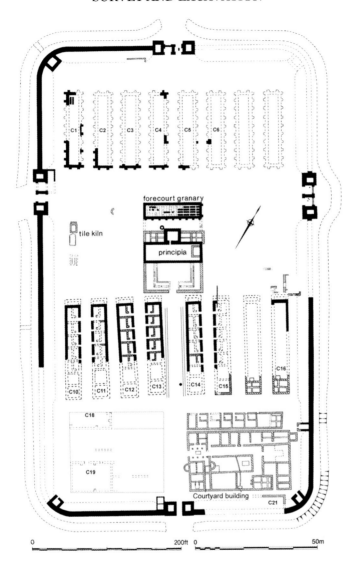

Figure 10. The late-Roman fort at South Shields (Period 7)

on a cruciform arrangement of streets. The replanning of the fort occurred in the period 286-c. 318 and signifies the arrival of a new and larger unit (possibly the *numerus barcariorum Tigrisiensium* of the *Notitia Dignitatum*) to replace *cohors V Gallorum*.

As in the preceding period, the fourth-century barracks contained five *contubernia*. As the complete complement of ten barracks is known, this allows the paper strength of the late-Roman unit to be estimated at around 400, divided into ten operational sub-units. The barracks were as formally arranged as their third-century predecessors, and even possessed officers' ends equipped with channelled hypocausts.

The courtyard house in the E quadrant, almost certainly the late-Roman commanding officer's residence, has been revealed as an architecturally ambitious peristyle house whose closest parallels occur in town houses in Mediterranean contexts as diverse as Ostia, North Africa and Syria. It functioned as an aristocratic residence until the period 350-80 and is of importance in demonstrating the high social status, and very probably the Mediterranean origins, of a fourth-century unit commander on Hadrian's Wall. The house in its original state has been partly reconstructed to full-scale *in situ* (opened 2001, with fresco painting and other internal decorations and furnishings going on since).

There was to be no further general replanning of the fort, although many alterations were made to existing buildings. The *praetorium* was maintained as a peristyle house of high status at least to the mid-fourth century. In 2003 excavation of the *via praetoria* SW of the house showed that it was still finely surfaced with limestone flags in the mid-fourth century. This was of a different character from the 40m length of the *via praetoria* NW of the main crossroads, re-excavated in 2002. SE of the crossroads the street did not have the elaborate kerbs or stylobates found on the N section, confirming that the portion leading from the crossroads to the *principia* was given special architectural emphasis. The mid-fourth century surface was contemporary with a hitherto unsuspected portico in front of the *praetorium* entrance. Opposite the *praetorium*, on the SW side of the street, a robber trench, enclosing a massive pitched stone foundation, indicated a large building which had originated in the mid-fourth century and encroached for a distance of 2m onto the *via praetoria*. After c. 350-80 the commanding officer's house was no longer maintained to its former standards, and some parts were demolished and others drastically altered, but a nucleus of rooms was retained as a residential area. On the evidence of coins running down to the Theodosian period, this was occupied until at least the early-fifth century. Similar alterations occurred in other buildings in the fort in the late-fourth century.

Outside the fort walls
A rescue excavation 125m WSW of the fort in 2002 found remains of second-to third-century timber *vicus* buildings at a depth of almost 2m, suggesting that the entire plan of the *vicus* may well survive intact beneath nineteenth-and twentieth-century housing. In common with other *vici* on the northern frontier, mainstream occupation seems to have finished before the end of the third century.

The existence of a sea-port guarded by the fort at South Shields is certain given the existence of the supply-base. Despite a number of archaeological interventions in advance of development at various points between the Mill Dam and River Drive, on the river frontage W of the fort, its whereabouts remains unknown. However, the use of the mouth of the Tyne by troop transports in the Roman period is indicated by objects from the Herd Sand on the S side of the river entrance. Finds since 1830 from the sands or dredged from their N edge include a shield-boss of the *Legio VIII Augusta*, a helmet cheek-piece, a patera, 67 coins, and other items. The finds are all remarkably close in date, falling in the second half of the second century, and the latest coin is of 176-80. It is probable that the objects and coins, which still come to light from time to time, are being washed out of the wreck of a ship that came to grief entering the mouth of the Tyne in the later-second century. The presence of a legionary of *VIII Augusta* (based at Strasbourg) would suggest a troop ship bringing reinforcements into the northern frontier zone, perhaps in response to the invasion attested in the early 180s. It may one day prove possible to locate the remains of this shipwreck.

After the Romans
There is evidence for a sudden dislocation in the life of the fort in the early-fifth century: this period saw the burial within the fort walls of victims of violent assault, whose remains have been radiocarbon dated. However, radiocarbon dating undertaken since 1999 also shows that a community was present, working objects out of antler, in the mid- to late-fifth century, and a cemetery developed outside the SW gate in this period. It is uncertain into what chronological context to fit the persuasive evidence that a church was constructed in the *principia* forecourt, although it seems to be of 'Roman' type. A table altar belonging to the probable church was found *in situ* in the 1875 excavation. An Anglo-Saxon occupation of the site is signalled by the recent recognition of a number of seventh- to ninth-century objects from immediately above the latest Roman levels in the E corner of the fort, which can be linked with larger numbers in the collections deriving from the 1875 excavations. There are now far more small objects of this period from South Shields than from the two monastic sites at Wearmouth and Jarrow. King

Oswin was said in a tradition recorded by Leland to have been born in the fort at South Shields; if true this would have been in the early 600s, and it is plausible that the Roman fort was a royal site in this period. Very few structural remains have been recognised that may possibly be associated with this occupation. What there is includes a timber portal inserted into the SW gate and a timber building over the ruins of a fourth-century barrack. The monastery at Jarrow was founded in 681/2 on land given by Ecgfrith which was presumably part of the royal estates attached to the settlement on the fort site. With the shift of this Anglo-Saxon power centre to another site by the ninth century, the fort at South Shields was abandoned.

N. Hodgson and P. Bidwell, TWM Archaeology

Reports since 1999
The history of the fort provided in Bidwell and Speak 1994 is now supplemented by Hodgson 2001. See also Hodgson 2005a (on the late-third century destruction deposit); Hodgson 2002a; Hodgson and Bidwell 2004 (on the barracks); Bidwell 2001; 2005b (shipwreck); Hodgson *et al.* 2001 (pre-Roman levels); Croom 2001a; 2001b; 2001c (finds); Croom and Caffell 2005 (human remains); Croom 2005 (sources for furnishing of reconstructions); Snape 2001 (Dacian brooches).

For a controversy over the place name *Arbeia*, see A. Breeze 2001; Hodgson 2002b; A. Breeze 2004; Hodgson 2005b.

The eastern terminus of the Wall and the Branch Wall from Wallsend fort

Robert Smith, who visited Wallsend in 1709, was the first person to note the existence of a wall running from the SE corner of the fort down to the River Tyne, the so-called Branch Wall. Almost every other antiquary who toured the Wall also mentioned it, with the notable exception of Horsley. On April 3rd 1783 John Brand and William Chapman 'caused many square stones, bedded in lime, to be dug out in several parts of it'. From the various accounts it is clear that the Branch Wall was at least 180m in length, continuing across the foreshore and into the river beyond the low-water mark. Its S end therefore was a sort of mole. Skinner and Wallis state that this part of the wall was built of very large, squared stones. These perhaps formed the base of a monument to mark the end of Hadrian's Wall, which could well be the origin of the famous inscriptions reused in the church at Jarrow (*RIB* 1051).

In 2000 part of the Branch Wall, running from the SE corner of the fort down to the river Tyne, was revealed for a distance of 12m and consolidated for permanent display. Its foundations were of the same width as the foundations of the fort wall (1.7-1.8m) which shows that, although the Branch Wall was effectively the final E length of Hadrian's Wall, it was built as an extension to the fort and not to the same specifications as the Wall. At the S end of the site mortared facing stones survived above the E side of the foundations. They were tilted forwards, indicating that the wall had collapsed, and were encased in a later foundation. This foundation was at least 6m long and consisted of a clay-and-rubble raft supporting a mortared wall 3.1m wide. There was a robbed E-W return at the NW corner of the foundation. These two features probably represent the E and N walls of a tower which was perhaps part of a gate giving access to the *vicus* and riverside areas S of the fort. There were indications of a third period of construction, when a narrower wall was built across the front wall of the probable tower, following its demolition. A trench carried 10.5m E of the Branch Wall failed to recover any traces of defensive ditches.

Paul Bidwell, TWM Archaeology

WALLSEND FORT – *Segedunum*

The excavations of 1975-84 by Charles Daniels are still being worked up for publication at the time of writing. The large scale digging inside the fort of 1997-8, of which an interim report was given to the last Pilgrimage, has been fully published (Hodgson 2003). The report arrives at the following salient conclusions:

The excavations of 1975-84 by Charles Daniels are still being worked up for publication at the time of writing. The large scale digging inside the fort of 1997-8, of which an interim report was given to the last Pilgrimage, has been fully published (Hodgson 2003). The report arrives at the following salient conclusions:

1. The fort was built directly over an Iron Age field system, still being actively cultivated on the eve of the selection of the fort site in the Hadrianic period.
2. Wallsend contributes our only complete plan of a Wall-fort as first built in the 120s. Within the stone defences the barracks were entirely of timber, the principal central-range buildings of stone. The Hadrianic fort accommodated a *cohors quingenaria equitata*. Its four cavalry troops (*turmae*) were housed in the four barrack blocks of the *retentura*, without any separate stables. This way of accommodating men and horses under the same roof is now recognised as the standard form of barrack accommodation for cavalry in the principate.
3. During the second half of the second century the timber barracks were rebuilt in stone. The fort plan (Fig. 11) remained unchanged except for the addition of a courtyard building, almost certainly a hospital, and a forehall fronting the *principia*.
4. The barracks were subsequently rebuilt and their plan rearranged to

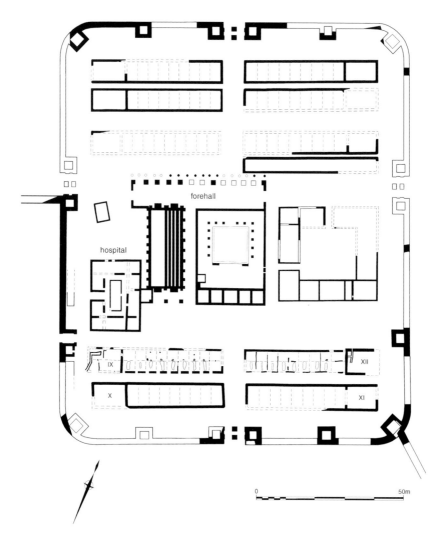

Figure 11. The second-century fort at Wallsend, with barracks rebuilt in stone in the mid-Antonine period (Period 2/3)

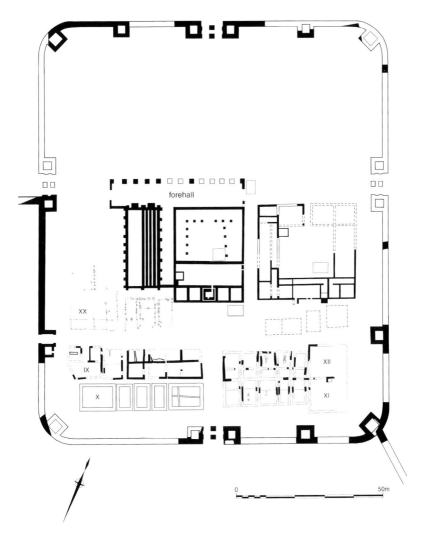

Figure 12. The fort at Wallsend with *retentura* barracks as re-planned in the mid-third century (Period 4)

reflect a major reorganisation of the garrison, attested by inscriptions and the *Notitia Dignitatum* as being *cohors IV Lingonum* in the third and fourth centuries (Fig. 12). This rebuilding is not closely datable but had occurred before the mid-third century. The reorganised barracks had only five *contubernia* (see further p. 33). The division of the fort into a cavalry half, with stable-barracks for the *turmae*, and a northern half with the barracks of the infantry centuries, was continued. The third-century barracks are the buildings described by Daniels as 'chalets' and assumed to be of broadly fourth-century date. But it now apparent that the fourth-century levels were largely removed by agricultural and industrial activity before Daniels excavated the site.

5. The new barracks included an additional insertion (re-excavated in 1998) of irregular plan and timber construction. This has been interpreted as accommodation for cavalry irregulars of a type widely attested on the Wall in the early-third century.

6. The *vicus* is fragmentarily known from excavations in 1997-8 and occupies the area S and W of the fort. The settlement was enclosed in whole or part in the third century by a system of defensive ditches and banks, seen 65m W of the fort, running S from Hadrian's Wall, and presumed to turn to front the river Tyne 75m S, where a section of defences was found in the Swan Hunter yard in 2001 (*Britannia* 33 (2002), 291-2). The extra-mural settlement and its defences had passed out of use by the late-third century.

7. Much of the evidence for fourth-century occupation has been lost, but the discovery of a zone of high coin-loss immediately inside the minor W gate (*porta quintana sinistra*), interpreted as a fourth-century marketing area that flourished after the *vicus* had passed out of use in the late-third century, shows that some key fourth-century deposits survive. In general, fourth-century street surfaces survive even where the building plots have been truncated.

The 1997-8 excavations confirmed that Daniels' work had left much of the surviving stratigraphy within the fort intact, particularly the earlier levels. A swathe of the fort lies untouched by modern excavation beneath the highway of Buddle Street, which transects the site.

A section excavated by the Archaeological Practice in 2006 across the NW ditches of the fort revealed a third ditch, additional to those noted in Hodgson 2003, 18-21) and Roman stone building beyond the defences, that is to the *north* of the Great Wall, a phenomenon already noted in the case of a timber building outside the E gate in 1998.

On a folding spoon from Wallsend: Sherlock 2007.

N. Hodgson, TWM Archaeology

FROM WALLSEND TO NEWCASTLE

The Wall at Buddle Street, immediately west of Wallsend fort

(Fig. 13)

Previous work at this site on Buddle Street has been described in Bidwell 1999a, 95-7 and Bidwell 2005a, 64-5, figs 7-8 (the latter discussing the emplacements for obstacles on the berm at the E end of the site). Hadrian's Wall, which crosses the head of a small valley 110m W of Wallsend fort, has now been exposed over a distance of 83m; excavations since 1999 on the W part of the site have revealed a complicated sequence of repairs not matched anywhere else on the Wall. The several collapses of the Wall are explained by the unstable nature of the subsoil, which is a boulder clay overlying saturated deposit of sand. Especially unstable, of course, are the valley sides which prudent builders would have avoided, as the Roman army eventually found to its cost.

Rig and furrow preceding the building of the Wall has been found to its S near its W end. The Wall was built to Narrow gauge with a width of 2.35m. What is at present taken to be the original fabric stands to a height of six courses or 1.10m near the W end of the site. There is a single offset 0.10m in width above the foundations; the core of the Wall is of rubble with some clay and the facing stones are bonded throughout with stiff compact clay. From the lowest point in the valley for a distance of 9.6m eastwards the S side of the Wall had collapsed and had been entirely rebuilt. Its new footings consisted of two offset courses of facing stones, above which the wall was faced with large rectangular facing blocks with lewis holes and clamp sockets associated with their previous use. Amongst these reused blocks are half of a monolithic semi-circular windowhead and a dentillated cornice moulding; nearby was a block chamfered on two sides which was probably from the central pier dividing a double carriageway. The reused masonry probably came from one of the main gates of the fort, possibly the S gate (*porta decumana*) which was out of use in the third century. The date of the repair is uncertain although deposits probably not long subsequent to the repair have produced late third-century pottery.

A culvert was inserted through the Wall when its S face was rebuilt. It discharged into a deep gully which suggests that at least on occasions there was a considerable flow of water through the culvert. It is possible that this represents the water supply for the fort baths which lay in the valley SW of the fort. Perhaps at the same time that the Wall face was repaired, a cutting 1.8m in width was dug along the S face of the Wall W of the rebuilt section. It seems that originally the Wall was constructed in a deep trench so as to even out the steep descent from the crest of the slope eastwards. The cutting was

Figure 13. The Wall under excavation at Buddle Street, west of Wallsend fort, looking east

perhaps a precautionary measure intended to relieve lateral pressure on the base of the Wall.

Not long after the first repair, the S face of the Wall immediately to the E collapsed, or showed signs that it was about to give way. A new face 32m in length was built to project beyond the original Wall face. Reused in its fabric was part of a stone relief showing a hound, and architectural fragments probably from a demolished shrine. Two fragments of altars were found nearby, but no large blocks of the type used in the earlier repair. This second repair was the result of a minor landslip, presumably caused by the collapse of the side of the valley to the S. A fissure opened up along the centre of the Wall and its S half subsided by at least 0.3m and slid 0.8m to the S. Probably at the same time the N face of the Wall toppled inwards; its remains are lying at an angle of about 45 degrees and seem to have been used as the footings for a rebuild at a higher level. This was perhaps not the first collapse to have taken place on the N side, for the facing stones in the tilted Wall face are very different in character to what is taken to be the original stonework of the Wall at the W end of the site.

The later repair on the S side added a projecting face to the Wall which is comparable with the insets and outsets visible in the S face of the Wall W of Housesteads. The robber trench of a similar repair was seen at Denton on the western outskirts of Newcastle. Associated finds of pottery show that this later repair is certainly post-Severan, as was the repair at Denton.

The story of collapse continued. Both of the repaired faces on the S side of the Wall gave way. The collapse of the first repair using the large blocks sealed a sequence of activity which began with the filling of the gully and its replacement with a small stone-lined channel associated with a series of metalled surfaces, the last of which covered over the channel. The fallen blocks of the Wall face lay directly on this surface which probably belongs to the end of the Roman period. It is likely that the collapse of the second repair to the E happened at the same time, although this cannot be proved.

Further to the W the N face of the Wall also gave way. Its stump remains to a height of five courses and as far as can be seen represents the original Wall fabric, although it seems to have been rebuilt at a higher level. Its collapsed face included notched voussoirs probably from the vault of a bath-house and other voussoirs from door or window openings. Below the collapse were two layers of metalling which at the W end of the site sealed a series of small gullies.

Some further excavations are required, and once the necessary funding is obtained all the remains on the site will be consolidated for permanent display.

Paul Bidwell, TWM Archaeology

Work at Wallsend fort, the branch wall and Buddle Street has been funded principally by the Heritage Lottery Fund, European Regional Development Fund, Northumbrian Water Kick-Start Fund, National Heritage Arts Sponsorship Scheme, Bellway Urban Renewal and North Tyneside City Challenge.

'Wall-Mile 0': From Wallsend fort to Stott's Pow

The last Pilgrimage book stated that 'The course of the wall is lost from the top of Byker Hill, along Shields Road and across the Ouseburn valley to the top of Stepney Bank...' Thanks to the increased amount of developer-funded archaeology that has taken place since 1999, this situation is reversed. A combination of excavation and desktop assessment has established with certainty or probability the exact alignment of the Wall between Wallsend and Newcastle.

The course of the Wall between Wallsend and the Ouseburn as currently understood is summarised in the fourteenth edition of the *Handbook* (2006). The new edition of the handbook adopts the milecastle positions identified by MacLauchlan and subsequently F.G. Simpson. These were rejected by Birley in 1960 when the argument was put forward that the structure formerly identified as Turret 0b was the N gate of Milecastle 1. This revised arrangement was featured on the Ordnance Survey Map of Hadrian's Wall in 1964 and accepted in HB12 and HB13. In returning to the older view HB14 follows Hill 2001 and the earlier arguments of G. Simpson (1975), although not to the extent of taking up Hill's suggestion that Milecastle 3 might be on the *west* side of the Ouseburn. Until remains of a milecastle or turret are actually found there will always be uncertainty, but the scheme based on the MacLauchlan positions at least gives an even spacing of structures between Wallsend and the beginning of the E extension of the Wall at the Lort Burn, and is better supported by archaeological observation than the 1960 alternative.

'Wall-Mile 1': From Stott's Pow to Tunstall Avenue

The first accurately recorded sightings of the Wall curtain along the stretch where it is followed by the Fossway were made in 2004. The Wall was found to run 2-3m S of alignment usually adopted on modern OS maps. The newly fixed fragments also confirm that the Wall was probably surveyed in a dead straight alignment all the way from Wallsend fort to the summit of Byker Hill *Britannia* 36 (2005), 403.

'Wall-Mile 2': From Tunstall Avenue to the Ouseburn

At Union Road on the summit of Byker Hill a watching-brief in 2005 revealed

Figure 14. Wall (left), berm-obstacles (centre) and ditch (right) under excavation at south side of Shields Road, Byker in 2001

the S lip of the Wall ditch and three rows of pits for defensive obstacles on the berm which were arranged in the same pattern as those at 224-228 Shields Road. At this point the Wall made a very slight turn to the N to take up its alignment along Shields Road. On the berm the obstacles were running in to converge with the Wall, as they are believed to do at turrets (p. 26); the change of alignment may therefore have occurred at Turret 2b which was probably placed at the summit of the hill. A representation of the Wall laid out in recent times immediately E of the cycle shop in Union Road is in fact some 10m N of the actual line (*Britannia* 36 (2005), 403).

Excavations at 224-228 Shields Road in 2001 in advance of the construction of a square in front of the Byker Library revealed a 29m length of Hadrian's Wall set back 10m from the street frontage (Fig. 14). This was the first modern observation of the Wall in this area, fixing its line to the S of Shields Road and confirming the accuracy of Stukeley's depiction of both Wall and ditch lying wholly to the S of, and running parallel to, the turnpike road. Only the foundations survived: a fragment has been displayed in the public square. The Wall was of standard narrow gauge with foundations 2.4-2.5m in width, and the berm strikingly occupied by three rows of pits to accommodate obstacles, separated from the ditch by a low mound raised on its S lip. This excavation is fully published (McKelvey and Bidwell 2005). 425m W at 24-46 Shields Road, further work in 2002-6 revealed a further 31m length of the Wall on exactly the same alignment, showing that the Wall runs parallel to Shields Road all the way to the Ouseburn. Again the berm was taken up with emplacements for defensive obstacles ((*Britannia* 38 (2007), 260-61). Excavation of only a small number of the pits was permitted. They appear to have followed the arrangement at Melbourne Street, but were probably of more than one period.

'Milecastle 3' (Ouseburn)
For the position of Milecastle 3, Bidwell (2003) has restated the antiquarian evidence which places it on the E side of the Ouseburn.

'Wall-Mile 3'
The Wall has not been seen in modern times in the Ouseburn valley, or in the vicinity of Stepney bank on the W side of the burn, but antiquarian sources beginning with Mackenzie (1827) specifically state that the Wall crossed the Ouseburn via the site of Beckington's steam-mill. This can be identified by comparing Oliver's map of 1830 and the first edition OS, and confirms that the Shield road alignment must have been followed at least to the burn crossing (Stobbs 2007). A single change of alignment on the W side of the burn at the bottom of Stepney bank (which probably follows the Wall ditch) would then

have brought the Wall to its next known point, at Crawhall Road.

Newcastle upon Tyne: Melbourne Street

Excavation at Melbourne Street in spring 2004 revealed a 13m section of Narrow Wall foundation, 2.4-2.5m wide. No facing stones survived above the foundation. This fragment was preserved because it lay in a shallow valley, where the depth of overburden deterred stone robbers. To E and W an intermittent robber trench marked the Wall line; the ditch survived across the full width of the site.

Three rows of oval pits for obstacles were found on the berm. Like the masonry, these only survived in the valley. All three rows ran parallel to the wall, with the middle row being offset. Most were filled with very stony silts; a couple contained possible post settings, though the evidence for this was unclear.

The valley was partly filled, with clay to the N and stone to the S of the Wall; there was no culvert. Since the valley was thus blocked, it appears that the stream was diverted into the Wall ditch. This is confirmed by early maps, which show the headwaters running S, then W along the line of the ditch, before turning S towards the Tyne. The Wall masonry was left in place and has been avoided by the piles of the hotel that now occupies the site; a panel describing the remains is being prepared. Work was supervised by Andy Platell.

Richard Annis, Archaeological Services Durham University

NEWCASTLE UPON TYNE – *Pons Aelius* (Fig. 15)

Excavations by the Tyne and Wear County Archaeology Section, the Newcastle City Archaeaology Unit, and Tyne and Wear Museums, spanning a period of twenty years from 1976, were prepared for publication by the last-named organisation (Snape and Bidwell 2002; Bidwell and Snape 2002). Four particular points of general interest were discussed in the report. First, the position and history of the fort add further weight to the suggestion that the medieval road running N from Newcastle (more recently, the Great North Road) had a Roman predecessor which joined the Devil's Causeway about 20km N of the Tyne crossing. Secondly, the construction date of the fort in the late second or early third century sets it amongst the very small number of completely new forts of comparable date which are known from the NW frontier provinces. The most reasonable estimate of its size suggests that it had an area within its walls of 0.64ha or 1.53 acres; the granaries and *principia* are of correspondingly small size. This will have been the result of reductions in the size of auxiliary units indicated primarily by earlier third-century barrack plans at other Wall-forts (cf. p. 33). There is no need to suppose that part of the first unit at the fort (presumably the *cohors I Cugernorum* mentioned in an inscription of 213) was detached for duty elsewhere.

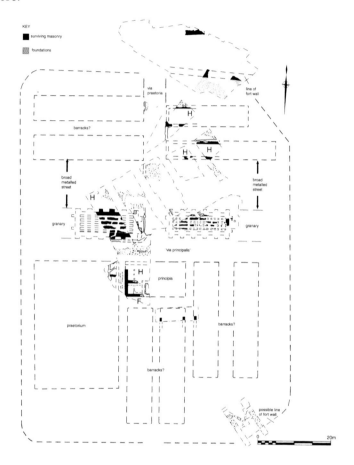

Figure 15. Known anatomy and conjectural reconstruction of plan of Newcastle fort

The plan of the fort is not fully understood but it seems to reflect the changes seen in the type of later-Roman, cruciform plan that occurs at South Shields. At Newcastle the exceptionally wide cross-street, bisecting the *via praetoria*, separates the granaries from what appear to be barracks to the N. The streets in front of the *principia* were probably isolated from the main areas of the fort and reserved for military ceremonials. In the fourth century a change of use is suggested by intensive coin loss concentrated on the *via praetoria*

and the area in front of the *principia*. The distribution of the coins has been taken to represent casual loss in the course of market-trading which lasted until the third quarter of the fourth century. There are signs that this part of the fort was subsequently restored to conventional military use. There is a clear Anglo-Saxon horizon at the Newcastle fort, lacking at every other fort in the Wall-system, when a cemetery was established on the site in the earlier eighth century; it was probably attached to a minster, as yet undiscovered. A forthcoming report on the cemetery is expected to shed further light on the fragmentary evidence for post-Roman and pre-cemetery activities.
Paul Bidwell, TWM Archaeology

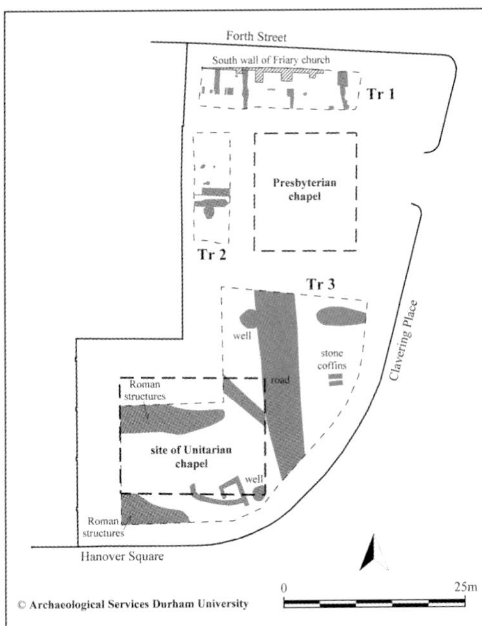

Figure 16. Bemco site, Clavering Place

Newcastle upon Tyne: BEMCO site, Clavering Place (Fig. 16)
Excavations were carried out at the former BEMCO building, Newcastle upon Tyne, between May 2008 and March 2009. The site is just S of the railway at the E end of Central Station, and is bounded by Forth Street, Clavering Place and Hanover Square. Following demolition of all buildings on the site except of the listed Presbyterian chapel, three areas were examined (Fig. 16).

85

The excavated evidence shows that there has been human activity at the site, at various times, since the Mesolithic period. Most finds date from the Roman, high medieval and modern periods, with little evidence of occupation before 140AD, or in the 5th-11th centuries AD. This area appears to have at one time been part of the *vicus*, but it seems that this part of the settlement was abandoned and the area was used for burials. No evidence of occupation in the early medieval period was found. A Carmelite friary was established here in 1262. This was investigated by Barbara Harbottle in the mid-1960s (Harbottle 1968).

The largest single feature was a fairly narrow Roman road running roughly N-S across the site to the S of the chapel, in Trench 3. This was flanked by broad, deep ditches and had been re-surfaced on at least two occasions. The basement of the Presbyterian chapel has destroyed the road, but the paved surface was not seen N or E of the chapel in Trenches 1 and 2. It must be assumed that the road turns E, towards the fort's W gate. Southwards, it heads directly towards the Tyne. It is possible that its route turns to the W: coins, roof tiles and two altars were found close to the Whitefriar tower on the town wall, SW of the excavation site, in 1843 (White 1861). It has been suggested that this line might allow for an easier ascent from the Roman bridge over the Tyne, avoiding the steep slope below the fort's S wall.

Occupation evidence was seen at the SW corner of the site, where a sequence of small stone structures and drains was uncovered. At depth, the clay subsoil permitted good waterlogged preservation. The chief features of this kind were two timber-lined wells found on the W side of the road. The N of these was lined with massive oak timbers that had been cut to a curve; other timbers were large second-hand boards. On the E side of the road, two massive sandstone sarcophagi lay in a large rectangular pit. They were aligned E-W, at right angles to the road. The pit extended further N but had been disturbed by modern intrusions. The sarcophagi were set at a height that would have left their lids above ground when the road was in use.

The coffins are made of point-dressed stone with drafted margins, but no smoothed surfaces or inscriptions. The S coffin is notably more even and symmetrical than the N one, and its floor has a shallow slope like a pillow at the head end. Each coffin has a coped lid fixed in place with four iron pins. Traces of an *opus signinum* seal were found on both, but this failed long ago and the coffins were filled with water. Despite this, the iron pins of the S coffin were intact and in good condition. Preservation of bone was very poor, apart from some molar crowns. The S coffin contained the skeleton of a woman in middle years; a jet hairpin with a faceted head and over 100 small circular jet beads were recovered from the coffin fill. Lead splashes from the sealing of the lid were found, together with a tiny piece of decorated lead with a filigree appearance. The N coffin contained the remains of a child of about six years of age, with (perhaps) another individual as well; some mineralised textile was also recovered. The lid of this sarcophagus was no longer fixed in place, so a secondary burial is a possibility, despite the obstacle of the great size and weight of the coffin lid. Close to the stone coffins, on the same side of the road, were three cremations in pots, buried in small pits. A fourth similar pit was found W of the road; here, a grey-ware vessel was covered with a similar inverted pot as a lid, but this contained no bone.The discovery of these burials is significant, as it confirms the suggestion that this is the site of a cemetery. Two stone coffins were found on the opposite side of Clavering Place in 1903 (Rich 1903); these were aligned N-S. Harbottle's excavations in the 1960s also produced funerary pottery a short distance N of the Trench 3 coffins.

Elsewhere the Roman features are more ephemeral. In Trench 1, on Forth Street, a series of ditches and gullies, generally aligned N-S, underlay the S wall of the Friary church and contemporary burials. To the W, in Trench 2, similar features were found.The finds assemblage is not large, but it is dominated by Roman material. It reflects both domestic and funerary activity, and includes a German lava quern, a small millefiori glass bowl, a handful of pottery counters and ten coins. Wood and leather were recovered from the fills of the wells.

The excavations were undertaken by Archaeological Services Durham University on behalf of the site's owners, Buccleuch Estates. The work was supervised by Matt Claydon; post-excavation assessment was under way as this article went to press.

Richard Annis, Archaeological Services Durham University

Since the above contribution was received assessment of the 47kg of coarse pottery from the Clavering Place site has confirmed that the main period of activity there was in the first half of the third century, with a possibility of later second century commencement and no occupation at all after *c.* 270.

GATESHEAD
Bottle Bank and 18-24 High Street, Gateshead (Fig. 17)

From January to April 2000, excavations were undertaken at Bottle Bank, Gateshead (NZ 2535 6355), by the Lancaster University Archaeological Unit (LUAU, now OA North), prior to redevelopment. Subsequently, a smaller investigation was carried out by OA North at 18-24 High Street, adjacent to the eastern edge of the Bottle Bank site, in January 2003. The work revealed evidence for Roman settlement on the plateau above the southern bridgehead of the River Tyne, directly opposite the fort at Newcastle.

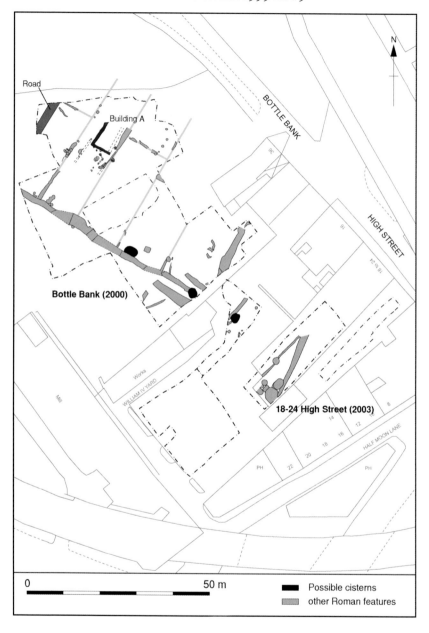

Figure 17. Roman settlement at Bottle Bank, Gateshead

Well over 3,000 sherds of Roman pottery were recovered from the two sites. At both, the diagnostic material was overwhelmingly of late second-third-century date. A very small amount of early second-century pottery (representing little more than 1% of the Bottle Bank assemblage, by weight) was present, but most of this was residual in demonstrably later contexts. On present evidence, therefore, it seems that the site may have formed part of a bridgehead settlement contemporary with the Newcastle fort, and was not related to any putative early fort at Gateshead. Small quantities of late third-fourth-century material were also recovered, including a single sherd of late fourth-century East Yorkshire calcite-gritted ware. The amount of samian was extremely low, at only 21 sherds in total, but Dressel 20 amphorae accounted for over 30% (by weight) of the Bottle Bank assemblage.

The earliest activity was represented by a few features that could not be closely dated, though some at least appear to have been Roman rather than earlier. Subsequently, most of the excavated area was subdivided into a number of NE-SW orientated rectangular plots, in excess of 30m long, defined by a rectilinear system of shallow ditches and gullies (Fig. 17). These may possibly have fronted a Roman road in the vicinity of modern Bottle Bank/High Street, leading down towards the southern bridgehead. Although individual ditches were frequently recut, sometimes on several occasions, the basic layout appears to have been retained throughout the settlement's existence. The two most northerly plots were seemingly c. 9m wide, but the others appear to have been somewhat wider, at approximately 13m. Evidence for occupation within them was fairly scant, however. There was some evidence, in the form of ditches aligned perpendicular to the plot boundaries, that the two most northerly plots at least had been subdivided laterally. In the southernmost of these, a possible second-century timber structure was replaced during the third century by a rectangular stone (or stone-footed) building (Building A), aligned NE to SW. This had unmortared rubble foundations faced with roughly squared stone blocks. It may have been c. 5.5m wide, externally, and was at least 7.4m long, but its N and E walls had been destroyed.

Also during the third century, a probable road at least 3.1m wide, with a stone-lined and stone-capped drain running roughly down its central axis, was laid out, running along the NW boundary of the most northerly excavated plot, c. 13m NW of the broadly contemporary stone building. Elsewhere, a few second/third-century stone-lined pits, possibly cisterns, were excavated, together with a number of unlined pits, postholes and at least one possible well. Fourth-century activity was evidenced only by the small number of pottery sherds. Most were residual in post-Roman contexts, but a few were stratified in the fill of one of the putative cisterns.

John Zant, Oxford Archaeology North

The original Eastern end of the Wall

For discussion of where the Wall may have originally terminated in Newcastle (which presupposes that the wall between the Lort burn and Wallsend was a later extension), see: Bidwell and Snape 2002, 260-2; cf. Bidwell 2003.

130m W of the Castle Keep the Wall was found in a test-pit in 2004, 1.7m below present ground level, in the former Hertz building on the N side of Westgate Road. The full width of the Wall was not seen but the 100mm thick flagged foundation and method of construction were of Broad Wall type. This is the easternmost sighting of the Broad Wall. It represents a continuation of the alignment recorded in front of the Mining institute, where the S face of the Broad Wall was found in 1952 (*Britannia* 36 (2005), 404).

Directly across the road from here, evaluation trenching in 2007 by North Pennines Archaeology within the former railway parcels office on Westgate Road, i.e. roughly 20-30m S of the Wall, confirmed the presence of Roman structural remains and recovered pottery of second to third century date.

See Macpherson and Bidwell 2001 for a probable slight southward change of alignment at the Westgate Road milecastle and for evidence that the Wall and ditch lay on the S side of the road as it ascended Westgate Hill. In the same area there was no sign of the Vallum, supporting the idea that it ran straight down to the Tyne from the top of Westgate Hill.

BENWELL – *Condercum*

Various watching-briefs in the area of the fort in recent years have shown that extensive remains of the fort are extant, often at a depth of only 400mm below modern ground level. Work by TWM Archaeology in 2005 contacted a solid flagged floor founded on pitched sandstone in the W granary, confirming that the S division of both granaries was floored in this way rather than being supplied with a raised floor (*Britannia* 37 (2006), 390-1).

On a silver spoon from Benwell fort: Sherlock 1999. On the rediscovery of RIB 1352 in the temple of Antenociticus: Wilson 2003a.

In 2003 trenching by TWM Archaeology found the Military Way in the grounds of Pendower Hall, 170m W of Benwell fort, 7.76m wide and 40m S of the West Road frontage, and therefore some 45-50m S of the Wall, which lies under the road. The Military Way was intact only 400mm beneath the modern ground surface. Three parallel rock-cut ditches ran along its S side. Between the Military Way and the Wall were two lesser metalled tracks, one 14m S of the frontage and 2.28m wide, the other 30m S of the frontage and 2.30m wide (*Britannia* 35 (2004), 272).

Further W of Benwell fort, opposite the crematorium, a fragment of the

Wall (of Broad constructional type) was seen in 2002 under the S carriageway of the road (*Britannia* 34 (2003), 310).

Milecastle 9 (Chapel House) (Fig. 18)

In 2000, a 'T' shaped trench was excavated in the SE corner of the milecastle. It was built on banded strata, representing pre-Roman occupation, and a double row of post-holes found by Birley (1930) may relate to such occupation. The walls (Birley 1930), like the Broad Wall here, were 3.1m wide. A stone building occupied the E side of the interior. A ditch, parallel to the walls and contemporary with their construction lay 4.54m to the E, and may have been part of a ditched enclosure around the milecastle. A previous trench

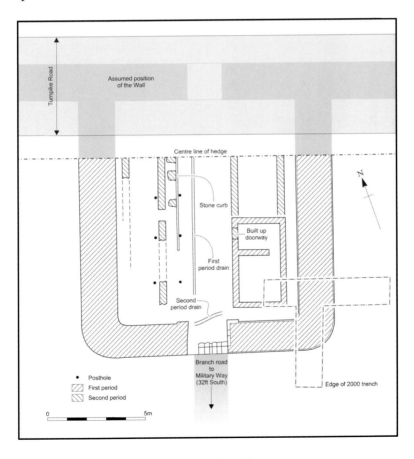

Figure 18. Milecastle 9

cut due S from the milecastle may have run through the entrance to such an enclosure (Wilmott 2009b, 144-52).
Tony Wilmott, English Heritage

Wall-Mile 9: Walbottle Campus
A trench by TWM Archaeology in the N carriageway of Military Road at the entrance to Walbottle Campus found the N face and part of the core of the Wall, standing three courses high. The face was mortar-bonded with a single offset course and a foundation of sandstone slabs and a core of clay and rubble – standard Broad Wall construction. The berm was inaccessible but 3.60m N of the Wall a bank, 2m wide and surviving to its complete original height of 0.60m, had been formed on the S lip of the wall ditch. This is similar to a bank at Byker, associated with obstacles on the berm (*Britannia* 37 (2006), 391).

Observation of Military Way at Walbottle Primary School: Archaeological Practice 2005.

Milecastle 10 (Walbottle Dene) (Fig. 19)
Two trenches excavated in 1999 confirmed that this milecastle, like Milecastle 9, was built with broad walls. These have been severely robbed, leaving only a single course. The milecastle measured 17.68m N-S by 14.76m E-W internally, and a large oven was found in the SE corner. Peter Hill's analytical study of the surviving stonework of the N gate shows differing standards of work and the possibility that this site witnessed a hiatus in construction followed by a resumption of work to a different standard (Wilmott 2009b, 152-59).
Tony Wilmott, English Heritage

Wall-Miles 10 and 11: Throckley to Heddon
A watching-brief in 2001-2 by TWM Archaeology on the renewal of a 2.2km length of water-main along the carriageway of the B6528 encountered a remarkable arrangement of obstacle-emplacement pits on the berm between Hadrian's Wall and the Ditch, similar to those found at Byker. The importance of these emplacements at Throckley is the confirmation that such defences were extensively provided rather than being localised features. In total 145 post-pits were identified over a distance of over 1km. There were many variations in dimension and alignment, but a typical row of pits consisted of rectangular slots 0.8m long, 0.4m wide and 0.5m deep, spaced at intervals of 0.5m between the narrow ends. Some of these long pits retained impressions of two uprights, square or sub-oval, some 200mm in diameter, one at each end of the emplacement. As at Byker, more than one phase of cutting was

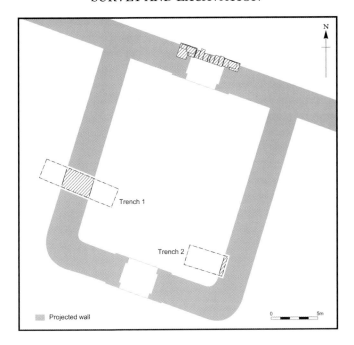

Figure 19. Milecastle 10

evident, so the obstacles must have been reconstituted at some time. In addition Hadrian's Wall itself was encountered at two points, fixing its line through Throckley and indicating that well-preserved stretches of the Wall survive beneath the B6528. A concentration of pottery of late-second to third-century date was probably discarded from Turret 11b, and at this point there was evidence that both the Ditch and the berm-obstacles had curved in towards the turret, although the ditch had been recut on an alignment parallel to the Wall at a later date, probably following the demolition of the turret. A N-S metalled surface of two levels may represent a road, probably of medieval origin, leading N of the Wall from Milecastle 11. This lay 50m W of the OS map position of this unlocated milecastle. These observations have been fully published: Frain *et al.* 2005.

Observations of the Military Way, with a surface of compact rubble and rough, sandstone kerbstones averaging about 0.4m in length and 0.23m wide, at Prospect House and Throckley Filling Station: Archaeological Practice 2006; 2007.

Wall-Mile 12 (Heddon on the Wall)

Heddon on the Wall
Monitoring and evaluation work was carried out in advance of development near the old police station on Hexham Road, at the W end of the village, in 2007-8. The N face of the Wall was seen under the road, and a small section of the Vallum was recorded. Its ditch was not bottomed, but a number of fills, including material introduced to level the ground, were recorded. Environmental evidence suggests that large-scale food-processing took place here in the tenth and eleventh centuries; there is a medieval kiln suitable for this kind of activity built into the Wall E of the village.
Richard Annis, Archaeological Services Durham University

RUDCHESTER – *Vindovala*
There has been no recent fieldwork. For discussion of the place name: A. Breeze 2002.

Milecastle 14 (March Burn)
In 2000, two evaluation trenches showed this to be the only example of a short-axis Broad Wall milecastle yet identified. This joins a small group of milecastles whose walls are all Broad Wall gauge (Symonds 2005). To E and W, Milecastles 13 and 17 have narrow side walls. It is probable that Milecastle 14 was one of Symonds' group of Broad Wall structures constructed at an early stage to protect potential weak points, in this case the steep defile of the March Burn valley. The site is almost totally robbed, but evidence for a stone building in the W side of the milecastle was recorded (Wilmott 2009b, 152-64).
Tony Wilmott, English Heritage

Milecastle 17 (Welton)
Two trenches excavated on the visible platform of the milecastle in 1999 showed that it had become deeply buried in colluvium. There was some small evidence for activity outside the walls in the form of a couple of cut features. Strata encountered within the milecastle were mostly post-Roman and included the walls of a medieval or post-medieval structure, possibly a field barn (Wilmott 2009b, 164-67).
Tony Wilmott, English Heritage

Wall-Mile 18 (West Deneside)
The profile of the Wall ditch and the counterscarp bank at West Deneside was surveyed in 2000 (LUAU 2000). The ditch is known to have an average

depth of 2.85m at this location, whilst the counterscarp bank survives to a maximum height of 0.9m. The survey concluded that the visible ditch was nearly 13m wide from the top break of slope on the S side to the crest of the counterscarp bank on the N. The surveyed profiles also demonstrated that the extant earthwork has a wide, U-shaped profile with an angle of slope of approximately 28° from the horizontal.

Ian Miller, Oxford Archaeology North

Milecastle 19 (Matfen Piers)
This was known to be a long-axis Narrow Wall milecastle before the excavation of two trenches in 1999 (Birley, E.B. *et al.* 1932, 1933, Simpson *et al.* 1936). Evaluation showed the site to have been heavily robbed and badly plough damaged. New detail on the interior layout was recovered. A cobbled surface occupied the W side, while on the E side one wall of a stone building with associated floor surfaces was recorded (Wilmott 2009b, 167-70).

Tony Wilmott, English Heritage

HALTON CHESTERS – *Onnum*
The major event here is the publication of the excavations carried out by J.P. Gillam in 1960-61 (Dore 2009). The excavations concentrated on the SW part of the fort, including the Hadrianic granary and a large building complex immediately to the W which displayed two principal phases, the first being destroyed by fire in the later-second or early-third century. Of particular interest are a description and assessment of the destruction deposit that has figured prominently in writing on the history of the Wall. Dore cautiously accepts that what was recorded represents a destructive fire affecting an extensive area of the fort, and concludes that although certainty is impossible, there is nothing to disprove contemporaneity with the nearby Corbridge destruction deposit. The later-Roman sequence is reassessed, convincingly dispensing with the idea of abandonment between 270 and 370 (see p. 36).

For the full publication of the geophysical survey of the fort *vicus* illustrated in the last Pilgrimage handbook, see Taylor *et al.* 2000.

Hodgson (2003, 119-20; cf. Hodgson and Bidwell 2004, 150-53) shows how the plan of the 'stables' recorded by Richmond in the *praetentura* can be restored to give a pair of third-century stable-barracks, arranged back to back 6 or 7 *contubernia* apiece (Fig. 20).

A narrow service trench excavated by TWM Archaeology in 1999 contacted stone strip buildings lining the road running S from the S gate at a distance of 240-260m from the fort, far beyond the limit of the stone structures evident

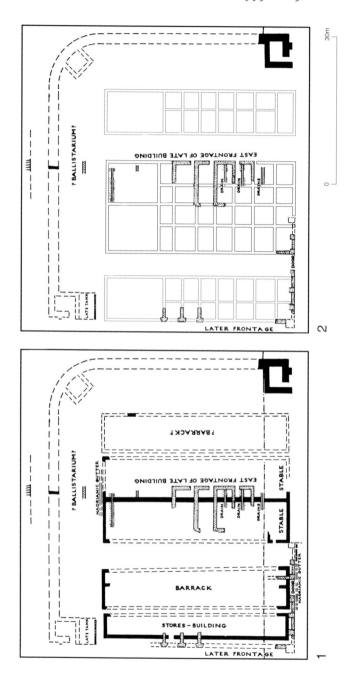

Figure 20. Plan of 'stables' at Halton Chesters after Simpson and Richmond 1937. 2. Restored as back-to-back stable-barracks

on the geophysical survey published in 2000. The excavation also showed that rather than veering to the E in this area, the Roman road continues to curve gently to the SW, crossing the line of the modern road on a course completely obscured by rig-and-furrow on the geophysical plot. The SW course suggests that the road branched from Dere Street somewhere between Corbridge and the Wall. All of the pottery recovered was of mid-second to mid-third century date.

Milecastle 22 (Halton Shields)
Evaluation in 2000- 2001 revealed 1-2 courses of Wall curtain just W of the site of Milecastle 20. The Wall was 3.15m wide overall with a narrow offset (*c.* 30-60mm) on the N side. The Wall core was of clay and stone. A space some 14m wide separated the S face of the Wall from the gully marking the N edge of the Military Way, which was surfaced with substantial stone slabs.
Alan Rushworth, the Archaeological Practice

Wall-Mile 22
Britannia 31 (2000), 436: a watching brief in 1999 on a service trench on the S side of the Military Road 500m W of Portgate found a buff sandstone building stone inscribed: COH VIII 7 HELLENI: 'Of the 8th Cohort, the century of Hellenius (built this).'

Milecastle 23
Publication of 1952 excavation of the Vallum causeway S of the milecastle: Heywood and Breeze 2008. Cf. p.28.

CORBRIDGE – *Coria* (Fig. 21)
Apart from watching briefs, which have not added materially to our knowledge, there has been no new excavation at Corbridge main site.

A joint project between Tyne and Wear Museums and English Heritage, carried out with funding from the North East Regional Museums Hub, has undertaken a survey and study of the large group of architectural fragments, found with many fragments of religious sculpture in excavations before the First World War and now stored at Matfen. These were mostly reused in a fourth-century resurfacing of the main 'Stanegate' road running through the centre of the Roman town. Close examination of the architectural fragments and the way they fitted together has allowed the appearance of buildings from which they came to be reconstructed. The collection includes a large number of decorated cornice fragments. These fall into a number of groups representing different buildings. A series of pedimented classical temples is undoubtedly represented. A number of column shafts, bases and foliate capitals in the collection are of the right order of size to be from the same buildings. The fragments can be used to reconstruct one of the temple facades in some detail. Long known at Corbridge is a series of stone slabs or panels carrying a repeated decorative motif shaped like the letter 'S' (Fig. 22). The motif is known elsewhere in the empire, most commonly run along the top of the raking cornice of pediments. At 350mm in height the Corbridge examples will have formed a bold decorative crest, certainly on the raking cornice of a full-sized pediment. From the proportions of the stones such a temple would

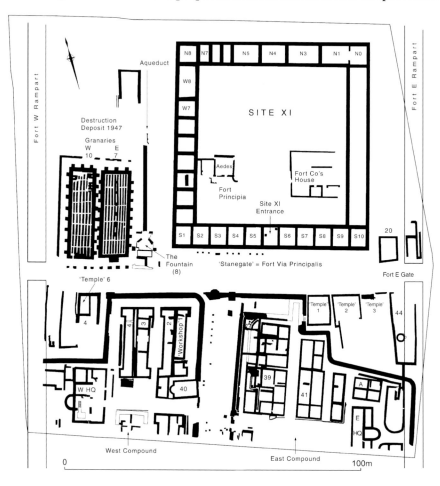

Figure 21. Corbridge: the central area with E and W ramparts of earlier fort indicated

Figure 22. Corbridge: architectural fragments from pediment

have had a facade around 6m wide (Fig. 23). Found with the architectural fragments was an inscription (RIB 1137), certainly from a temple, dedicated by the Sixth Legion to Sol Invictus under Calpurnius Agricola, governor in the mid-160s. It seems reasonable to group this stone with the architectural and sculptural fragments found with it and to suggest they came from a common source – a legionary sanctuary, which must have been in existence by the 160s and can be associated with the conversion of Corbridge to a base for legionary detachments at that time. The sanctuary in question is not to be identified with the buildings at Corbridge which Richmond identified as temples. These cannot be as early as the 160s and are better interpreted as third-century stores or shops. The sanctuary that provided the source of the architectural fragments probably lay outside the central area of the site at Corbridge. A second group of fragments can be associated, with less certainty, with the well-known fountain whose remains can still be seen. The survey and study of the Corbridge architectural fragments will be published as Hodgson forthcoming.

A by-product of this research, in order to understand the historical context of the postulated sanctuary, was a study of the development after c. 160 of Corbridge from a fort to a legionary detachment base (Hodgson 2008a). As well as discussing the date and character of the second- and third-century legionary bases at Corbridge, this paper revisits the problem of the date and function of the great courtyard building, Site XI, concluding that it was for the storage and marketing of goods, as well as the question of the date and

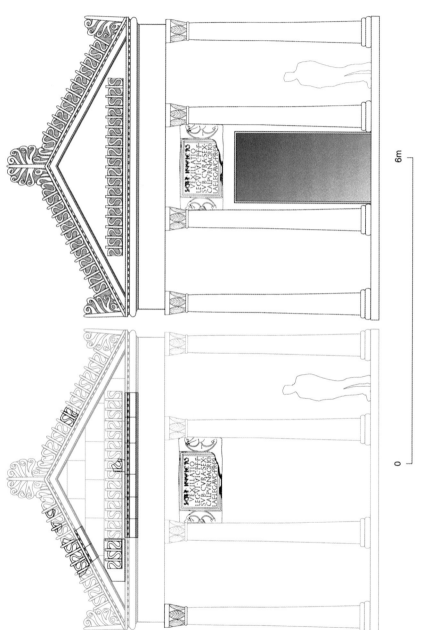

Figure 23. Corbridge: 1. extant architectural fragments from one of the temple facades 2. Reconstruction of the same temple facade

significance of the 'Corbridge destruction deposit' (see p. 31-2).
N. Hodgson, TWM Archaeology

For a controversy over the Roman name of Corbridge, see A. Breeze 2001;
Hodgson 2002b; A. Breeze 2004; Hodgson 2005b.

IX legion tile stamp formerly attributed to Corbridge, but really from Carlisle:
Bishop 2007.

THE ROMAN BRIDGE AT CORBRIDGE (Fig. 24)

In prehistoric times the River Tyne flowed to the S of its present course
across what are now the Dilston Haughs. By the beginning of the Roman
period it had moved further N and its line has continued to change in more
recent centuries. The southern part of the Roman bridge still lies on the river
bed, but gradual erosion was threatening to destroy the road ramp which was
preserved in the river bank. Expert opinion was that the only way to save these
important remains was by recording them in detail and then dismantling the
stonework and re-assembling it on a site nearby where it would be safe from
erosion. The road ramp was excavated in 2004 (Fig. 25). Over 300 blocks,
some of them weighing more than a tonne, were removed and have now been
re-assembled a short distance from the present river bank. The result is an
impressive mass of masonry standing to a height of more than 3.5m. The
project was made possible by funding from the Heritage Lottery Fund, Tyne
and Wear Museums and English Heritage.

  The Roman bridge consisted of perhaps as many as eleven stone arches
and stood to a height of perhaps as much as 9m above the river. The road
ramp was built to take Dere Street up to the level of the carriageway across
the bridge by means of a gentle gradient. The road, which appears on recent
aerial photographs of Dilston Haughs, approached the bridge at right angles
from the E. The N side of the ramp was formed by a massive wall along
the river bank, which also served to protect the S abutment of the bridge
from erosion. It is this wall which has been dismantled and re-assembled.
The stone blocks which form the wall are an excellent example of *opus
quadratum*, a Roman technique of construction used for major engineering
works. The blocks were fitted together with very narrow joints and without
the use of mortar. To save time and effort, the centres of the faces were cut
back roughly leaving raised bands around the edges which were carefully
worked to a flat surface (band anathyrosis). The visible faces show decorative
finishes, often consisting of feathering (curved lines of tooling arranged in
intersecting zones). The blocks also have sockets for dowels and iron clamps
set in lead. Some of their upper surfaces have lewis-holes for the insertion of

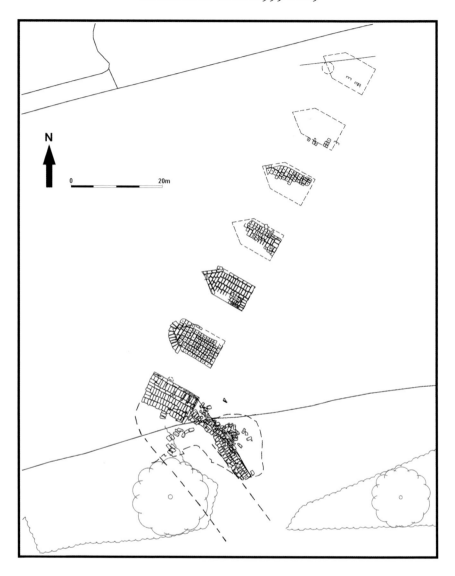

Figure 24. Plan of Roman bridge at Corbridge

lifting devices, showing that cranes were used in the building of the bridge, and slots to take the ends of the crowbars which were used to lever the blocks into position.

The road ramp had been entirely rebuilt during the Roman period, probably following a flood which had not only destroyed the original ramp but also part of the bridge. All the blocks in the revetting wall were reused, and they included elements which were probably from the pointed end of a bridge pier and architectural fragments from the carriageway. The latter included cornice blocks with mouldings similar but not identical to those from the bridge at Chesters. There was also a square-sectioned upright with a cushion-like cap which on analogy with the superstructure of other bridges would have been set in the parapet; lead dowels in two opposite sides of the upright would have joined it to the vertical slabs which formed the main part of the parapet. These slabs and uprights were set in grooves cut in the top of the cornice blocks, although some have sockets for wooden posts rather than grooves. The details of the parapet are very close to those at Chesters and reinforce previous arguments, depending on the identical techniques of construction, that the bridge at Corbridge and the road-bridge at Chesters were built at the same time, perhaps by the same team of masons or under the direction of the same architect. The bridge at Chesters is now known to be of mid-Antonine date (Bidwell 1999a, 120).

Nothing was found to indicate where the river crossing was before the building of the mid-Antonine bridge. There was also nothing to date the rebuilding of the road ramp, although the original external faces of the reused masonry were fresh and unweathered which suggests that it took place no more than a few decades after the bridge was completed. A most unusual find was a large octagonal capstone, now displayed in the Corbridge Roman Site Museum. It was heavily weathered and, to judge from its findspot, had been part of the superstructure of the ramp. It had sat on top of an octagonal shaft and may have been part of an itinerary stone which listed on its faces the names of the places and their distances along each of the roads which radiated out from the bridge. Stones of this type are known from Tongres in Gallia Belgica and from Junglinster, on the road from Trier to Rheims. They belong to a wider class of itinerary inscriptions on marble, stone or fired clay, not otherwise known in Britain.

The work on the S side of the river produced no evidence for the date at which the bridge went out of use. A mortared wall seen in a watching brief SE of the ramp now seems to have been part of a post-medieval strengthening of the river bank rather than a secondary ramp of late-Roman date as claimed in previous interim publications. However, an important excavation on the N side of the river by R.P. Wright (1941) in 1938-9 has been overlooked in subsequent discussions of the bridge. He examined the abutment of a small bridge over the Cor Burn just to the W of the river bridge. It sealed what seems to have been a small lime kiln which contained a piece of Crambeck

Figure 25. The S road ramp of the Roman bridge at Corbridge, under excavation in 2004

parchment ware no earlier than *c.* 370. The bridge was probably built following the re-routing of the Stanegate to the N when its original line along the bank to the N end of the river bridge had been destroyed by flooding. In the last quarter of the fourth century resources were thus still being expended on keeping the main routes open, and presumably the river bridge was still being maintained. For the post-Roman robbing of the bridge, see the section on Hexham Abbey.

The reused Roman stonework in the Anglo-Saxon crypt at Hexham Abbey (Fig. 26)

Part of the Corbridge Roman Bridge project included a survey of the Hexham crypt which was intended to identify the sources of the reused Roman stonework in its fabric. The crypt was built by Wilfrid in the 670s as part of the church of St Andrew. Many of the blocks were identical in their range of sizes and the details of their often very elaborate tooling with those examined at Corbridge. However, it seems that the whole church, and not just the crypt, was built with reused Roman blocks. A quantity survey has shown that it was most unlikely that the bridge would have supplied a sufficient number of blocks: although it was an enormous structure, much of the fabric of the bridge remains on its original site, either *in situ* or scattered across the bed of the river, and other parts of it were removed in the earlier nineteenth century. The other main source of reused stone was almost certainly the E abutment and road ramp of the bridge at Chesters, which underwent the same systematic robbing as the revetting wall of the road ramp at Corbridge.

In addition to the two bridges, another structure was demolished to provide materials for the Hexham church. It is represented by sections of fluted pilasters which would have had a height, including their bases and capitals, of 5.6m (19 Roman feet); by four different but stylistically similar decorative friezes with various combinations of leaf-and-berry ornament, dentils, and cable and bead-and-reel motifs; and by a number of undecorated blocks with smooth, rubbed faces from ashlar masonry of the highest quality. The only structure known at Corbridge which could have been the source of these architectural fragments is the Shorden Brae mausoleum, originally situated near the N bank of the Tyne (now flowing much further to the S), 700m W of the Corbridge main site. The monument consists of the foundation of a tower-tomb, *c.* 10m square, set in a precinct *c.* 40m square which was enclosed by a wall set on a massive foundation. It is now apparent, following reinterpretation of the surviving stonework and original report published in 1961 by Gillam and Daniels, that the precinct wall took the form of a massive stone screen decorated with stone pilasters of exactly the same size as those reused at Hexham, although their shafts are plain rather than fluted. The

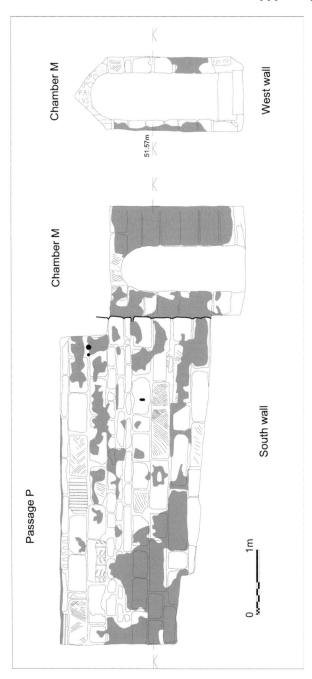

Figure 26. Sample Elevation of crypt at Hexham, as surveyed in 2004-5, showing re-used Roman masonry and inscription

style of the friezes suggests that the monument is of Antonine date. It is of exceptionally large size; whether it was erected to commemorate some high official of the empire or served as a cenotaph cannot be determined.
Paul Bidwell, TWM Archaeology

Snape (2003) has demonstrated that the conspicuous structure of timber and Roman stones visible when the water is low on the N side of the river, downstream from the N abutment, is not Roman but the remains of a rare horizontal-wheeled watermill of Anglo-Saxon date, making extensive re-use of blocks from the Roman bridge.

Turret 26b (Brunton)

The Pilgrimage of 2009 will visit this well-known monument with an additional objective. Paul Bidwell has shown (2005a; cf. p. 26) that there is evidence that the Wall ditch converged with the Wall at the sites of turrets, the extra-wide berm that accommodated obstacles narrowing at these points and the obstacles themselves being omitted immediately in front of the turret. This phenomenon is not usually to be seen on the ground, because in later times the Wall-ditch seems to have been recut on an alignment parallel with Wall. At Turret 26b, however, it is possible that an apparent inward curve of the ditch is a remnant of the original arrangement. No systematic study of the ditch here has ever been undertaken.

Wall-Mile 26

Where the A6079 crosses the Wall at Brunton, excavation by TWM Archaeology in the road in advance of water-main insertion found the Vallum ditch, 70m from the Wall, the Military Way (7.5-9m wide) immediately N of where the Vallum N mound would have been and some 45m from the line of the Wall (TWM Archaeology 2007).

Chesters bridge

There has been no further work on the site since 1991, but progress has been made in understanding some of the details of its construction. Metallurgical analysis (unpublished) by Mr Ted Morgan has shown that the tie-bars are of pure lead; it was thought that the lead might have been alloyed with tin to improve its tensile strength. The sequence of robbing has also been reassessed in connection with the Hexham and Corbridge studies. The demolition of the E abutment and road ramp was almost certainly undertaken to obtain stone for Hexham. Demolition of the superstructure of the bridge and perhaps the arches might have been carried out earlier, its purpose not to obtain stone but to recover lead and iron from the fabric. It can be calculated that 7 or 8

tonnes of lead were used for the tie-bars in the abutments and piers. The metal was used extensively in roofing early Anglo-Saxon churches.
Paul Bidwell, TWM Archaeology

CHESTERS – *Cilurnum*

Geophysical survey (Fig. 27)

A geophysical survey was undertaken of the fort and surrounding areas using magnetometry and resistivity techniques in 2001 and 2003. The survey to the N and NE of the fort showed few significant features and there was little evidence of a road leading out of the N gate.

As the fort was built astride the Wall it has always been evident that a road from the Wall bridge would lead to the lesser E gate and its line can be made out visually. The latter feature is probably the build-up of stone needed to create the ramp leading up from the bridge. The Wall itself can be seen as an area of high resistance, with the Wall ditch identifiable further away from the fort. At a position *c.* 28m from the river bank, a large stone building *c.* 10m square is apparently located immediately S of the Wall. This would have been of monumental proportions and would seem to be a unique feature in this position. A circular feature *c.* 50m in diameter appears just outside the lesser E gate. It could be interpreted as a *gyrus*, but it would have blocked the road between the bridge and the gate.

The survey suggests buildings in the area between the fort and the baths and the size of one suggests that it was built around a courtyard. The extent of the anomalies along the riverside S of the baths and curving round to the W suggests the presence there of *vicus* buildings. Evidence of possible enclosures or field systems indicates that agricultural activity took place prior to the construction of the fort or on the fringes of the *vicus* during its occupation.

The line of the Vallum is indistinct. [Editor's note: does a ENE-WSW trending wide linear band, 50m S of the baths, visible on both resistance and magnetic surveys, represent the beginning of a Vallum diversion around the fort? Its E end would align perfectly with Vallum on the E side of the N Tyne, and the angle is typical for a Vallum diversion]. A number of features close to the river bank cannot be assumed to be Roman and a modern origin should not be discounted. However, some probable exposed Roman masonry can be seen.

The survey shows that when both the resistivity and magnetometry surveys are viewed together, the site is extremely complex. Without the application of both geophysical survey techniques it is unlikely that some of the anomalies would have been recognised and would not have been placed

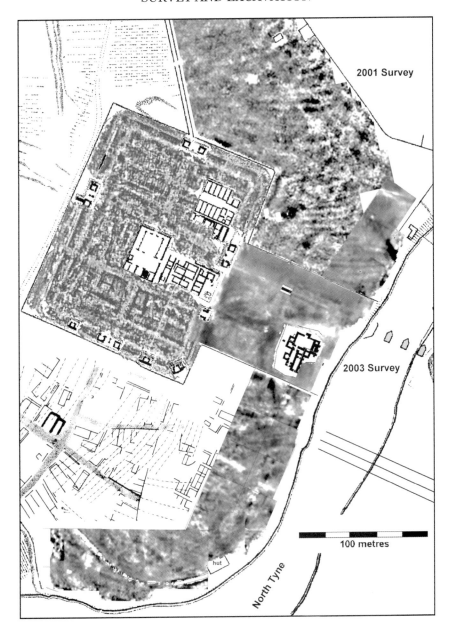

Figure 27. Chesters magnetic survey, courtesy of English Heritage and Timescape Surveys

in their appropriate context.
Publication: *Britannia* 35 (2004), 273-274; *Archaeology in Northumberland
2003 -2004* (Northumberland C.C.).
J. A. Biggins and D. J. A. Taylor, Timescape Surveys

On ceramic vaulting tubes (probably from the baths) at Chesters: Wilson 2003b.

Inscription
In 2004 an inscription was found in the North Tyne, just downstream of the
baths (*Britannia* 36 (2005), 480-1), and is now in the site museum. This is a
fragment of a monumental dedication from a temple of Jupiter Dolichenus.
Unfortunately the dedicator and military unit involved cannot be read with
certainly: R.S.O. Tomlin reads *symmacharii* (allied or irregular troops).
The great importance of this inscription is its late date: the named consuls
Maximus and Aquilinus establish this as 286. This is the latest evidence for
the cult of Jupiter Dolichenus, formerly supposed not to have outlasted the
250s when the cult-centre of the deity (in modern Turkey) was destroyed by
the Persians. It is also the latest consular date on an inscription from Roman
Britain, and of great interest in showing that traditional epigraphic practice
and an extra-mural temple at Chesters were still active in the changed
conditions of the late-third century. The location of this temple can now be
pinned down: Paul Bidwell points out that RIB is in error is attributing RIB
1452, also a *dolichenum* dedication, to the fort interior: HB3 makes it clear
that this was found during the unearthing of the extra-mural baths in 1884,
very close to the findspot of the new inscription. The *dolichenum* presumably
stood on the terrace overlooking the river just S of the baths, where much
possible masonry shows on the geophysical survey.

Wall-Mile 28
In 2008 an evaluation trench in the grounds E of Walwick Hall uncovered
the well-preserved remains of the Roman Military Way. The road was seen
to lie slightly N of the line projected on the modern Ordnance Survey, and
was formed of smooth but irregularly shaped and sized stone slabs, blocks
and cobbles. Although the S flank of the roadway within the trench had been
disturbed, the N edge survived and was formed of substantial kerb stones. A
cut feature running on the same alignment as the roadway on the N side may
have formed a roadside gully or ditch.
*Richard Carlton, The Archaeological Practice and Alan Williams, Alan
Williams Archaeology*

A small trench excavated to the E of Milecastle 29 (OA North 2002a), revealed that the Narrow Wall, here 2.2m wide, had been built on clay-and-cobble foundations 2.4m in width. Clay had also been applied as a bonding material in the lowest course of the facing stones on the S, which was actually set below ground level, as the Wall is cut into the hillslope at this point. Conversely, the lowest course of the N face had been bonded with mortar, with no evidence of clay having been used.

The excavation also provided some evidence for two phases in the general deterioration of the Wall. Numerous tumbled facing stones N of the Wall were probably the result of natural collapse, but their absence from a stone spread of a stratigraphically later date to the S of the Wall was suggestive of stone-robbing activity. Moreover, the approximate centre of the robber trench, which survives as a distinct E-W aligned hollow, coincided with the position of the S face of the Wall, whereas the surviving elements of the N face lay beyond the N lip of the hollow.

Ian Miller, Oxford Archaeology North

Milecastle 29 (Tower Tye)

The site is distinctly marked by robber trenches. There has been no excavation since the time of Clayton (1857). It is one of very few milecastles apparently surrounded by a ditch.

Wall-Mile 29: Black Carts.

Excavations on the Wall and Vallum in 1998, which were reported in the last Pilgrimage *Handbook* (Bidwell 1999a, 120-22) have been published (Wilmott 2009a, 78-102).

Milecastle 30 (Limestone Corner)

Publication of 1951 excavation of the Vallum causeway S of the milecastle, found not to be primary: Heywood and Breeze 2008. Cf. p. 28.

From Tower Tye to Limestone Corner most elements of the Wall can be seen: two milecastles (29 and 30), the remains of one turret (29a) and the site of another (29b), Vallum, ditch, upcast mound and the Military Way, and the Wall itself (here Narrow Gauge, 7' 3" wide above the offset, on Broad foundation), cleared of overburden (without much archaeological record) as recently as the 1970s (Fig. 28).

Wall-Mile 34

The precise line of the Wall in the vicinity of Sewingshields Farm was resolved by the excavation of five small trenches between 1999 and 2002 (LUAU 1999; OA North 2002b). The Wall (2.5m wide, with no evidence of

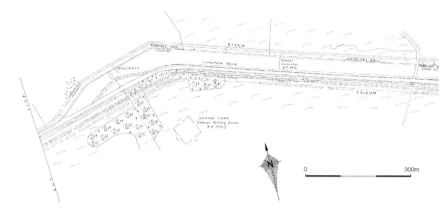

Figure 28. The Wall in Wall miles 28-30, as drawn by Brenda Heywood

Broad Wall foundation: *Britannia* 31 (2000), 390), was found several metres to the S of the line projected on the Ordnance Survey.
Ian Miller, Oxford Archaeology North

HOUSESTEADS – *Vercovicium*

There has been no excavation at Housesteads since the last Pilgrimage. At the time of writing the definitive publication of the excavations at Housesteads by John Gillam, Charles Daniels and Jim Crow, as well as other research and survey in the period 1954-1995, was imminent (Rushworth 2009). Note also: a revised edition of J. Crow's *Housesteads* (Crow 2004c). On the water collection tanks: Beaumont 2008.

Geophysical survey (Fig. 29)

A geophysical survey of the *vicus* to the S and W of the fort was undertaken in April 2003. Magnetometry was used over the whole of the survey area whilst some targeted resistivity was undertaken to the W of the fort. The presence of the Whin Sill outcrop had significant implications for the magnetometry survey as it was severely affected by the magnetic characteristics of this igneous rock.

It would seem probable that the outcropping rock had been broken up and reused in retaining walls and boundaries for the many small field enclosures which formed a large part of the survey area to the W (1). This series of fields followed the slope and had conjoining boundaries, with the long boundaries usually running along the slope. It is not possible to identify those built within the period of the Roman occupation.

The *via decumana* (3) leading W out of the E facing fort is well defined with

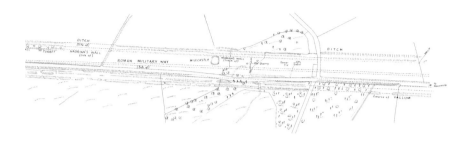

ditches, probably representing property divisions, running at right angles to each side. Some buildings can be seen within the limits of the boundaries. A series of defensive banks and ditches (4) close to the W side of the fort have been cut by the road and are almost certainly the late defensive features formed in front of the W gate seen by Hodgson in 1833.

The road leading to the S (15), on the line of the *via principalis,* is not well defined but that leading to the SW and probably to the fort at Vindolanda, can clearly be seen (16) entering the annexe via a gate. Excavation has identified the presence of many buildings to the S of this gate and the survey confirmed the complexity of the remains. This concentration of buildings is bounded by ditches to the E (10) and W (9) and the line of the Vallum to the S. These features suggest that this enclosed area measuring *c.* 105m by 97m was clearly set out and did not develop amorphically and was possibly an annexe to the fort or a defended *vicus* attached to the fort. Excavations within the SW sector of this enclosure identified several buildings (18) which were described by Birley *et al.* as 'nothing but hovels of the poorest description'. He went on further to suggest that the pottery found showed native characteristics.

Towards the E of the E ditch and 20m S of the curtain wall is a large building *c.* 10m by 8m (21). A drain runs from the curtain wall through this feature and onto a building further to the S. It is suggested that the large building could possibly be a bath-house and is sited in a similar position in relation to the fort to that shown by survey at the fort of Halton Chesters. A further drain to the E (24) is that running S from the latrine block exposed within the SE angle of the fort. The line of the footpath leading to the fort (29) cuts the corner of the enclosed settlement and overlies the identified buildings.
Publication: Biggins and Taylor 2004b.
J. A. Biggins and D. J. A. Taylor, Timescape Surveys

VINDOLANDA (Fig. 30)
In the past ten years, the Vindolanda Trust has purchased some 38 acres of additional land, including the important field to the N of the main site, and a

Figure 29. Housesteads magnetic survey, courtesy of Timescape Surveys

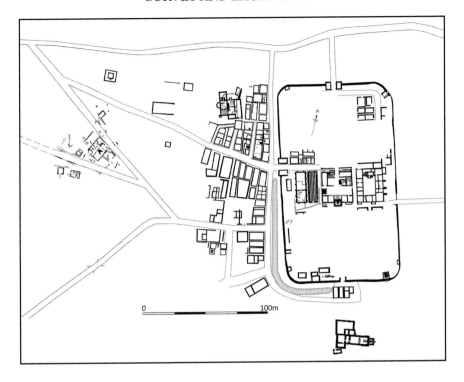

Figure 30. Vindolanda: general plan of excavated stone buildings

part of the field to the W. Magnetometer surveys, by Alan Biggins of Timescape Surveys, has proved that there had been significant activity there in the past, and it will be possible to test this in the course of 2009-2012. There have also been significant improvements to the Museum and other site facilities, and a major £6.2 million project will start at the end of 2009, to further upgrade the displays, provide accommodation for volunteers, and improve the access routes from the Roman site to the Museum. The bulk of the Roman stone structures examined since 1999 have now been consolidated for permanent display, and in 2009 the granary and stores building excavated in 2008 will be treated. Six months of excavation have taken place each year since 1999, summarised below, with up to 400 volunteers annually assisting the three site archaeologists.

In-house research has been enhanced by the work of many specialists elsewhere, notably Richard Brickstock (coins), Deb Bennett (faunal remains), Jacqui Huntley (environmental material), Elizabeth Greene (intaglios and jewellery), Elise Marliere (amphorae); Geoff Dannell (samian), Rob Sands (wooden objects), Anthony Birley and Roger Tomlin (inscriptions and graffiti), Alan Bowman and David Thomas (writing tablets), Kay Hartley (mortaria stamps), Will Higgs (bricks and tiles), Alan Biggins (magnetometer surveys), and Ian Tyers (dendrochronology). Research reports on the work of 1999-2006 have been published, and the 2007 results will shortly be available on the Trust's web site.

The pre-Hadrianic occupation
Vindolanda Tablet 155, dated to period II (*c.* AD 90-97), had listed '18 builders to the bath house', and the structure was certainly not that later built for the Fourth Cohort of Gauls (or their immediate predecessors), lying to the NW of the Stone Fort. Excavation in 2000 (Birley, A. 2001) located the building some 20m to the S of the stone fort's walls, on the edge of the small plateau above the sharp descent down to the Doe Sike rill. The baths had been ruthlessly demolished by a later garrison, who recovered the bulk of the expensive door sills, jambs, thresholds and voussoirs, as well as many of the large flagstones, probably for use in a successor building. But after demolition, the site was abandoned, and it was possible to recover the complete original plan. It proved to be an example of the *Reihentyp* variety, similar to the officers' baths at Inchtuthil, rather than the block type which dominated the Hadrianic forts. On at least two occasions the building had undergone substantial modifications and repairs, perhaps when the First Cohort of Tungrians replaced the Ninth Cohort of Batavians in AD 105, and when the effects of high temperatures below the floors of the *tepidarium* and *caldarium* had weakened the stone walls and hypocaust bricks. Construction and maintenance of the building had required a massive quantity of bricks and wall flues, and it is likely that these had been produced in a Vindolanda tilery nearby, making use of the good quality local clay. Other evidence, in the shape of wasters, identified in analysis by TWM Archaeology and by Kay Hartley (personal communications), strongly argued for the local production of pottery as well. In the course of production, the bricks and tiles had been laid out to dry in an area accessible to dogs, cattle and cats, whose prints survived on many examples.

In 2001-2004 pre-Hadrianic levels were examined to the NW of the previous areas (Birley, A. 2003; Birley, A. and Blake 2005) with the identification of a probable *schola* and a possible hospital dating to Vindolanda's period IV (AD 105-*c.* 120), together with evidence for period I (AD *c.* 85-*c.* 90) multiple ditches to the W of the contemporary small fort. The periods II and III remains had been largely removed by Roman re-building in the areas examined, and the period V material had been almost obliterated by later second century activity. There were some ink and stylus writing tablets amongst the period

IV material, including an important document detailing the issue of weapons to a number of named individuals (T01/39), and another quotation from Virgil, this time from his Georgics (Georgics 1.125). A part of the wooden water pipeline, first discovered in 1988 near the Cerialis period III residence, was encountered beneath the possible hospital floor, and one of the timbers produced a felling date of AD 97.

On the western fringes of the extramural area, in the course of work on the remains of possible temples (Birley, A. and Blake 2007), wooden structures with massive oak posts (some 600mm x 500mm and still standing up to 1.6m high) were encountered, associated with one or more buildings. Two of the timbers produced felling dates: one was AD 97, the same date as the timber in the pipe-line, and the other had been felled between AD 102 and 112. In due course further work will be devoted to these structures, which were on a scale very much larger than any of the buildings so far examined in the pre-Hadrianic forts. They evidently date to the periods III and IV occupations, but their function remains uncertain. A closing date for period IV and the precise dates of period V require more evidence.

The second century occupation
On the stone fort site the most important results concerned the period VI structures (AD *c*. 130-200), previously known as Stone Fort 1 (Birley, A. and Blake 2007). A detailed examination of the rampart mound and fort wall, to the S of the Stone Fort Two W gate, revealed that the fort, whose W gate had been discovered by Ian Richmond in 1932, had initially been constructed with turf and timber defences. But when the stone wall was added, the gate was moved to the position later occupied by the Stone Fort Two gate. The builders of the stone fort wall had failed to provide it with the depth of foundations required for such a heavy structure on ground that had already seen considerable disturbance, and the failure was compounded by the use of small facing stones without good tails to embed in a core which had been built with rubble and clay. As a result, there had been several major collapses, with one 14m section abandoned on the berm when re-building took place. The construction dates for the period VI fort remain uncertain, although the conversion to stone wall defences was probably in the AD 160s.

Further work on this occupation period did not form part of the excavation programme, but a chance discovery in 2007 finally solved a problem which had puzzled archaeologists for many years. The remains of the NW wall of the fort were located, extending over 20m to the N of the Stone Fort Two NW corner, and almost reaching the field wall that now bounds the S edge of the current Stanegate road. This discovery carried with it the certainty that this modern line of the Stanegate was not the original Roman route, because a fort ditch must have been sited at this point. Aerial photography and the magnetometer survey suggest that the original line lay some 50m further to the N.

When excavation of the structures underlying the third century extramural buildings between the contemporary military bath-house and the wall of Stone Fort Two was undertaken in 2007, it was revealed that there had been what amounted to a small reservoir there in the second century, whose construction had almost entirely obliterated pre-Hadrianic remains.

Excavation on the western fringes of the extramural area in 2004-6 (Birley, A. and Blake 2007) revealed a number of rectangular stone buildings of second century date, with considerable furnaces associated with the processing of iron ore, an activity which was also found in third century levels elsewhere in both the extramural areas and within the stone forts. The local supplies of iron ore were extensive enough to attract extraction in the nineteenth century, and it was not surprising to find that the Roman army had made good use of them – and the local coal seams.

Severan

Little fresh information has been added to the interpretation of the unorthodox military establishment to the W of the stone fort, dated to the late Severan period (AD 205-211), but it would appear that it had adopted the W wall of Stone Fort One as its E defences, when the former fort site was given over to the orderly ranks of circular buildings. Another series of these native-style huts was found in the SW corner of the ground later occupied by Stone Fort Two, suggesting that there may have been nearly 200 of them in all (Blake 2001). Work on the S rampart of the Severan defences discovered a well which had been back-filled with rubble when that establishment was abandoned, and it produced a votive altar dedicated to the god Hvvetir. Another altar to the same deity or deities was found in the civilian settlement nearby, bringing the number of such dedications at Vindolanda to 11 (Birley, A. 2003). A section across the ditch to the S of this southern rampart produced a mass of leather goods, including 90 items of footwear, and a considerable volume of pottery, and the ditch had been sealed before the construction of civilian buildings early in the third century.

Stone Fort Two

In 1999-2002 excavation concentrated on the S fort wall, a latrine in the SE corner and the South Gate (Birley, A. and Blake 2000). The fort wall, 1.83m wide, showed evidence for repeated re-builds, especially in the SE corner, where inefficient foundations had allowed the structure to slip 0.5m southwards, causing the latrine inside to collapse, probably before the end of the third century, and its site was then covered with clay. To the W of the S gate, three irregular structures had been built into the rampart mound and across the intervallum road, but they had been badly disturbed by stone robbers. Pottery (mainly Huntcliffe wares) and coins (including a worn and clipped *siliqua* of Arcadius, minted in 393/4) suggested a late-fourth or early-fifth century date for this phase. At the SW corner the heavily robbed remains of a small angle turret and another latrine were examined, and the latter's sewer included in its drain, just outside the fort wall, a plinth with a dedication to the goddess of Gaul, set up by 'the Gallic citizens in agreement with the Britons' (Birley, A. and Blake 2007) (Fig. 31).

Outside the SW corner of the fort, a patch of flagging across the silted-up ditch suggested the remains of another late structure, which contained a small stone plaque inscribed with the Celtic form of the *chi-rho*, probably dating to the late sixth century.

Further work within the S guard-chamber of the W gate proved that the primary doorway facing onto the gate passage – always the position in every military establishment – had later been blocked and a new door had been placed in the E wall. At a similar date the guard-chamber had

Figure 31. Vindolanda: dedication by *cives Galli* to *de(ae) Galliae concordesque Britanni*

been provided with an oven and hearths. This may have happened in the late fourth century, when other buildings had also been converted into accommodation.

Close to the S guard-chamber, a late fourth century rectangular building had been inserted into the rampart mound, with two ovens outside its S wall. An explicit sculpture of Priapus lay nearby. The fourth century *via principalis* to the N of the granary and stores building sites had been surfaced with massive flags, which were littered with mid- to late-fourth century coins. A total of nearly 500 were recovered, and are now being studied by Richard Brickstock. Anthony Hedley had found some 300 mid-fourth century coins when he examined the ruins of the W gateway in the 1830s, and it would appear likely that markets had been held on the broad roadway in front of the stores buildings in the mid- to late-fourth century.

In 2008 the area between the *principia* and the intervallum road to the W was examined, and the material recovered, including over 1,000 environmental samples from the granary building, is now being studied. It was anticipated that there would be two granaries there, but only the E of the two buildings possessed under-floor ventilation, and the W structure appears to have been designed for non-grain supplies. Both buildings had been destroyed by fire at some time, and the W building was turned into accommodation when it was re-built in the late fourth century. The recovery of fifth to seventh century bronzes from the site suggested lengthy post-Roman occupation here, as elsewhere on the fort site.

Important finds included two fragments of the dedication slab honouring Caracalla, found by E. Birley in 1933 (RIB 1705) in a nearby *principia* drain, and a remarkable fragment of a bronze perpetual calendar, recording details for the month of September. Outside the S walls of both buildings there were considerable deposits of iron slag, similar to those found in large quantities in the extramural area.

On the N side of the *via principalis* excavation of anticipated barracks started in 2008 and will continue throughout 2009. A large kerb stone on the N side of the road, in front of a late fourth or fifth century building, had been inscribed RIACVS, a rare inscription at that late stage.

The extramural area
Three large stone buildings, with courtyards and, in two cases wells, were examined in the S parts of the area, suggesting that they had been the properties of relatively wealthy civilians, but there and elsewhere there was no evidence for occupation in the fourth century (Birley, A. 2003). The extreme SW of the area revealed further fragmentary remains of structures,

mainly devoted to industrial activities, where finds included a votive altar dedicated to the Syrian God, normally only found at Carvoran. Just outside the fort's S gate the remains of three rectangular structures were examined. They had been severely robbed, but there were no traces of hearths or cooking benches in them, and they may have been used as military stores buildings. Their position effectively debarred wheeled traffic from entering the fort by this gate.

In the far W of the extramural area, a number of industrial premises of possible third century date were examined, with two small rectangular temples to the W of them (Blake 2003). They could not be dated closely, and some may have originated in the later second century. Finds near the temples included several fragments of statuary (Birley, A. and Blake 2007), perhaps from tombs rather than temples. This area had been intensively ploughed by the occupiers of the nearby Wellmeadow Close croft, demolished in the early twentieth century, whose foundations lie below the present Admissions building. Work will continue in the extramural area in 2009-2012.

Reports 1999-2009
S defences of stone fort 2, circular structures: Birley, A. and Blake 2000; Blake 2001
Pre Hadrianic baths: Birley, A. 2001
Civil settlement, pre-Hadrianic levels and work at Carvoran: Birley, A. 2003
Excavations of 2001-2002: Blake 2003
Excavations of 2003-2004: Birley, A. and Blake 2005
Excavations of 2005-2006: Birley, A. and Blake 2007
Excavations of 2007: Birley, R. forthcoming
General: Birley, R. 2000; 2005; 2008; new overview: Birley, R. 2009
Writing tablets: Birley, A.R. 2002a; 2002b; Bowman and Thomas 2003
Cives Galli de(ae) Galliae concordesque Britanni inscription: Birley, A.R. 2008a; Jewellery: Birley, B. and Greene 2006; Footwear: van Driel-Murray 2001
Robin Birley, Vindolanda Trust

Geophysical survey (Fig. 32)
Magnetometry surveys were carried out by Timescape Surveys of the extant Stone Fort 2 together with areas to the N and W of the fort in 2000 and 2007-8. This is published with extensive commentary in: *Britannia* 39 (2008), 280-3. The survey reproduced here has been supplied courtesy of

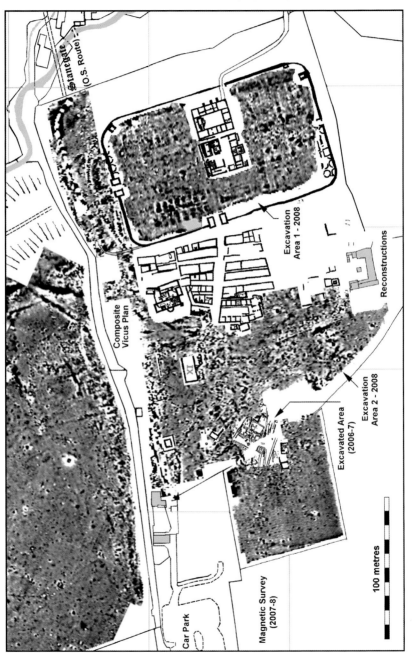

Figure 32. Vindolanda magnetic survey, courtesy of Timescape Surveys

J. A. Biggins,. J. Biggins, P. Shipley and D. J. A. Taylor. Note particularly: The back-to-back pair of barracks in the NW quadrant of the fort, evidently having only around six *contubernia* each, like the examples on the opposite side of the *praetentura* excavated by Bidwell in 1980; the suggestion of many buildings lining the N side of the Stanegate; a cluster of possible roundhouses on the W side of the field N of the road; in the field W of the *vicus* two rows of black squares probably represent the massive timbers found in that area continuing to the W.

On a new quarry-face inscription on Barcombe Hill: Wilson 2003a.

Wall Mile 39 (East Bog)

In 2003 two evaluation trenches were excavated across the Vallum ditch at East Bog, Northumberland (NY 7486 6687). The work was undertaken in advance of improvements to the field drainage system within the ditch, which survives as an earthwork feature. The sequence of filling was similar in both trenches, though in neither was the base of the ditch reached. The earliest recorded deposit, at a depth of approximately 2m below the modern ground surface, comprised a fine, pale grey silty clay, probably water-lain, which was sealed by a build-up of highly organic peaty material, approximately 0.5m thick. A further accumulation of silty clay was followed in one trench by a limited episode of deliberate infilling, probably during the post-medieval period. Palaeoenvironmental assessment of the ditch fills revealed rich assemblages of pollen and waterlogged plant and insect remains. Three radiocarbon determinations were also obtained. The base of the peat provided a date of 40 cal BC-cal AD 140, suggesting that it began to accumulate almost immediately after the Vallum was constructed. The top of the same deposit yielded a date of cal AD 80-330, whilst the secondary accumulation of pale silty clay overlying the peat was dated to cal AD 560-670.
John Zant, Oxford Archaeology North

The 2009 Pilgrimage will ascend Winshields Crag from the E, walking up from Steel Rigg Car Park to the site of Milecastle 40. The objective is to examine an example of the previously unobserved variation in the form of the Wall ditch that has been described by Humphrey Welfare (2004; cf. p. 24). At this point, rather than ending suddenly, the ditch and glacis (spread-out upcast bank) are replaced by a counterscarp bank (formed from the scraped-up overburden from a 'minimal ditch', and then by a single extended scarp, before fading into the precipitous crags. This shows how much can still be learned from examining existing remains that have been visited by Pilgrims – and other archaeologists – many times in the past.

Milecastle 42 (Cawfields)
Publication of 1958 excavation of the Vallum causeway S of the milecastle: Heywood and Breeze 2008. Cf. p. 28.

GREATCHESTERS – *Aesica*
There has been no recent fieldwork.

Wall-Mile 44
In 2008, excavations in advance of footpath work associated with the Hadrian's Wall Path National Trail, revealed the remains of a rectangular, stone-built structure immediately adjacent to the S face of the Wall at King Arthur's Well, in the nick close to Walltown Farm (NY 6806 6664). The structure, which was retained largely *in situ*, was aligned perpendicular to the Wall and was seemingly built up against its inner face, though this relationship was not established by excavation.

The building was approximately 5m wide and over 5m long, with a central hearth and walls of unmortared whinstone. Pronounced bowing and leaning of the walls, together with evidence for attempted repairs, suggested that the building experienced structural problems that may have resulted in its eventual collapse. Preliminary analysis of the associated pottery indicates a mid-late second-century date for the entire assemblage, and an intaglio was also recovered. A radiocarbon determination of cal AD 80-240, obtained from alder charcoal recovered from the central hearth, seemingly provided confirmation that the building was of Roman date. However, a fragment of burnt animal bone apparently associated with the same feature yielded a much earlier date of 540-380 cal BC.
Jeremy Bradley, Oxford Archaeology North

CARVORAN – *Magna*
A 12 hectare magnetometer survey in 1999 by Timescape Surveys, for the Vindolanda Trust and English Heritage, included the stone fort and the bulk of the extramural area to N, S and E. Some details of the internal fort buildings were revealed, but only excavation can determine whether the data indicated surviving masonry or merely robbers' trenches. Unexpectedly extensive traces of buildings were revealed to the SE of the fort, on the line of the Stanegate road.

Excavation of the fort S gate and sections across the E and W walls in October and November 2002 (Birley, A. 2003) confirmed the scale of the destruction of the remains by stone robbing. Carvoran had been the lords of Blenkinsopp's only available Roman remains, and many of its stones were incorporated in their castle in the early fourteenth century, half a mile to the S. Structures that remained were gradually removed by the farming family of Carricks, as they endeavoured, in John Hodgson's words, 'to bring the site of the station into a profitable state of bearing' (Hodgson 1840), and, to the dismay of the historian Wallis, the builders of the military road were granted access to the land for stone robbing. The section across the fort's E wall found only the foundation course, 1.63m wide, with a ditch to the E some 4 to 5m wide, and the section across the S wall produced similar results. In the latter section, the rampart mound was found to be 3.50m wide. The W fort wall lay below the later field wall, but a section across it revealed no surviving traces.

Stone robbing had been equally severe at the S gate, where no more than the rubble core of the foundations remained, but there was sufficient to demonstrate that it had been a single portal 5m wide, with the guard-chambers constructed flush with the outer face of the fort wall.

In the course of preparing for the construction of a cycle path for Sustrans, in 2006, on land leased from the Vindolanda Trust, Pennine Archaeology undertook a limited investigation of potential archaeology on the route. The path site, close to the N edge of the adjacent military road, was found to lie above a substantial Roman rubbish dump, with material preserved in anaerobic conditions.
Robin Birley, Vindolanda Trust

Geophysical Survey (Fig. 33)

A magnetometry survey of the fort and *vicus* encompassing *c.* 15 hectares was undertaken in May 2000. The previously suspected total destruction of the fort has not been confirmed by the survey, although areas of disturbed masonry were recorded together with well-preserved buildings within the fort. The depth of the archaeological deposits is very considerable, being possibly 2-3m.

The extent of the S-facing fort and its defences are clearly defined and it can be seen that a large part of the *latera praetorii* (3) has been extensively robbed. Barrack and other buildings in both the *praetentura* and *retentura* are evident with those in the latter (5) being well defined. The NW corner turret is presently exposed.

The survey confirmed the route of the Stanegate (15) described by Horsley as it passes to the S of the fort in a straight line outside the defences. Although the survey definitively established the presence of many substantial buildings fronting the Stanegate, the full extent of the *vicus* has not yet been

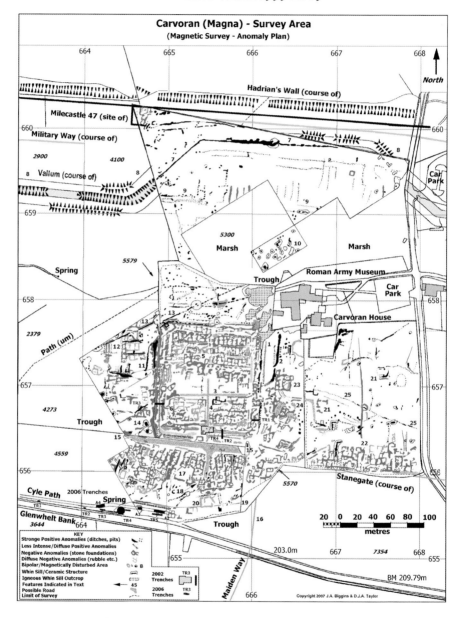

Figure 33. Carvoran: magnetic survey anomaly plan

established. It is expected that the settlement is much more extensive to the S, SE and SW of the fort in an area which was not surveyed. The routes of both the Stanegate from the E and the Maiden Way from the S have not been fully characterised. The line of the *via praetoria* leads S out of the fort in the direction of a further possible road (20), which can be seen in the natural hollow to the S of the fort where rows of buildings fan out down the slope.

The evidence indicates that buildings forming the *vicus* appear to have developed to the E and S of the fort along the route of the Stanegate. The scale and form of the buildings suggest that some have been either workshops or had storage functions as well as residential use. Outside the E gate of the fort two particularly large buildings (23 and 24) can be seen, one of which would appear to have an internal courtyard. Further to the E, N of the Stanegate, there would appear to be little evidence of buildings. Towards the W only isolated buildings and field boundaries were identified, however, the survey in this area was limited and it is likely that the field boundaries extended much further as has been identified at the fort of Castlesteads. No evidence of buildings associated with the settlement was recorded N of the fort.

The route of the Vallum (8), with its diversion, is clearly shown to the N of the fort and the location of Milecastle 46 was confirmed by the survey. Strong circular magnetic anomalies (19) were also recorded which corresponded with surface mounds in an area between the fort and the Vallum. These surface mounds can be compared with similar features at High Rochester where burials have been identified.
Publication: *Britannia,* 32 (2001), 330-332.
J. A. Biggins and D. J. A. Taylor, Timescape Surveys

Milecastle 47 (Chapel House): Robbing of the milecastle using explosives in the nineteenth century noted (Wilmott 2006c).

BIRDOSWALD – Banna
The major excavations of 1987-92 (Wilmott 1997) and of 1996-98 (Wilmott, Evans and Cool 2009) reported in the last Pilgrimage Handbook (Bidwell 1999a, 145-57) have been published. The work confirmed that there was a definite early-third century replanning and remodelling of the buildings of the *praetentura* (Fig. 34), which confirms the 'Severan' phase identified during the excavations of 1929 (Richmond and Birley 1930).

Two small projects have taken place since the last Pilgrimage, and these are also now published (Wilmott *et al.* 2009) (Fig. 35). The first of these took place in 1999, when an evaluation of the extramural settlement to the W of the fort, and of the cremation cemetery beyond this, was undertaken by the Channel 4 *Time Team* TV programme. The three trenches in the W *vicus* showed that the known geophysical anomalies were representative of buried stone-founded buildings including hearths, cobbled surfaces, pits and ditches. The work demonstrated that these features had complex structural histories. Pottery from these trenches was mostly second century, but the, admittedly small, assemblage showed that occupation ceased by the early fourth century.

In the cremation cemetery a number of burials disturbed by medieval

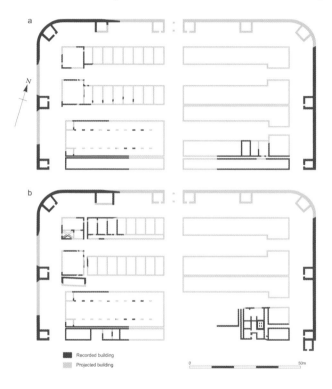

Fig 34. Birdoswald *praetentura*

ploughing were found, and a complete cremation deposit containing two pottery vessels. The cremation urn contained the cremated remains of a woman aged 18-40. Also within the urn were part-burned remains of decorated bone plaques which had adorned the bier of the deceased. Evidence from here and the Brougham cemetery implies a major industry in the production of these highly intricate plaques.

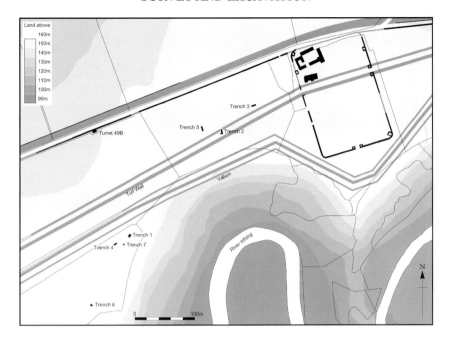

Figure 35. Birdoswald: trench locations

The second project, undertaken in 2000, had the aim of clarifying the place of the pottery known as 'Housesteads ware' in the Birdoswald sequence, by re-examining the feature from which the material first came. The feature, recorded as a 'native hearth' (Simpson and Richmond 1934, 123) proved to be a re-used Roman well, and the work confirmed the third century date of this material, which has been found only to the S of the fort in an area of timber buildings dissimilar from the stone-built *vici* to E and W.

Continued land slippage and erosion of the river cliff in the area of the cemetery has prompted the initiation of a project to excavate a strip of the cemetery before it is lost. A trench was excavated by North Pennines Archaeology under the direction of F. Giecco in January 2009 in order to evaluate the line of a new fence sited well to the S of the cliff. Within the trench eight features containing cremated bone and other burnt material were located, though whether these were deposits of pyre debris or disturbed, un-urned cremations was unclear. The area within this fence is to be totally excavated in a new partnership project by English Heritage and the University of Newcastle upon Tyne beginning in September 2009, shortly after the Pilgimage.
Tony Wilmott, English Heritage

Geophysical survey (Fig. 36)
A geophysical survey of the fort and *vicus* was undertaken in 1997 and 1998, which was reported in the Hadrian's Wall 1989-1999 Pilgrimage summary of sites (publication: Biggins and Taylor 1999). Further survey of the cemetery and two areas in the Irthing Valley, below the escarpment on which the fort is sited, was undertaken in 2000. These limited surveys are designated as sites 2, 3 and 4 and are summarised below:

Site 2
The area of the cemetery revealed many small anomalies any of which could indicate cremation burials; most were concentrated near the NE sector of the field. At the time of survey the entire E area of the cemetery had been badly disturbed by farming machinery, up to a depth of 600mm. Further to the SW, very large anomalies were detected which may indicate large pits.

Site 3
The NW portion of the site includes a level platform which is being encroached upon by landslip from the unstable escarpment below the fort. Part of a large building with two or more compartments can be seen in the NE part of the survey with magnetic responses suggesting that further parts of the building lie to the E. The high level of the magnetic readings could suggest a bath-house. Evidence of further unidentified buildings was seen. On the flood plain below the river platform some evidence of enclosures was identified.

Site 4
The W part of the site is located to the NW of Underheugh Farm at the foot of the escarpment below the fort. Positive magnetic anomalies suggested the position of three conjoining field boundaries. There is no assurance that these boundaries are of Roman date. The field to the E of Underheugh Farm revealed fewer magnetic anomalies.
Publication: Biggins and Taylor 2004c.
J. A. Biggins and D. J. A. Taylor, Timescape Surveys

Taken together the geophysical survey plans of Birdoswald now offer a remarkable overview of the pattern of extra-mural building and cemetery development outside a Wall-fort, yet all except the fort itself is invisible on the ground. Indicating the extent of the known but invisible remains on an open site like this is a valuable exercise, serving to remind pilgrims that as techniques of excavation and remote survey progress, the familiar visible remains become a smaller and smaller part of the whole picture.
Also on Birdoswald, note: Wilmott 2001; Wilmott 2002

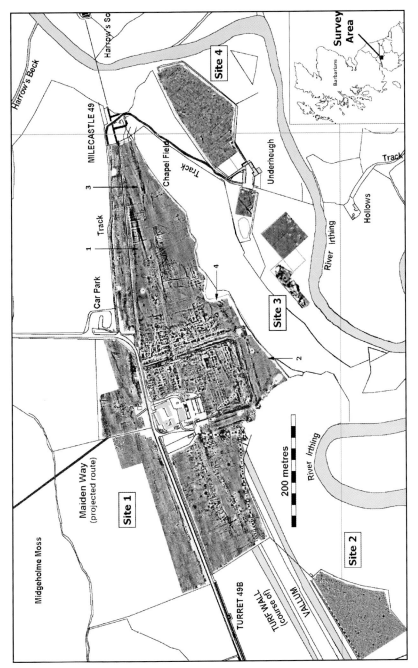

Figure 36. Birdoswald magnetic survey

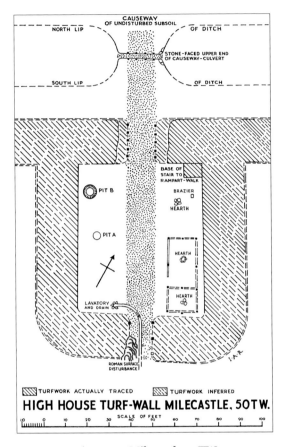

Figure 37. Milecastle 50TW

Milecastle 50TW (High House) (Fig. 37)

Here is one of only two surviving and visible causeways across the Wall ditch in front of a milecastle (the other is at Milecastle 25, Codlaw Hill). That the High House causeway was of undug earth, and therefore original to the construction of the Turf Wall, was proven by excavation in 1934. Humphrey Welfare (2000; cf. p.24) has surveyed the field archaeological evidence for other original causeways in front of milecastles. The question is crucial to our understanding of the intended function of the Wall. See Fig. 38 for a map of the frontier works between milecastles 49 and 55.

Wall-Mile 50 (Appletree)

The Turf Wall Cutting at Appletree, exposed for every Pilgrimage since the Fourth in 1906 in a tradition which is not now to be repeated, was excavated in order fully to contextualise the Turf Wall with the other earthworks of the system. A trench 100m long within which the Turf Wall, its ditch, the N, S and marginal mounds of the Vallum and the Vallum ditch were located was excavated and viewed by the participants of the Twelfth Pilgrimage in 1999. The structure of the Turf Wall was recorded. When the Stone Wall was built, on a different course, the Turf Wall Ditch was partially backfilled with material from the demolished Turf Wall. Between the Turf Wall and the Vallum a narrow stone-metalled track was found. This was primary to the Turf Wall, as it was built on land stripped of turf for construction. The Vallum mounds were similarly built on stripped land, including the marginal mound. This shows that the Vallum was constructed before vegetation had a chance to regenerate after the building of the Turf Wall. This work has been published (Wilmott and Bennett 2009, 103-120).
Tony Wilmott, English Heritage

Wall-Mile 53 (Hare Hill)

Immediately E of the great upstanding fragment of Wall at Hare Hill an additional 12m length of the wall has recently been included within the English Heritage guardianship area. In 2004 English Heritage commissioned TWM Archaeology to evaluate the remains with a view to displaying the Wall. The remains of the Roman Wall were at a much greater depth than expected, being overlain by a boundary wall of much later date. The Hadrianic Turf Wall was seen, but its full width could not be established. There was no cobble foundation. Overlying its levelled remains was the flagged foundation for the later-Hadrianic stone wall, 2.88m wide. The facing stones had been robbed, but fissures in the slabs on both sides allowed the width of the Wall above the footing to be determined at 2.32m. The core was clay and rubble, with a light adhesion of mortar where the facing stones had been. The superstructure had been demolished in post-Roman times, perhaps to provide stone for Lanercost Priory, the N extent of whose estate is formed by the Wall here.

In the later-medieval period a narrow stone wall was reinstated over the line of the Roman Wall; this is the wall consolidated following the 2004 excavation. Its existence suggests the irony that, having demolished the Roman wall for building material, the canons of Lanercost were confronted with the need to re-fortify the boundary of their estate, perhaps sometime after the onset of border warfare in the early-fourteenth century. As well as being seen here and at Hare Hill Turret, the boundary wall can still be traced on the ground at many points along the levelled line of Hadrian's

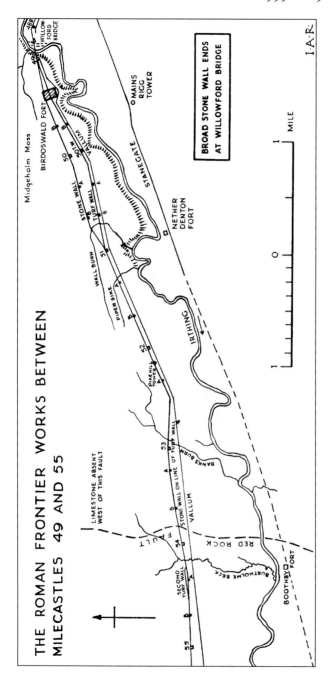

Figure 38. Richmond's map of the Roman frontier works between milecastles 49 and 55

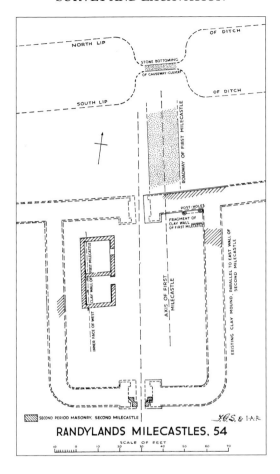

Figure 39. Milecastle 54 (Randylands)

Wall running westwards to Burtholme Beck, which was certainly the western boundary of the Priory lands. Immediately W of Burtholme Beck there still stand three impressive, if overgrown, fragments of the Roman Wall. The E end of the estate parcel was probably, though not certainly, at Banks Burn, and beyond here also the Roman Wall was not dismantled in the same way: a huge fallen fragment, still possessing a few facing stones on the S side, lies in the field immediately E of the burn (W end of Wall-Mile 52). The particularly thorough dismantling of the Wall exemplified at Hare Hill is thus firmly linked to the Lanercost estate. The massive standing fragment at Hare Hill itself probably survived because it was

135

incorporated into a building in the medieval period.
Publication: Hodgson and McKelvey 2006.
N. Hodgson, TWM Archaeology

Milecastle 54 (Randylands) (Fig. 39)

Wall-Mile 54
Immediately W of Burtholme Beck is a rare sight: the core of the Roman Wall in its natural ruined and unconsolidated state, still 1.5m high but overgrown and prized apart by tree roots. Just beyond the beck, near the bottom of the slope, the core is of rubble set in hard white mortar. In the fragments towards the top of the slope, nearer the next field boundary, the core is of a very distinctive herringbone pattern set in a white and pink mortar. Before the advent of the national trail this was a little-visited part of the Wall, which has not been walked on recent pilgrimages.

Turret 54a (Garthside) (Fig. 40)

Wall-Mile 55 (High Dovecote Farm)
In 2003 an evaluation trench at the N end of the green lane N of High Dovecote Farm, near Walton, Cumbria (NY 5309 6436), revealed no trace of either the Wall or the ditch, and the natural subsoil was encountered at a shallow depth beneath the modern topsoil. It appeared that the Wall and its foundation had been entirely removed by the green lane, which had eroded the natural slope at this point. On the estimated line of the Wall ditch, a thick layer of colluvial material containing one small fragment of BB1 was found. It is therefore possible that, rather than excavating a ditch in this area, a large counterscarp bank was created to the N of the Wall, accentuating the natural topography to form a wide, ditch-like feature. The earthwork remains of this putative counterscarp bank are visible immediately E of the site.
John Zant, Oxford Archaeology North

CASTLESTEADS – *Camboglanna*

Geophysical survey of the *vicus* (Fig. 41)
The site of the fort at Castlesteads was levelled in 1791 when the walled garden was formed. This area is now enclosed by woodland. The *vicus* was sited below the fort on a SE sloping site above the River Irthing.

The survey shows the extent of a *vicus* clustered around the S of the fort with a road running from E to W. A further major (and previously unknown) road runs to the SE some 200m to the W of the *vicus*. This road is heading

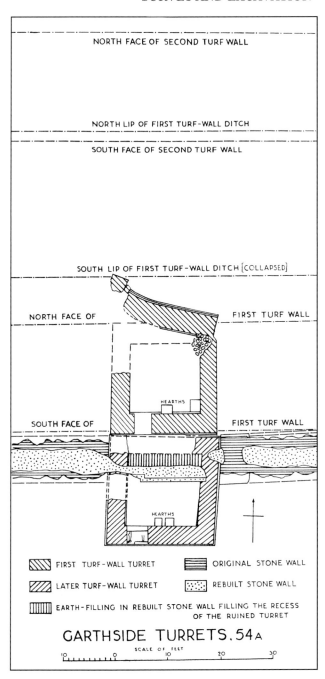

Figure 40. Garthside turret

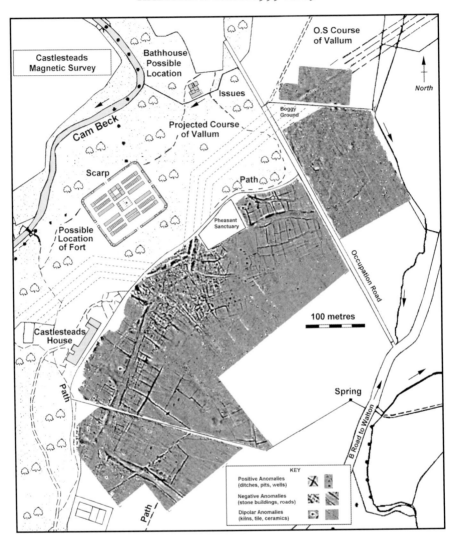

Figure 41. Castlesteads magnetic survey

in the direction of the river Irthing and the line of Stanegate. A possible cemetery can be seen to the NE of this road in the last complete field within the survey. It is significant that this major road is not aligned on the known fort and it could suggest that an earlier fort remains to be located to the W of the accepted site.

The buildings to the *vicus* are grouped to the S of the Vallum and evidence of a further ditch can be seen outside this feature. Between this and the Vallum itself are four substantial buildings, the larger of which is *c*. 8m square and is subdivided. A series of lanes run between the buildings, which are generally stone built. Some evidence can be seen of buildings between the Vallum and the fort. It is likely that a substantial number of buildings lie to the E and W of the fort outside the gates, within the woodland.

The strength of the magnetic response of the Vallum suggests that it remained open for a considerable period, perhaps for the greater part of the life of the fort. A crossing of the Vallum was identified to the NE of the fort.

To the E of the *vicus* and divided from it by a culverted stream are a series of Romano-British fields seen to be of two phases. These contrast markedly with the regular shaped fields to the SW of the *vicus*. This field pattern can also be seen to run below some of the field systems to the W of the stream where several roundhouses can also be identified. This marked change in character could suggest a boundary defining the E limit of the *vicus*, and perhaps different land use or allocation.

Publication: Biggins and Taylor 2007.
J. A. Biggins and D. J. A. Taylor, Timescape Surveys

Wall-Mile 57

In 2002 limited archaeological work on the line of Hadrian's Wall NE of Newtown, Cumbria (NY 502 629) revealed the very badly damaged remains of the Wall and a possible laid surface of compacted sandstone fragments, 1-1.5m wide, situated immediately in front of the N face. This deposit was poorly preserved, but appeared to form a possibly linear feature aligned roughly parallel to the Wall itself.

John Zant, Oxford Archaeology North

Milecastle 62 (Walby East)

Nine test pits were excavated on the site of the milecastle in 1999, guided by geophysical evidence (Gater 1981). No previous excavation had taken place here. The site was heavily robbed. There were traces of the original turf Wall and its milecastle beneath surviving stonework. Cobbling in a gap in the N wall seems to represent the site of the N gate. The inner face of the E wall of the milecastle was identified, as was the W wall of an internal building on the E side of the installation. The internal dimensions of this long axis milecastle were in the region of 16.5m x 24m (Wilmott 2009b, 170-74).

Milecastle 63 (Walby West)

In 2000 a trench excavated on the supposed site of Milecastle 63 and guided by geophysical results (Gater 1981) failed to identify the milecastle, but found

139

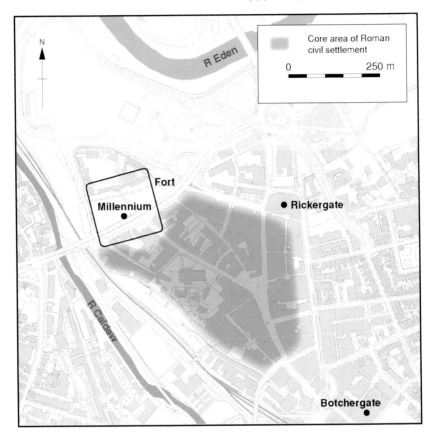

Figure 42. Carlisle, site locations

the bottom course of Hadrian's Wall beneath a field boundary (Wilmott 2009b, 174-77).
Tony Wilmott, English Heritage

STANWIX – *Petriana*
There is little new work. Note a publication of observations in *vicus* 180m W of fort (Caruana 2000), with an important discussion of the sizes of the successive forts at Stanwix.

CARLISLE – *Luguvalium*
Since publication of the last edition of the Handbook in 1999, a number of important excavations have been undertaken within the Roman fort and the

associated civil settlement at Carlisle (Fig. 42). Several of these were already underway at the time of the 1999 Pilgrimage, but work was insufficiently advanced for summaries to be included in the Handbook. Within the fort, Carlisle Archaeological Unit/Carlisle Archaeology Ltd (CAU/CAL) undertook a phased programme of excavation from November 1998 to March 2001, in association with Carlisle City Council's Gateway City (Millennium) Project (Zant 2009; Howard-Davis 2009). During the same period, CAU/CAL was also responsible for two important excavations within the Roman town, at Botchergate, adjacent to the main road S, and at Rickergate, in proximity to a road leading N to the crossing of the River Eden. Additional fieldwork was undertaken on the Botchergate site by the Lancaster University Archaeological Unit (now Oxford Archaeology North) between May and July 2001.

The fort

The Millennium project (NY 397 561) greatly enhanced understanding of the origins and development of the fort, building upon earlier work at Annetwell Street (Caruana in prep). The excavations were located largely within the S part of the fort (probably, but not definitely, the *praetentura*), but a small area of the *latera praetorii* was also investigated for the first time. The work, whilst essentially confirming the sequence of development, has necessitated the reinterpretation of several aspects of the stratigraphic sequence.

Flavian site development

Few dendrochronological dates were obtained from the earliest phase of occupation, but the evidence as a whole is consistent with the construction date in the autumn/winter of AD 72-3 established for the S defences (Caruana in prep). The known positions of the S and W ramparts and the S gate, together with certain topographical considerations, indicate that the fort was approximately 600 Roman feet square (*c.* 3.2ha) (Fig. 43), considerably larger than previously thought. In spite of its comparatively large size, the fort, or at least the investigated S portion, seems to have been crammed with buildings. In addition to a series of N-S aligned barracks (each *c.* 48 x 8-8.5m), of which five have been partially excavated (Fig. 44.1), rampart-back buildings were erected in the intervallum areas, and the frontages of two principal roads (probably the *via praetoria* and *via principalis*) were also occupied with free-standing buildings. Some of these appear to have been *fabricae*, though others were perhaps used for storage or additional accommodation. In the *latera praetorii*, fragments of two buildings, probably the *principia* and *praetorium*, were exposed. Too little of the former was seen for it to be characterised, but most of the excavated area of the *praetorium* appears to have been given over to bronze- and leather-

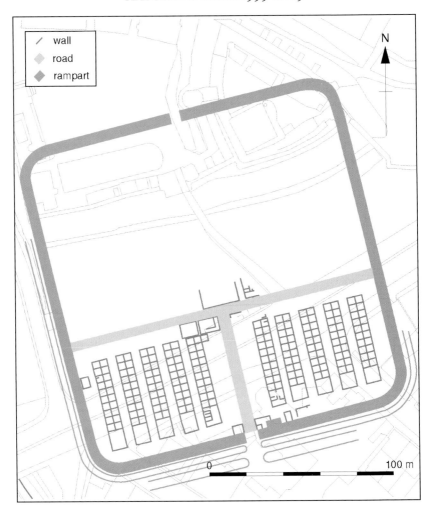

Figure 43. Carlisle: reconstruction of plan of primary fort

working, suggesting that this part of the structure may have been a *fabrica* serving the commander's household. Most of the excavated early Flavian buildings incorporated much timber other than oak, particularly alder but also ash. Such non-durable material was not confined to the 'lesser' buildings or to minor structural components, but was utilised for principal wall-posts in the barracks and the probable *praetorium*. However, it is noteworthy that oak was extensively used in the defences.

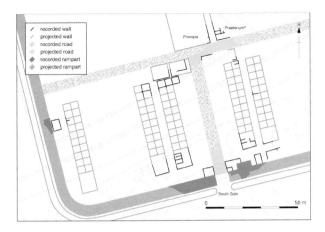

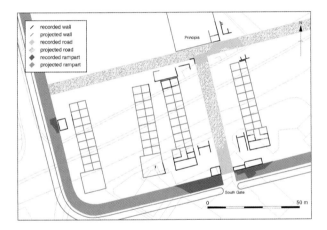

Figure 44. Carlisle:
1. Fort of 72/3
2. Fort of 83/4

Ceramic evidence suggests that the fort may have been built and/or garrisoned by a unit or units with connections to the legionary fortress at Nijmegen on the Rhine (Swan 2008, 52). It is possible that the construction detail may have been a detachment of *Legio II Adiutrix*, which occupied Nijmegen before being brought to Britain by Petillius Cerialis *c.* AD 71 (Holder 1982, 104), and which was stationed at Chester by the mid-70s (Philpott 2006, 63). A writing tablet records a trooper of the *ala Gallorum*

Sebosiana at Carlisle during Agricola's governorship (Tomlin 1998, 74–5), but since this individual was seconded to the governor's mounted guard it is not clear if the entire regiment was in garrison at this time. It may be no coincidence, though, that the unit was also seemingly transferred from the Rhine in AD 71 (Jarrett 1994, 41), and other writing tablets record the presence of an unnamed quingenary *ala*, probably but not certainly the *ala Sebosiana*, in the later Flavian period (Tomlin 1998, 76). Furthermore, the fragments of the Cerialian barracks that have been excavated indicate that they may have been of the 'stable-barrack' type (Hodgson and Bidwell 2004). The provision of ten *contubernia* seems likely, with the officers' suite on the S (Caruana in prep), but in the only barrack for which sufficient evidence is available, the northernmost *contubernium* appears to have been larger (Fig. 44.1), probably comprising three rooms (one projecting) rather than two. This compartment may therefore have had a specialised function, leaving nine 'standard' *contubernia*, each of *c.* 30m², for the rank-and-file.

Dendrochronological dating indicates that a reconstruction of the fort within its defensive perimeter (or at least those areas subjected to excavation) occurred during the autumn/winter of AD 83-4, with almost all the excavated buildings rebuilt in more-or-less their original positions (Fig. 44.2). In contrast to the original work, major structural elements were fashioned exclusively from good-quality oak. There is no evidence for work on the defences at this time, a testament, perhaps, to the durability of the oak used in their original construction. The new barracks were similar in size to the earlier structures (47 x 9m), with (probably) nine larger *contubernia* (*c.* 36m²) and wider officers' quarters. Again, they may have been of the 'stable-barrack' type, and presumably accommodated the *ala* that is known to have occupied the fort at some stage prior to *c.* AD 105.

After AD 83-4, there is little evidence for internal alteration prior to the demolition of the fort *c.* AD 103-5. Two of the *fabrica*-type detached structures were rebuilt around AD 93-4 using large oak sill-beams into which the wall-posts had been mortised. This contrasted with the technique employed both in earlier and subsequent phases, where post-in-trench construction was the norm for load-bearing walls. A strong Gallic influence in the late Flavian garrison (be it the *ala Sebosiana* or some other unit) is indicated by a significant group of pottery imported from northern *Gallia Belgica*.

The fort in the Trajanic and Hadrianic periods

The fort was rebuilt around AD 105, again seemingly wholly in timber (Fig. 45.1). The excavated evidence suggests a high degree of continuity in layout from the Flavian period. However, it is not clear whether this extended to the entire installation, and consequently the size and shape of the new fort

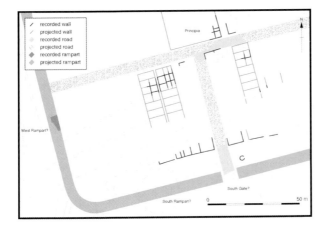

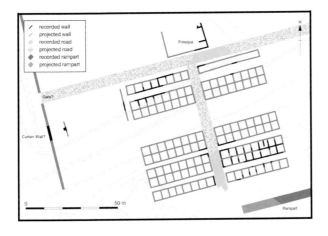

Figure 45. Carlisle:
1. Fort of c. 105
2. The stone fort

cannot be estimated. The S and W ramparts and the S gate were probably reinstated in their earlier positions, although the remains were poorly preserved. The two major roads also lay on their former alignments and N-S aligned barracks were erected in the ?*praetentura*. In the *latera praetorii*, a new *principia* was built and a structure erected on the site of the Flavian *praetorium*. The small part of this building excavated was seemingly used as a *fabrica*, but it is unknown if this was free-standing or formed part of a larger building complex, perhaps the Trajanic *praetorium*.

It has been suggested (Swan 2008, 59) that the Trajanic fort was built by *Legio IX Hispana*. The Ninth was manufacturing stamped tiles at Scalesceugh, *c.* 6km SE of Carlisle, around this time, and all the known examples were stamped from one die, indicating a single phase of production. This may have been related specifically to the reconstruction of *c.* AD 105.

The identity of the Trajanic garrison is not known, but the S part of the fort seems to have been less crowded than before (Fig. 45.1). Swan (2008, 54-5) notes the strong showing of a type of bi-conical beaker produced in northern *Gallia Belgica*, probably for the consumption of beer, which, together with other north Gaulish forms, suggest that the Gallic influence apparent in the late first-century fort was maintained into the second century. However, the barracks, though of similar width (*c.* 8.5-9m) to the Flavian structures, were seemingly shorter (less than 40m) and probably had no more than seven or eight *contubernia* (allowing space on the S for officers' quarters), each of approximately 35m². Two of the three partially excavated structures appear to have been built almost back-to-back.

The fort was not abandoned following the construction of Hadrian's Wall, but sometime during Hadrian's reign a marked change in the character of occupation, accompanied by a widespread internal replanning, occurred. In the *latera praetorii*, the *principia* and *fabrica* continued in use, although the nature of the activity within both changed. In the *principia*, this was reflected by, amongst other things, the deposition of numerous projectile heads. In the *fabrica*, a build-up of dark soils occurred; these contained much rubbish, including a cache of armour, perhaps destined for recycling, comprising several laminated limb defences, two scale shoulder-guards, a greave and many other fragments. To the S, all the known buildings, including the barracks, were demolished and replaced with new structures, some of which had an industrial function, or with cobbled surfaces. The amount of smithing debris also increased greatly at this time. The significance of these developments is difficult to assess, though they imply a change, in part at least, in the function of the fort. The catalyst for this remains unclear, but it was probably associated with the construction of Hadrian's Wall, and in particular the presumed primary Wall-fort at Stanwix, less than 1km to the N. The evidence suggests that the site may have become less a base for a regular military unit than something akin to a works depot. The installation was demolished around the middle of the second century, perhaps as a consequence of the Antonine reoccupation of southern Scotland.

The fort site in the second half of the second century
The second half of the second century is perhaps the most obscure period

in the history of the fort. Quite complex sequences of deposits have been excavated, but the nature of the occupation remains poorly understood. It is not even clear if the site was occupied by a conventional fort at this time, although this seems increasingly unlikely. Initially, widespread silting occurred, suggesting complete or near-complete abandonment. In the SE quadrant, a stone-footed courtyard building was erected sometime after AD 165 (Caruana in prep). This was associated with a road to the W, roughly on the line of the main N-S road of the earlier forts, and a turf-and-clay rampart to the S. A large ceramic waterpipe some distance to the N might possibly have been associated. Elsewhere, a few small timber buildings, some associated with cobbled roads and gravelled surfaces, were erected. Further silting in the *latera praetorii* occurred prior to the construction of the stone fort, but to the S occupation seems to have continued, uninterrupted, up to that time.

The stone fort
Ceramic evidence (Swan 2008, 64-71) indicates that the fort was rebuilt in stone during the early third century, and an *in situ* building stone in the E wall of the *principia* demonstrates that the work was undertaken by *Legio VI Victrix*. What is known of the internal layout suggests a fort of more-or-less conventional type (Fig. 45.2). Key elements, including both of the major roads and the (S-facing) *principia*, occupied the same positions as in the earlier forts (though no trace of the *praetorium* was located), whilst the SE and SW quadrants continued to house barracks, now aligned E-W. However, the defences pose a problem, for whilst the rampart associated with the late second-century courtyard building was retained on the S (Caruana in prep), a stone wall 1.1m wide was constructed inside the Flavian/Trajanic W rampart.

The fort buildings were probably stone-built to roof height, externally, though some internal partitions may have been timber-framed on stone sleeper walls. There was space for at least eight barracks to the S, though only two have been substantively excavated; these measured 35 x 10m and were divided into eight two-room *contubernia*. Additionally, four half-width buildings, similar but comprising eight single-room compartments, have been recorded; the significance of these remains uncertain. In the SW quadrant, a small fragment of a possible granary has been observed (Fig. 45.2).

That the fort was garrisoned by legionary troops in the first half of the third century is amply demonstrated by epigraphic evidence. However, whilst *Legio VI* may have been responsible for construction, the evidence suggests that the garrison, the strength of which is unknown, comprised detachments from *Legio II Augusta* and *Legio XX Valeria Victrix*.

Few structural changes seem to have been made before the fourth century, when a heated room was inserted into the E range of the *principia*. An external latrine-pit, served from within the E range, yielded seeds from a range of medicinal plants. In the second half of the fourth century, the *principia*'s colonnaded portico was remodelled using large, socketed foundation slabs reminiscent of the 'park railing stones' known from late contexts at Haltonchesters and Rudchester (Gillam 1961, 164; 1962, 164; Gillam *et al.* 1973, 82–4; Dore 2009). In the external area E of the *principia*, a timber 'lean-to' was erected, on coin evidence, after AD 388.

Following demolition of this the area, and also the main E-W road directly in front of the *principia*, were surfaced with broken sandstone rubble and cobbles. This was in turn cut by a few shallow pits prior to the accumulation of 'dark earth' over almost all the latest Roman levels. Precisely what timescale is represented by this sequence cannot be determined, but it seems probable that occupation pre-dating the 'dark earth' extended well into the fifth century.

Approximately 250 coins, the latest issued after AD 378, were recovered from these levels, but none came from the *principia* itself. A close parallel for this is known from Newcastle and a similar phenomenon, albeit on a much smaller scale, has been recorded at Wallsend (cf. p. 37). The patterns of coin loss can best be explained by envisioning the development of a cash-based market within these forts during the second half of the fourth century, and it seems highly probable that Carlisle provides a third example.

In the S part of the fort, at least one of the third-century barracks was partially reconstructed during the fourth century (Caruana in prep). The other excavated structures underwent a variety of internal modifications before being demolished. For the most part, the levelled remains of the fort were sealed by 'dark earth'. However, part of the E wall of the *principia* probably stood into the twelfth century, and substantive elements of some of the barracks remained upstanding for centuries, with many walls being robbed to ground level only in the medieval period (Caruana in prep).

The town
Approximately 300m E of the fort, excavations in 1998-9 by CAU/CAL on the E side of modern Rickergate (NY 340 556), which is believed to lie on or close to the line of a Roman road leading N from the town to the river crossing (Fig. 42), revealed an ancient channel of the River Eden, some 300m S of the river's present course (OA North 2002c). Radiocarbon dating of organic material from the channel's alluvial fills indicated that it had become choked with silt and vegetation by the beginning of the Roman period. Probably in the early third century AD, that part of the channel adjacent to the road

appears to have been deliberately infilled prior to the construction of timber buildings on the street frontage, several structural phases being recorded. The walls of the latest surviving structure, though of timber, were provided with substantial clay-and-cobble foundations.

On the modern street, the latest Roman strata were removed by modern construction works. However, to the rear, a sequence of external deposits and boundary ditches, probably the remains of yards/gardens and property divisions associated with the frontage buildings, extended, on pottery evidence, into the second half of the fourth century.

Approximately 800m S of the fort, excavations in 1998-9 (Giecco *et al.* 2001) and 2001 (Zant *et al.* forthcoming) revealed a sequence of activity E of Botchergate (NY 404 555), which follows the line of the main Roman road S (Fig. 42). Amongst the earliest features were four late first-early second century cremation burials, two of which were of the *bustum* type. Probably during the reign of Hadrian, a marked change occurred, seemingly involving the imposition of a planned layout of regularly-sized building plots, most containing one or more timber structures. The full extent of this development is unclear, but it almost certainly extended along the street for at least 175m. Behind the street frontage, activity tailed off sharply, although there was evidence for the continued deposition of cremation burials.

The occupation was seemingly largely industrial in character; and reached a peak of intensity during the second half of the second century. An Antonine 'strip' building contained a large lead-smelting furnace, and also yielded limited evidence for iron-smithing, and several other structures also contained large ovens or furnaces and metalworking debris. The development appears to have been swept away in the late second-early third century, after which the area reverted to cemetery use.

John Zant, Oxford Archaeology North

For an excavation by North Pennines Archaeology in the Botchergate area (NY 4053 5533) revealing second to third century activity: CW[3], 7 (2007), 252.

Fisher Street Pottery

For the excavation of an important pottery production zone of the late-first and earlier-second centuries at Fisher Street, about 150m E of the fort, see Johnson and Anderson 2008; Johnson *et al.* forthcoming; and discussion in Swan 2008.

The Southern Lanes

A report has been issued on this area of the E part of the Roman town, excavated in the 1970s, where timber and stone strip buildings housing craft activities, and associated yards and fences were in use throughout the third and fourth centuries (McCarthy 2000).

See also: McCarthy 2002 (overview of Roman Carlisle in its regional setting); McCarthy 2003 (general discussion of town); Shotter 2001 (early-Flavian coins); Henig 2004 (sculpture); McCarthy *et al.* 2001 (armour).

Wall-Mile 67

In 2008-9 excavation took place in advance of the construction of a new road bridge over the River Eden near Knockupworth Farm (NY 372 568), where the Wall occupies the steep cliff forming the S bank of the river. Probable evidence for the Turf Wall, together with remains of the Stone Wall and the Vallum, were recorded. The Turf Wall and the Vallum overlay a field boundary ditch, aligned perpendicularly to the Wall. The Turf Wall had been slighted prior to construction of the Stone Wall, which was seemingly built directly on top of its remains. The Stone Wall proved to be poorly preserved, for the most part only the rubble core remaining, together with some of the S facing stones, to a maximum height of two courses. The N face had been completely eroded, and it seems likely that much of the masonry had fallen down the steep river bank in antiquity. The Vallum ditch was largely obscured by the remains of the Carlisle and Silloth Railway, which followed the route of the Carlisle Navigation Canal. The Vallum N mound comprised deposits of gravel and clay, presumably upcast from the ditch, above a layer of cobbles laid directly on the underlying turf.

Fraser Brown, Oxford Archaeology North

Milecastle 69 (Sourmilk Bridge)

Two possible locations have been proposed for Milecastle 69, one on a high point W of Grinsdale village (marked on the 1972 edition of the OS map of Hadrian's Wall), the other further W, near Doudle Beck, where Henry MacLauchlan (1858, 80) saw a large quantity of stone. Both sites were subjected to geophysical survey during 1999 and 2000, but no clear sign of the milecastle was visible. A possible anomaly was sampled by a trench in 2000 on the Grinsdale site, and this proved to be the bottom course of Hadrian's Wall preserved under a collapsed plough headland. The milecastle remains unlocated (Wilmott 2009b, 177-82).

Tony Wilmott, English Heritage

Wall-mile 69: dimensions of Vallum recorded in 2007 at Millbeck Farm (*Britannia* 39 (2008), 283).

Milecastle 70 (Braelees)

Geophysical survey in 2000 around the measured site of Milecastle 70 failed to locate it. Such was the uncertainty that no excavation trench was attempted. Excavation on Milecastle 71 showed it so completely robbed that no geophysical response could be expected. This is probably also the case for Milecastle 70 (Wilmott 2009b, 182).

Milecastle 71 (Wormanby)

Five evaluation trenches were opened on the site of this milecastle in 2000. Hadrian's Wall survived as two partial courses of stone overlying a remnant of turf Wall. The E wall of the milecastle was located, although only a few small fragments of stone survived in a linear deposit of sparse crushed sandstone 2.98m wide. There was a hint of the location of an interior building on the E side of the milecastle (Wilmott 2009b, 182-86).
Tony Wilmott, English Heritage

Wall-Mile 71

In 2002 ten evaluation trenches were excavated in the field to the E of the Wall-fort of Burgh-by-Sands II, between the projected positions of turrets 71a and 71b, and across the line of the Wall as depicted on Ordnance Survey mapping (OA North 2002d). A geophysical survey carried out in 1991 (Linford 1992) identified a linear anomaly that corresponded to this projected line, although the excavation proved this to be the road leading to the Wall fort, and concluded that the Wall actually lay some distance to the N.

The excavated trenches also provided evidence for an extramural settlement that extended for at least 200m to the E of Burgh II. Whilst *in-situ* remains were left unexcavated, the stone foundations of at least one building, metalled alleyways at right-angles to the main road, internal floors, and several hearths were all clearly recognisable. The presence of metalworking slag indicated that some of the hearths had been used for secondary iron-working, whilst the remains of a probable kiln and associated molten glass suggested that there may have been a glass workshop in the immediate vicinity. A wide range of other material was also recovered from the excavated trenches, including several relatively unusual high-status objects, such as a cast and ground polychrome mosaic glass bowl, a face jug, a triple pot, a *tazza*, and several miniature jars.
Ian Miller, Oxford Archaeology North

BURGH-BY-SANDS – *Aballava* (Fig. 46)

A project to publish the air survey and excavations carried out by the late

G.D.B. Jones in and around Burgh-by-Sands in 1977-82 has been carried out by David Breeze and David Woolliscroft, and the report is now published (Breeze and Woolliscroft 2009). Taken in conjunction with other recent surveys and excavations in the Burgh area, this work has greatly clarified our understanding of the complex sequence at this fort, although a number of outstanding problems remain.

It has now been known for 30 years that the Wall-fort at Burgh-by-Sands had a predecessor, Burgh I (1.58ha), that lay 1km SSW. An important advance in the new publication is the first proper study of the pottery from Burgh I, which found some pre-Hadrianic material, but more from the Hadrianic period. The pottery suggests that the southern fort may have had pre-Hadrianic origins but was certainly occupied in the Hadrianic period and up to the mid-second century (with only a few pieces suggesting continued activity after that). Burgh I would thus seem most likely to be the Hadrianic fort at Burgh, and Burgh II, the fort in the village on the line of the Wall, a later addition. Burgh I is best interpreted as a square fort on the Brampton Old Church model, with turf rampart on stone base, stone central range buildings and timber barracks, with an annexe attached to its SE side. As at Old Church, the sheer distance from the Wall might suggest an origin in the later-Trajanic period, as a post on a route from Carlisle to Kirkbride. Excellent air-photographs of the site are to be found in Jones and Woolliscroft 2001, Fig. 30 and Plate 9. The absence of an actual Wall-fort at Burgh in the Hadrianic period possibly explains the omission of *Aballava* from the list of names on the Staffordshire Moorlands pan (p.22).

Burgh II straddles the original line of the Turf Wall, but that does not mean that it was necessarily ever a projecting fort of the early-Hadrianic type. This is because geophysical survey (published for the first time in the Breeze and Woolliscroft report) has clearly shown a realignment of the Wall to bring it up to the N corners of the fort (as at Birdoswald). It is possible that this realignment of the Wall was contemporary with the first building of the fort. A ditch discovered E of the fort in the vicarage garden excavations, aligning with a ditch seen W of the fort in 1978 (Austen 1994, 49) may represent the Vallum, running under the fort and therefore confirming a late-Hadrianic or later date for Burgh II: the identification as the Vallum is not certain, but seems possible in the light of a further sighting on the alignment W of the fort (Walker 2007).

A settlement apparently lining a road from the S gate of Burgh II has been investigated at Amberfield, 200m S, on a number of occasions (Hodgkinson 1993; Reeves and McCarthy 1999; Reeves 2002; Masser and Evans 2005; Mitchell forthcoming). This settlement is probably a *vicus* of Burgh II. The pottery from this area is generally of second-century date, not later. The

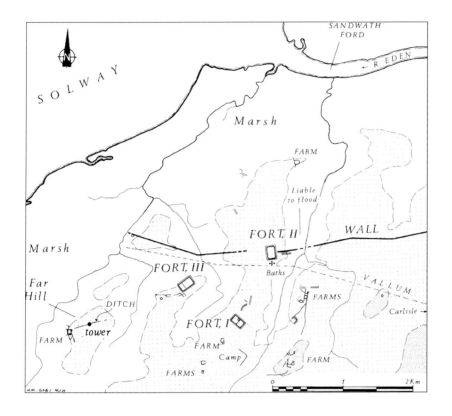

Figure 46. Sites in the Burgh-by-Sands area, after G.D.B. Jones

most detailed pottery report is in Masser and Evans 2005. This indicates Hadrianic samian occurring in no greater quantity than one would expect for a site founded in the mid-second century. The report suggests the 'late-Hadrianic period' as the most likely start date (Masser and Evans 2005, 61). The Amberfield material, if associated with Burgh II, certainly rules out the early-third century start date for the fort suggested by Paul Austen in 1994 and in the last Pilgrimage handbook. On the other hand from this assemblage of pottery it is not possible to make a sharp distinction between say *c.* 140 on one hand and *c.* 160 on the other.

The simplest interpretation of the Burgh evidence is that in the Hadrianic period the fort (Burgh I) lay detached 1km S of the Turf Wall. Either at the end of Hadrian's reign (*c.* 138) or, more likely, when the Turf Wall was rebuilt in stone, perhaps around 160, Burgh II was built, and the Wall realigned to join its N corners. Burgh III, a site of 3.35ha in its largest form, identified by Jones as a fort 1km to the W, could in this case represent either a pre-Hadrianic fort earlier than Burgh I, or, more likely, a camp.

The closing date of the Amberfield *vicus* development coincides roughly – in the late-second or early-third century – with the start of the *vicus* development excavated immediately outside the SE part of the fort (vicarage garden) in 1980-2. Rather than signifying the beginning of Burgh II, then, this date seems to be that of a movement of the *vicus* closer to the fort, encroaching on the N side of the Vallum (itself already overlain by the fort if correctly identified at the vicarage garden). As many as 17 distinct buildings of timber or stone, possible property divisions, and a road were identified ranging in date from the late second century to the late third century. Evidence for metalworking was found in four successive third century buildings. The *vicus* was abandoned by the later-third century.

The Breeze and Woolliscroft report accepts a circular enclosure underlying the SE rampart of Burgh I as a pre-fort Roman watchtower, as Jones had suggested, and also accepts three further sites claimed as watchtowers by Jones, to the W of Burgh, at Far Hill (NY 303580), Easton (NY 274 579) and E of Burgh at Monkhill, near Kirkandrews (NY 344 584) as likely to be Roman. Certain lengths of ditch and alignments of postholes in the vicinity of these features and running parallel to the NE rampart of Burgh I are also accepted as pre-Hadrianic frontier works or '*clausurae*.' See in general Jones and Woolliscroft 2001, 62-71 and, also, Woolliscroft and Jones 2004, for publication of a trench across a road and running ditch accompanied by fence-lines, 2.5km S of Drumburgh. The ditch and fences are argued to be of Roman character, but there is no decisive indication that they are not part of the pre-Roman Iron Age agricultural landscape.

Milecastle 73 and Hadrian's Wall at Burgh-By-Sands: geophysical survey (Fig. 47)

A magnetometry survey was carried out on Watch Hill from Turret 72b to the edge of Burgh Marsh, which included Milecastle 73. The survey shows the line of the Stone Wall running some 7m to the S of the route shown on the current OS maps. Some indication of the Wall ditch can be seen but the feature is not well defined. The end of the Wall at the edge of the marsh was seen as a very high negative feature. This is a far greater value than is expected for a stone wall. It is possible that this feature and the headland on which it sits represent the terminus of the Wall and show that it was not built across the marsh.

The line of the Vallum runs behind the present field boundary to the N of

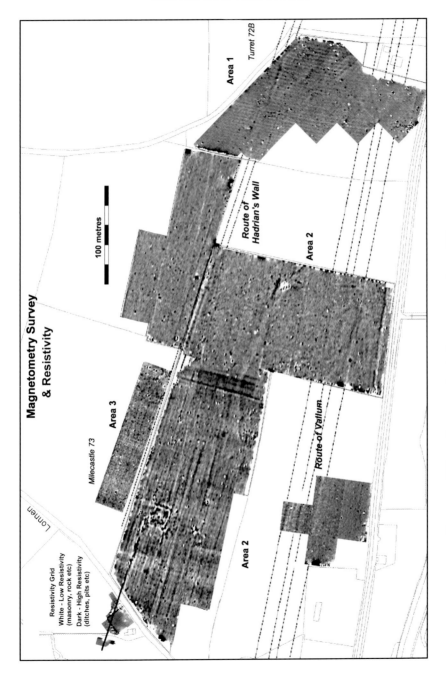

Figure 47. Milecastle 73 geophysical survey, courtesy of Timescape surveys

the unclassified road and is some 45m to the S of its plotted course.

There is little evidence of Turret 72b to be seen in the magnetic response. However, the remains of Milecastle 73 are greater than some of those this far W, e.g. MC 69 and 70. The milecastle was seen to be 496m (542 yards) to the W of Turret 72b, measured from the estimated centre of each structure, assuming a planar distance. The external dimensions were, E-W 26.0m (85.3ft) by N-S 24.75m (81.2ft).

There is some indication of a road at the milecastle running N of the Wall ditch with a funnel near the crossing. However the Wall ditch does appear to be continuous at this point. Two contiguous enclosures were built onto each of the E and W walls of the milecastle with a further one in stone built to the W of the western enclosure. Some evidence of buildings and divisions can be seen in both western enclosures. A trackway runs E-W to the S of the milecastle. [Bidwell 2005a, 68 points out that this survey shows a wide berm (10m) between the wall and ditch throughout, except at the site of Turret 72b, where there is an indication that the Wall ditch swings S to converge with the Wall.]

Publication: Biggins *et al.* 2004.

J. A. Biggins, S. Hall and D. J. A. Taylor, Timescape Surveys

DRUMBURGH – Congabata

The Staffordshire-Moorlands Pan confirms that the place name (previously only known from the Notitia Dignitatum) is correctly applied to Drumburgh (see p. 00).

Milecastle 78 (Kirkland) (Fig. 48)

The three trenches excavated on this site in 2000 were extremely informative in locating for the first time the E and W walls and the SW corner of the milecastle. The flagstone wall foundations survived in the bottom of robber trenches, and some internal surfacing was also in evidence. The long-axis milecastle measured 19.2 x 20.74m externally, and its walls were 2.35m wide. The S exterior corners were curved, but the internal corners were square. A truncated burnt feature, possibly the base of an oven was located in the SW corner (Wilmott 2009b, 186-93).

Milecastle 79 (Solway House) (Fig. 49)

This milecastle was evaluated in 1999. Two trenches confirmed the results of previous work on this installation, which is one of the most thoroughly excavated of the milecastles (Richmond and Gillam 1952), and the fact that the well-preserved remains of both the turf and stone milecastles survived. In the stone phase a timber building occupied the E side of the milecastle (Wilmott 2009b, 193-97).

Tony Wilmott, English Heritage

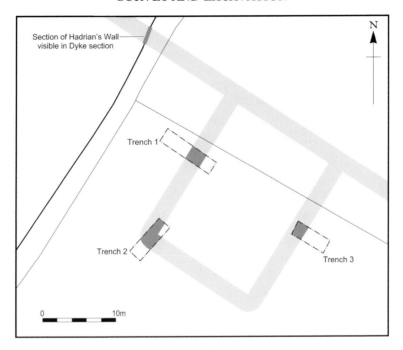

Figure 48. Milecastle 78

Wall-Miles 77 and 78

Work in 2006-7 during improvements to the waste water treatment system between Bowness-on-Solway and Drumburgh, revealed possible traces of Hadrian's Wall at three locations. In Wall-Mile 78, what may have been the spread remains of the Turf Wall were observed in section in the roadway immediately S of Hesket House, Port Carlisle (NY 323 562). These comprised a sequence of clay and turf layers 0.25m thick and approximately 8m wide, NW to SE. What may have been the poorly-preserved sandstone foundation for the Stone Wall was also recorded, c. 15m to the NW. This survived as a cut, 0.45m deep and at least 2.3m wide, filled with compacted sandstone rubble. Approximately 2.5m NW of the putative foundation, what was probably the S edge of the Wall ditch, in excess of 10m wide at the lip and over 2m deep, was seen. Elsewhere, possible traces of the Stone Wall foundation, similar in character to those recorded at Port Carlisle, were observed in the roadway NW of Kirkland House (NY 324 561), also in Wall-Mile 78, and in Wall-Mile 77, c. 200m W of Westfield House (NY 325 561).

John Zant, Oxford Archaeology North

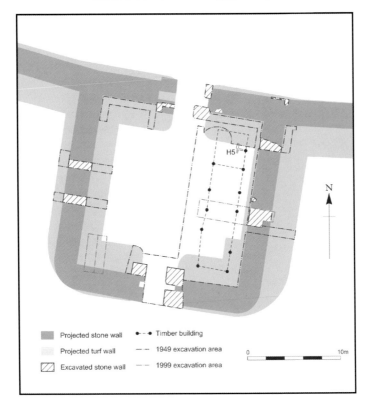

Figure 49. Milecastle 79

BOWNESS ON SOLWAY (*Maia*)

No recent work. Metal object from foreshore: Cracknell 2004.

THE CUMBRIAN COASTAL SYSTEM

Introduction

Since 1999 there has been no further extension of the regular system of milefortlets and towers on the Cumberland coast beyond the southernmost known tower (Risehow, 25b), two miles S of Maryport, and there is general agreement that the system may have extended no further than a postulated 'terminal' milefortlet at Flimby (MF26).

The principal research development in this area has been the publication in 2004 of *Romans on the Solway*, a collection of studies in honour of Richard Bellhouse, the indefatigable pioneer who from 1954 almost single-handedly traced the system of coastal fortlets and towers from the Cardurnock peninsula to just S of Maryport. The book is prefaced with a judicious overview of the Solway frontier by Roger Wilson (Wilson 2004) which should be a starting point for all who embark on the study of the Cumberland coast. Also of great utility is a discussion and comprehensive schedule of the sites, with bibliographical references (Breeze 2004). It should be noted that Breeze follows Daniels (1990) in rejecting Bellhouse's schedule for the Maryport area and S. This had been based on the belief that the system was scaled N and S from notional towers (23b and 24a) at the NW and SW angles of the supposedly pre-existing Maryport fort, meaning that there was no MF24. A return is effectively made to the schedule given in Birley's *Research on Hadrian's Wall*, in which T23b would be under the fort at Maryport.

In the same volume there is a study of coastal erosion and change and its effect on the Roman installations (Clare 2004); a discussion of the long-standing problems of the Roman names of the Cumberland coast forts, now to some extent resolving, thanks to the discovery of new evidence (Holder 2004); a discussion of the coin finds and their significance (Shotter 2004a); and a biographical note on Joseph Robinson, one of the earliest pioneers of research on the Cumberland coast, who carried out much fieldwork in just two very productive years between 1879 and 1881 (Harbottle 2004). The remaining papers deal with individual sites, noted below in their proper places.

Milefortlet 1, Biglands: air photograph of fortlet and running ditches: Jones and Wooliscroft 2001, 123, Fig. 74.

Tower 2b, Campfield
The late G.D.B. Jones' report on excavations here, originally published in the *Manchester Archaeological Bulletin* (1993, 8, 31-9) have been republished in the *Romans on the Solway* volume (Jones 2004). His claim that there were two successive timber predecessors to the stone tower is critically assessed and dismissed by Breeze (2004, 74), Caruana (2004b) and Wilson (2004, 22-3): 'the overwhelming body of evidence at present points to the conclusion that no such timber towers ever existed'. For discussion of the running ditches observed here: Wilson 2004, 24-5.

Milefortlet 5, Cardunock: air photograph of fortlet and running ditches: Jones and Woolliscroft 2001, 125, Fig. 76. For discussion of the running ditches observed here: Wilson 2004, 24-5.

KIRKBRIDE
There has been no recent work on the ground at this pre-Hadrianic fort at the mouth of the river Wampool, but see Jones and Woolliscroft 2001, 66-7 for informative air photographs, one apparently showing an enclosure outside the fort.

Milefortlet 9, Skinburness: air photograph of fortlet and running ditches, the latter thought unlikely to be Roman: Jones and Woolliscroft 2001, 126, Fig. 77. For discussion of the running ditches: Wilson 2004, 24-5.

Coastal Mile 10 – Silloth
An excavation in 1994 investigated features in Silloth school playing fields seen from the air in 1975 and interpreted as a pair of running frontier palisades and a road. The palisade trenches were found to be modern field drains. The character of the road was consistent with a Roman date (Woolliscroft and Jones 2004; Jones and Woolliscroft 2001, 127-8 and Fig. 78).

BECKFOOT – ?*Bibra*
In 2006, Oxford Archaeology North undertook an evaluation *c.* 350m SW of the fort at Beckfoot, on the Cumbrian coast (NY 087 486), in an area of coastal dunes long known to be the site of a Roman cemetery presumably associated with the fort (Caruana 2004a). The work was carried out at the request of English Heritage, in order to assess the extent and survival of the cemetery, which has suffered, and continues to suffer, severe erosion by the sea, and to seek evidence for the existence of Milefortlet 15, the measured position of which falls within the evaluated area (Bellhouse 1957, 21-2; 1962, 71-2).

No evidence for the milefortlet was found, supporting Bellhouse's assertion (1957, 21-2) that it has been completely destroyed by coastal erosion. Features and deposits relating to the cemetery were, however, plentiful. In total, eight definite or probable cremation burials were recorded, though only four were fully excavated. Additionally, several shallow ditches and a few pit-like features of indeterminate character were located. No inhumation burials were present, nor was there any evidence for pyre sites similar to those excavated elsewhere in the cemetery in 1948 and 1954 (Hogg 1949; Bellhouse 1954, 51-3). However, quite extensive spreads of probable pyre debris, comprising dark soils containing much charcoal and some cremated bone, were present in the central part of the site, suggesting the likely proximity of one or more pyres outside the excavated areas. Two of the cremations were sealed by these layers, whilst a third had been dug through the material; the others had no stratigraphic relationship with the deposits.

Of the four excavated burials, two were of adults (one probably female), whilst the others contained the bones of a juvenile/sub-adult and an infant. Both of the latter were contained within Black Burnished ware Fabric 1 jars, which had been utilised as burial urns, though in both cases far more burnt bone and charcoal was recovered from the burial pit itself, surrounding (and, in the case of the infant grave, beneath) the urn, than from within the vessel. None of the other burials yielded evidence for containers, but the presence of iron strips, tacks and rivets amongst the spreads of pyre debris indicated the likely presence of wooden containers and/or furniture on the funeral pyres, such as the 'funeral beds' found at the pyre sites in 1948 and 1954 (Hogg 1949, 34-6; Bellhouse 1954, 51-3). However, some of these objects might also have derived from pieces of scrap wood used as fuel. The placing of other goods, such as footwear and fine tableware, on the pyres was suggested by the recovery of many hobnails and numerous burnt samian ware sherds (three-quarters of the small samian assemblage had been intensely burnt). The two Black Burnished ware urns were both moderately burnt, indicating that they may have been placed at the edge of the pyre.

The infant burial and one of the unexcavated graves were enclosed by penannular ditches 2.5-3m in diameter, similar to those known from the cemetery associated with the fort at Low Borrow Bridge (Hair and Howard-Davis 1996). The ditch surrounding the infant grave yielded cremated bone from a probable sub-adult, almost certainly a different individual to the one interred in the other urned grave. Some of the other, linear, ditches on the site might have been burial plot boundaries, but none could be characterised with any certainty. The charcoal assemblages from the burials and the pyre debris comprised material derived from a wide range of species, including oak, alder/ hazel, ash, birch/maple, blackthorn/cherry, pine and hawthorn/apple-type.

With the exception of one South Gaulish samian sherd and a coarseware fragment of possible Flavian/Trajanic date, the pottery from the site was entirely Antonine or later. Overall, the ceramic assemblage suggested a *floruit* for this part of the cemetery during the third century, though some second-century material and a few sherds of possible late third-fourth-century date were also recovered.

John Zant, Oxford Archaeology North

For important air photographs of the fort, see Jones and Woolliscroft 2001, 128-30. Of particular note is the road issuing from the *portae principales*, which can be traced over a considerable distance and demonstrates that similar observed stretches of road on the Cumberland coast, as at Silloth, above, could represent a 'Military Way' or road connecting the frontier installations.

Milefortlet 17, Dubmill Point: air photograph in Jones and Woolliscroft 2001, 130, Fig. 81.

Milefortlet 21, Swarthy Hill: this milefortlet, excavated in 1990-91, is fully published and was reported on in the last Pilgrimage handbook. It measures overall 29.5m E-W by 27m N-S and has the usual arrangement of gates in both seaward and landward sides. On the S side of the central road there was a range of three buildings of turf or timber beam construction; postholes and occupation levels indicated a timber building on the N side. The fortlet was surrounded on all but the seaward side by a single ditch 7.5m wide. The site was of single period and not occupied after the reign of Hadrian.

T22b, Club House: the tombstone of a child, found here in the 1950s, has been published: *Britannia* 31 (2000), 435.

Milefortlet 23, Sea Brows: air photograph in Jones and Woolliscroft 2001, 131, Fig. 82.

MARYPORT – ?*Alauna*

For this fort, *Romans on the Solway* (Wilson and Caruana 2004) offers an important supplement to the earlier essays in *Roman Maryport and its Setting* (Wilson 1997). The introductory discussion by Wilson (2004) reconsiders many aspects of Maryport and its problems. Most notably, the *vicus* and the environs of the fort have been revealed in spectacular detail by a geophysical survey (Biggins and Taylor 2004a) of which the directors give a summary below. There are commentaries on this survey by Wilson (2004) and, particularly importantly, by Sommer (2006), especially valuable on the form of the *vicus*. In addition see Waldock 2002 for a discussion of the various suggested parade grounds at Maryport, important because it severs the link between buried altars and parade-grounds that still exists in many minds. Frere (2000) discusses the unit based at the fort and the possible sequence of commanders under Hadrian.

Occurring too late to be taken into account in the discussions in the *Romans on the Solway* volume, the only excavations to be carried out at Maryport in the last decade have been by the Maryport & District Archaeological Society in fields to the SW and SE of the fort earthworks in Camp Field. It has been claimed (*Britannia* 37 (2006), 392) that these excavations have encountered an earlier fort than the visible one, indicated by a stone-based rampart, 5.5m wide, intervallum road and timber buildings. The rampart was joined at right angles by another, also 5.5m wide, supposed to represent an annexe. Little dating evidence was recovered. The discovery of a predecessor to the known fort at Maryport would indeed be a major development, but the excavations in question were on a very small scale, and judgement on the significance of these results will have to be withheld until a detailed report is available.

Funding has been made available, from the Heritage Lottery Fund, Hadrian's Wall Heritage Ltd and the Senhouse Museum Trust, to develop further programmes of archaeological research at Maryport.

Geophysical Survey (Fig. 50)
Geophysical survey was carried out in 2000, commissioned by the Trustees of the Senhouse Museum. The survey covered an area of 75 hectares (188 acres) and at the time represented the largest carried out on the northern frontier.

It is clear from the survey that considerable erosion has taken place to the cliff edge and archaeological evidence has been lost. Within the fort, the *principia* with its well (5) can be identified together with some buildings in the *retentura*.

The road leading NE from the fort is bounded on each side by buildings for a distance of over 400m. In many cases property divisions run along the sides of the buildings to a ditch running to the rear. Many of these buildings are large in size. On the SE side of the road at a distance of *c.* 85m from the fort a substantial building *c.* 30m long by *c.* 11m wide can be seen (15). On the other side of the road *c.* 150m from the fort a further building *c.* 26m long by *c.* 11m wide is sited (16). This building has what appears to be buttresses to its long walls – a possible granary?

Adjacent to the SE field boundary of the field to the NE of the fort, at its highest point, was the site of the rectangular and circular buildings, probably both temples together with two others nearby, excavated by Robinson in 1880. This possible sanctuary site (19) can be seen to be within an irregular enclosure of which only part remains.

The field to the NE of this temple site was where seventeen altars were uncovered in 1870 (20). This area has been extensively ploughed and few archaeological features are identifiable, but a possible minor road and enclosure may be present.

At a point approximately 690m from the NE gate of the fort the spine road of the *vicus* crosses a ditch (32). This ditch can be seen to enclose an open area to the NE of the *vicus* and it is possible that it defines the *territorium* of the fort.
Publication: Biggins and Taylor 2004a.
J. A. Biggins and D. J. A. Taylor, Timescape Surveys

Milefortlet 25 (Risehow Bank) and Towers 25a (Rise How) and 25b (Risehow Tower = Fothergill): mark the southernmost known of

Figure 50. Maryport geophysical survey, courtesy of Timescape surveys

the fortlets and towers of the Cumberland coast, T25b possibly being the final tower, just two miles S of the fort at Maryport. Only a further 3 miles down the coast is the site of:

BURROW WALLS (Fig. 51)

Excavation in 1955 suggested a small fort with an estimated area of 1.2ha, equipped with a stone wall on clay-and-cobble foundations, some 2.5-3m wide, and two ditches. Immediately within the fort wall was the ditch of an even smaller and later installation: this inner, late ditch produced large quantities of post-370 pottery. Although nothing is known of the history of the earlier fort, a group of five altars found in 1852, one inscribed (RIB 806), clearly attests second- or third-century occupation.

'It has a large prospect into the sea, but little towards the land' (Horsley, *Britannia Romana* (1732), 483).

MORESBY – ?*Gabrosentum*

A 1.42ha fort whose S and W ramparts are visible. A churchyard covers the E half of the fort platform. The building of the fort is dated by a building inscription of Hadrian as *pater patriae*, that is of 128-38. The site has produced inscriptions of *cohors II Lingonum* and *cohors II Thracum*, the latter placed by the Notitia Dignitatum at *Gabrosentum*. There has been no recent archaeological work except for some Time Team trenches at Moresby Hall in 2003 which recovered Roman finds.

An engraving of 1816 by Samuel Lysons (Fig. 52) shows Moresby viewed from the S, with church (rebuilt 1822), Moresby Hall, and in the background Lowca Hill, which was later obscured by the spoil heap of Harrington colliery. In the distance across the Solway is SW Scotland and Burnswark.

'The fort...lies on a low, flat hill-top overlooking the sea to the W and the Lowca Beck to the N...it must always have had the appearance of lying in a slight saucer with higher land on three sides. To the N the outlook could never have been further than Lowca Hill...to the S the headland of St Bees is clear, 5 miles away' (Charles Daniels, HB13, 281-2).

David Woolliscroft has pointed out (1994, 57) that while Beckfoot and Maryport are in elevated positions, Burrow Walls and Moresby are low-lying locations and are not placed upon the adjacent headlands. This, he suggested, supports the idea that the two southern forts were not integrated into the system of fortlets and towers along the Cumberland coast, which therefore did not extend this far S. The Pilgrimage will visit Moresby in 2009 with the specific objective of examining the setting of this little-studied fort.

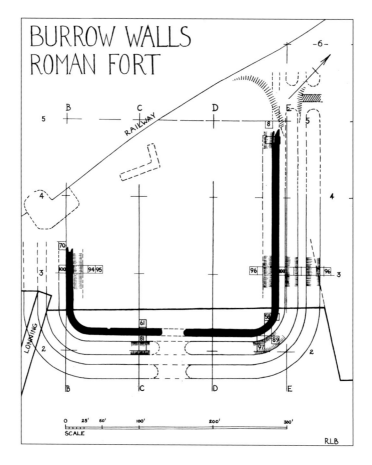

Figure 51. The fort at Burrow Walls

RAVENGLASS – ?*Itunocelum*

An analytical earthwork survey of the fort has been published (Blood and Pearson 2004). It should be noted that the wood which covered the site at the time of the survey has now been cleared. The S defences were recorded for the first time, and the likely position of the S gate – suggesting that the fort faced E, inland. For a discussion of the function of this fort, and a suggestion that the full-sized fort here replaced the known fortlet to guard the entrance to Eskdale when the inland site at Hardknott Castle was abandoned in the late-Hadrianic period, see Bidwell *et al.* 1999, 69-72.

166

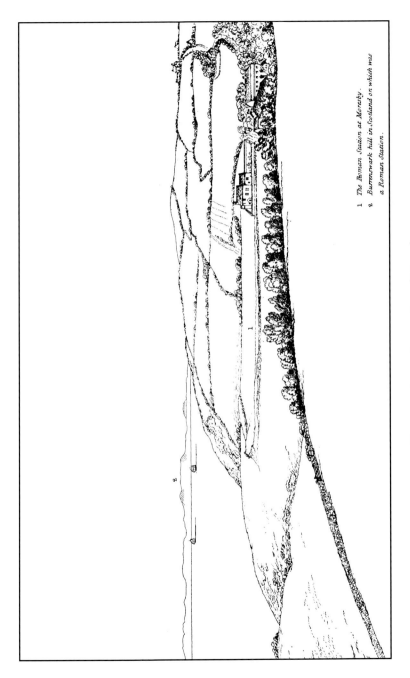

1 The Roman Station at Moresby.
2 Burrowmark hill in Scotland on which was a Roman Station.

Figure 52. Lysons' engraving of Moresby

THE OUTPOST FORTS

HIGH ROCHESTER – *Bremenium*

Geophysical survey (Fig. 53)

A magnetometry survey was carried out at High Rochester Roman Fort in 2003, concentrating on the field W of the fort. The survey was designed to complement and extend previous geophysical survey work, and to investigate the nature and extent of the fort annexe(s).

The survey established the existence of a complex multi-phase annexe. It confirmed the presence of the smaller annexe A (18) associated with the Flavian turf and timber fort. A more prominent annexe B was discovered, possibly dating to the Antonine reoccupation. The extent of this annexe is marked by defensive ditches (15), two to the W and three to the N. The features at its S perimeter suggest various re-alignments (27 – 29, 15B), progressing outwards over time. The defences of annexe B include an entrance passage on its N side (16) which appears to connect with a minor road from the N (9A). There is also a possible projecting tower (17) at its NW angle, uncommon for annexe defences; and an apparently substantial gateway with one or two flanking towers on the W side (22). The fact that the projecting tower and gateway are set forward of the annexe rampart implies that they may be later additions or reconstructions.

Structures found in the southern sector of annexe B indicate possible buildings (19, 25), presumably used for storage or as workshops, the linear features (21) imply roads. The comparative absence of features in the N sector suggests that this large area of open space was used as a wagon park, corral or for temporary storage.

Outside the SW angle of the annexe, a secondary enclosure or sub-annexe was located protected by a ditch and a rampart with a palisade fence (36). While the southern extent of this sub-annexe and its function are unknown, the N half is dominated by a large building complex (34) with an associated entrance area (35). The overall size of this building is about 30 by 40m, and from its location, its layout and a characteristic sub-circular feature, it may well be identified as the garrison bathhouse. This bathhouse could pre-date the internal bathhouse which was built after AD 213. It may even pre-date the Antonine annexe, as it shows another entrance-like passage at its S end (37), which, when extrapolated, extends straight to the fort's W gate.

Publication: Hancke *et al.* 2004.

T. Hancke, B. Charlton and J. A. Biggins

[Further magnetic survey shows possible buildings lining Dere Street as it

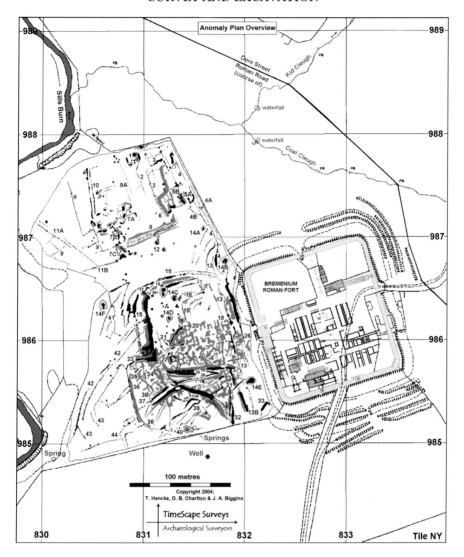

Figure 53. High Rochester geophysical survey

passes immediately E of the fort.]

See also: On survey and excavation 1992-8: Crow 2004b; on the 'Officer's tomb': Wilson 2004.

Lead sealings of *cohors I Lingonum*, attested at High Rochester in the early-Antonine period (RIB 1276), and QLOLLI (Q. Lollius Urbicus?) were found in 2002: *Britannia* 35 (2004), 343.

BEWCASTLE – *Fanum Cocidii*

Geophysical survey (Fig. 54)

A magnetometry survey was carried out in 2000, 2002 and 2003. The survey extended over the accessible region of the fort together with five surrounding areas and covered a total area of 9.25ha. The survey within the fort walls, identified the *principia* and *praetorium*, together with the *via praetoria* and *via principalis*, though these are hard to recognise without reference to the excavation plans of the 1930s. It was found that the buildings in the *praetentura* were built parallel with the E facing fort wall. The buildings in the *retentura* (barracks?) are well defined and are set out parallel to the NW fort wall. Further S, a strip of buildings is set out parallel to the SW wall.

There is little evidence of any buildings in the field directly to the E of the fort. A road, however, leads from the N gate of the fort, increasing in width some 65m N, to pass to the W of a rectangular enclosure. The enclosure is surrounded by a substantial ditch to the W and S sides, but the boundaries to the N and E are not clearly defined. Traces of buildings, some of stone, can be seen outside the N gate.To the S of the W gate is a natural platform overlooking Hall Sike where several disturbed features can be seen. In the side of an unfinished silage pit a large stone block of Roman masonry can be seen.

Significantly no evidence was seen around the fort of any field enclosures as seen at forts on the Wall. The lack of any significant *vicus* at Bewcastle implies that the fort was sited in an unstable location unsuited to a civilian settlement. This is supported by the fort's position, which was not chosen for its defensive situation, being in the valley bottom and the fact that the garrisons to the outpost forts in the second and third centuries where known comprised a milliary cohort.

A. J. Biggins and D.J.A. Taylor, Timescape Surveys

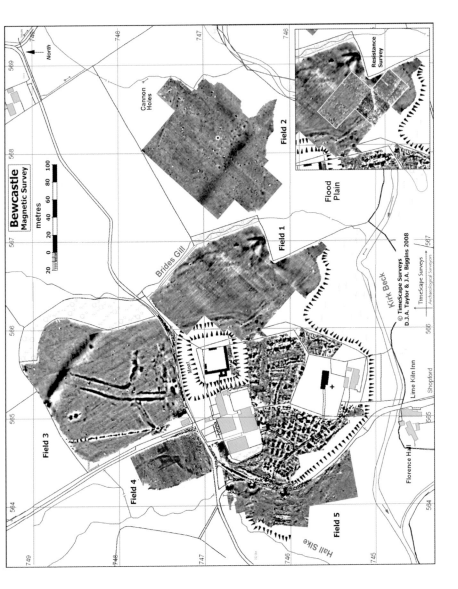

Figure 54. Bewcastle geophysical survey

BIBLIOGRAPHY

The bibliography includes references to all substantial publications on Hadrian's Wall which have come to my notice between 1999 and May 2009, but excludes annual summaries – unless they are the main or primary publication – and interim reports superseded by definitive publications. Certain 'grey literature' reports are cited. These comprise laboratory reports, some academic theses and developer-funded reports produced for clients as part of the planning process. Their entries are enclosed in square brackets to distinguish them from conventional publications. They are generally available from the County Historic Environment Records (formerly Sites and Monuments Records) or the relevant universities, and access may be subject to certain restrictions. Publications before 1999 are included where cited in the text. For full bibliographies of the sites, readers are referred to the various editions of the *Handbook to the Roman Wall*.

Abbreviations:

AA^{1-5} *Archaeologia Aeliana, series 1-5*
Arbeia J.   *Arbeia Journal*
Arch. J. *Archaeological Journal*
BAR   *British Archaeological Reports, British and International Series*
CW^{1-3} *Transactions of the Cumberland and Westmorland Antiquarian and Archaeological Society, series 1-3*
JRS   *Journal of Roman Studies*

Abdy, R., 2003 'Museum Notes 1: A Roman coin hoard from Longhorsley', AA5, **32**, 189-191
Allason-Jones, L., 1999 'Health care in the Roman North', *Britannia*, **30**, 133-146
Allason-Jones, L., 2002 'The material culture of Hadrian's Wall', in Freeman et al. 2002, 821-24
Allason-Jones, L., 2004 'Mithras on Hadrian's Wall', in Martens, M. and de Boe, G. (eds), *Roman Mithraism: the evidence of the small finds,* Archeologie in Vlaanderen, **4**, Brussel: Instituut voor het Archeologisch Patrimonium, 183-89
Allason-Jones, L., 2008 'Finding significance in the finds', in Bidwell 2008a, 41-47
[The Archaeological Practice, 2000   *Halton Shields Archaeological Evaluation,* unpub. report]
[The Archaeological Practice, 2001   *Halton Shields Additional Archaeological Evaluation,* unpub. report]
[The Archaeological Practice Ltd., 2005   *St. Cuthbert's Roman Catholic Primary School, Walbottle: Report on an Archaeological Evaluation,* unpub. report for St. Cuthbert's School]

[The Archaeological Practice Ltd., 2006 *Prospect House, Throckley: report on an archaeological evaluation*, unpub. report for Blaydon Builders]

[The Archaeological Practice Ltd., 2007 *Throckley Filling Station, Archaeological Evaluation*, unpub. report for Vision Developments]

[ASDU (Archaeological Services Durham University), 2008 *East and West Brunton, Newcastle – plant macrofossil and pollen analysis* (Report 1794) unpublished report for TWM Archaeology]

Austen, P.S., 1994 'Recent excavations on Hadrian's Wall, Burgh-by-Sands', *CW²*, **94**, 35-54

Austen, P.S., 2008 'Some problems of projecting forts on Hadrian's Wall', in Bidwell 2008a, 113-118

Bates, C., 1886 'Heddon-on-the-Wall: The Church and Parish', *AA²*, **11**, 240-294

Beard, M., 2008 'A very modern emperor', *Guardian Saturday Review, 19.07.08*, 2-3

Beaumont, P., 2008 'Water supply at Housesteads Roman Fort, Hadrian's Wall: the case for rainfall harvesting', *Britannia*, **39**, 59-84

Bellhouse, R.L., 1954 'Roman sites on the Cumberland coast, 1954', *CW²*, **54**, 28-55

Bellhouse, R.L., 1957 'Roman sites on the Cumberland coast, 1956', *CW²*, **57**, 18-26

Bellhouse, R.L., 1962 'Moricambe in Roman times and Roman sites on the Cumberland coast', *CW²*, **62**, 56-72

Bennett, J., 2002 'A revised programme and chronology for the building of Hadrian's Wall', in Freeman *et al.* 2002, 825-34

Bidwell, P.T., 1999a *Hadrian's Wall 1989–1999: a summary of recent excavations and research prepared for the Twelfth Pilgrimage of Hadrian's Wall, 14-21 August 1999*, Carlisle

Bidwell, P.T., 1999b 'Hadrian's Wall 1989-1997', in Gudea 1999, 55-65

Bidwell, P.T., 2001 'A probable Roman shipwreck on the Herd Sands at South Shields', *Arbeia J.*, **6-7** (for 1997-98), 1-23

Bidwell, P.T., 2003 'The Original Eastern Terminus of Hadrian's Wall', *AA⁵*, **32**, 17-24

Bidwell, P.T., 2005a 'The systems of obstacles on Hadrian's Wall: their extent, date and purpose', *Arbeia J.*, **8**, 53-76

Bidwell, P.T., 2005b 'Additional notes on a probable shipwreck on the Herd Sand at South Shields', *Arbeia J.*, **8**,132-133

Bidwell, P.T., 2005c 'The dating of Crambeck Parchment Ware', *J. Roman Pottery Stud.*, **12**, 15-21

Bidwell, P.T., 2005d 'Connections between the military units of Spanish origin in Britannia and their homelands', in Fernández Ochoa and García Díaz 2005, 35-38

Bidwell, P.T., 2007 *Roman Forts in Britain*, Stroud

Bidwell, P.T. (ed.), 2008a *Understanding Hadrian's Wall*, Kendal

Bidwell, P.T., 2008b 'Did Hadrian's Wall have a Wall-walk?', in Bidwell 2008a, 129-143

Bidwell, P.T. and Snape, M.E., 2002 'The history and setting of the Roman fort at Newcastle upon Tyne', *AA⁵*, **31**, 251-81

Bidwell, P.T., Snape, M.E. and Croom, A.T., 1999 *Hardknott Roman Fort, Cumbria* (CW Res. Ser. **9**), Kendal

Bidwell, P.T. and Speak, S.C., 1994 *Excavations at South Shields Roman Fort Volume 1*, Soc. Antiq. Newcastle upon Tyne Mon. Ser., **4**

Biggins, J.A. and Taylor, D.J.A., 1999 'A survey of the Roman fort and settlement at Birdoswald, Cumbria', *Britannia,* **30**, 91-110

Biggins, J.A. and Taylor, D.J.A., 2004a 'The Roman fort and *vicus* at Maryport: geophysical survey, 2000-2004', in Wilson and Caruana 2004, 102-133

Biggins, J.A. and Taylor, D.J.A., 2004b 'A Geophysical Survey at Housesteads Roman Fort, April 2003', *AA⁵*, **33**, 51-60

Biggins, J.A. and Taylor, D.J.A., 2004c 'Geophysical survey of the *vicus* at Birdoswald Roman fort, Cumbria', *Britannia,* **35**, 159-178

Biggins, J.A., and Taylor, D.J.A., 2007 'The Roman Fort at Castlesteads, Cumbria: A Geophysical Survey of the Vicus', *CW³*, **7**, 15-30

Biggins, J.A., Hall, S. and Taylor, D.J.A., 2004 'A Geophysical Survey of Milecastle 73 and Hadrian's Wall at Burgh-By-Sands, Cumbria', *CW³*, **4**, 55-70

Birley, A., 2001 *Vindolanda's Military Bath Houses,* Greenhead

Birley, A., 2003 *Vindolanda Research Report 2003, vol. 1: The Excavations of 2001 and 2002: Civilian settlement, second-century forts, and the pre-Hadrianic occupation, with a report on the trial excavations at Carvoran,* Bardon Mill

Birley, A. and Blake, J., 2000 *Vindolanda 1999 Excavation Report on the work on the Southern Defences of Stone Fort Two,* Bardon Mill

Birley, A. and Blake, J., 2005 *Vindolanda: The Excavations 2003-2004,* Bardon Mill

Birley, A. and Blake, J., 2007 *Vindolanda Research Reports: The Excavations of 2005-2006,* Bardon Mill

Birley, A.R., 2001 'The Anavionenses', in Higham, N. (ed.), 2001 *Archaeology of the Roman Empire: a tribute to the life and works of Professor Barri Jones* (BAR Int. Ser., **940**), Oxford, 15-24

Birley, A.R., 2002a *Garrison Life at Vindolanda: a Band of Brothers,* Stroud

Birley, A.R., 2002b 'The Roman army in the Vindolanda writing tablets', in Freeman *et al.* 2002, 925-930

Birley, A.R., 2005 *The Roman Government of Britain,* Oxford

Birley, A.R., 2008a 'Cives Galli de(ae) Galliae concordesque Britanni: a dedication at Vindolanda', *L'Antiquité Classique,* **77**, 171-187

Birley, A.R., 2008b 'Some Germanic deities and their worshippers in the British frontier zone', in Börm, H., Ehrhardt, N. and Wiesehöfer, J. (eds), *Monumentum et instrumentum inscriptum: beschriftete Objekte aus Kaiserzeit und Spätantike als historische Zeugnisse* (Festschrift für

Peter Weiss zum 65. Geburtstag), Stuttgart, 31-46

Birley, B. and Greene, E., 2006 *Vindolanda Res. Reports, N.S. IV.5 The Roman Jewellery from Vindolanda: Beads, Intaglios, Finger Rings, Bracelets and Ear-rings*, Greenhead

Birley, E.B., 1930 'Excavations on Hadrian's Wall west of Newcastle upon Tyne in 1929', *AA⁴*, **7**, 143–178

Birley, E.B., Brewis, P. and Simpson, F.G., 1932 'Excavations on Hadrian's Wall between Heddon on the Wall and Newcastle upon Tyne in 1931', *AA⁴*, **9**,

Birley, E.B., Brewis, P. and Charlton, J., 1933 'Report for 1932 of the North of England Excavation Committee', *AA⁴*, **10**, 97–101

Birley, R., 2000 *Chesterholm: from a clergyman's cottage to Vindolanda's Museum 1830-2000*, Greenhead

Birley, R., 2005 *Vindolanda: extraordinary records of daily life on the northern frontier*, Greenhead

Birley, R., 2008 *Vindolanda's Treasures: an extraordinary record of life on Rome's northern frontier*, Greenhead

Birley R., 2009 *Vindolanda: a Roman frontier fort on Hadrian's Wall*, Stroud

Birley R. (ed.), forthcoming *Report on the excavations at Vindolanda in 2007*

Bishop, M.C., 2007 'Nodding Scholars, or how an old tile-stamp from Carlisle became a "new" tile-stamp from Corbridge', *AA⁵*, **36**, 366

Blake, J., 2001 *Vindolanda Excavations 2000: The southern defences of Stone Fort Two, with the circular huts and other features*, Greenhead

Blake, J., 2003 *Vindolanda Research Report 2003, vol. II: The Excavations of 2001-2002*, Bardon Mill

Blood, K. and Pearson, T., 2004 'The Roman fort at Ravenglass: a survey by RCHME', in Wilson and Caruana 2004, 95-101

Bowman, A.K. and Thomas, J.D., 2003 *The Vindolanda Writing Tablets (Tabulae Vindolandenses) III*, London

Breeze, A., 2001 'The British-Latin Place-names *Arbeia, Corstopitum, Dictim* and *Morbium*', *Durham Arch. J.*, **16**, 21-25

Breeze, A., 2002 'Plastered walls at Rudchester? The Roman place-names *Vindovala* and *Nemtovala*', *AA⁵*, **30**, 49-51

Breeze, A., 2004 'The Roman place-names *Arbeia* and *Corstopitum*: a Reply', *AA⁵*, **33**, 61-64

Breeze, D.J., 2002a 'A Pannonian soldier on Hadrian's Wall and the manning of milecastles', *Zwischen Rom und dem Barbaricum*, Archaeologica Slovaca Monographiae, **5**, 59-63

Breeze, D.J., 2002b 'The edge of the world: the imperial frontier and beyond', in P. Salway (ed.) *Short Oxford History of the British Isles: the Roman Era*. Oxford: Oxford University Press, 173-201

Breeze, D.J., 2003a 'Warfare in Britain and the Building of Hadrian's Wall', *AA⁵*,

32, 13-16

Breeze, D.J., 2003b 'Auxiliaries, Legionaries, and the operation of Hadrian's Wall', in Wilkes, J.J. (ed.), *Documenting the Roman Army: essays in honour of Margaret Roxan* (BICS Supplement, **81**), London, 147-151

Breeze, D.J., 2003c 'John Collingwood Bruce and the Study of Hadrian's Wall', *Britannia*, **34**, 1-18

Breeze, D.J., 2004 'Roman military sites on the Cumbrian coast', in Wilson and Caruana 2004, 66-94

Breeze, D.J., 2005a 'Why was Hadrian's Wall built across the Tyne-Solway isthmus?' in Beutler, F. and Hameter, W. (eds.), *Eine ganz normale Inschrift ... und ähnliches zum Geburtstag von Ekkehard Weber am 30. April 2005*, Wien (Vienna), 13-16

Breeze, D.J., 2005b 'Destructions on Hadrian's Wall', *Arbeia J.,* **8**, 1-4

Breeze, D.J., 2005c 'Death or decay: interpretations of destructions on Hadrian's Wall' in 'Archäologie der Schlachtfelder – Militaria aus Zerstörungshorizonten': Akten der 14. Internationalen Roman Military Equipment Conference, *Carnuntum Jahrbuch,* 33-42

Breeze, D.J., 2006a *J. Collingwood Bruce's handbook to the Roman Wall* (fourteenth revised ed.), Newcastle upon Tyne

Breeze, D.J., 2006b *Hadrian's Wall* (English Heritage Guidebooks), London

Breeze, D.J., 2007 'The making of the *Handbook to the Roman Wall*', *AA⁵*, **36**, 1-10

Breeze, D.J., 2008a 'Civil government in the North: the Carvetii, Brigantes and Rome', *CW³*, **8**, 63-72

Breeze, D.J., 2008b 'To study the monument: Hadrian's Wall 1848-2006', in Bidwell 2008a, 1-4

Breeze, D.J., 2009 'Did Hadrian design Hadrian's Wall?', *AA⁵*, **38**

Breeze, D.J. and Dobson, B., 1976 *Hadrian's Wall*, Harmondsworth

Breeze, D.J. and Dobson, B., 2000 *Hadrian's Wall* (fourth revised ed.), Harmondsworth

Breeze, D.J. and Hill, P.R., 2001 'Hadrian's Wall began here', *AA⁵*, **29**, 1-2

Breeze, D.J. and Jilek, S., 2008 *Frontiers of the Roman Empire: the European Dimension of a World Heritage Site*, Edinburgh

Breeze, D.J. and Woolliscroft, D.J. (eds.), 2009 *Excavation and survey at Roman Burgh-by-Sands, Excavations by the late Barri Jones and a geophysical survey by English Heritage*, Cumbria Archaeological Research Reports, **1**, Carlisle

Brickstock, R.J., 2000 'Coin supply in the North in the late Roman period', in Wilmott and Wilson 2000, 33-37

Brickstock, R.J., 2005 'Currency circulation in the north-east of Britannia', in Fernández Ochoa and García Díaz 2005, 229-233

Burton, A., 2003 *Hadrian's Wall Path*, London

Caruana, I.D., 2000 'Observations in the vicus of Stanwix Roman Fort on the site of the Miles MacInnes Hall, 1986', *CW²*, **100**, 55-78

Caruana, I.D., 2004a 'The cemetery at Beckfoot Roman fort', in Wilson and Caruana 2004, 134-173

Caruana, I.D., 2004b 'Timber towers on the Solway frontier?', in Wilson and Caruana 2004, 184-185

Caruana, I.D., in preparation *The Roman forts at Carlisle: excavations at Annetwell Street 1973–84*

Charlesworth, D., 1978 'Roman Carlisle', *Arch. J.*, **135**, 115-137

Charlton, J., 2004 'Saving the Wall: quarries and conservation', *AA⁵*, **33**, 5-8

Clare, T., 2004 'Coastal change and the western end of Hadrian's Wall', in Wilson and Caruana 2004, 39-51

Collins, R., 2008 'The Latest Roman Coin from Hadrian's Wall: a small 5th century purse group', *Britannia,* **39**, 256-261

Collins, R. and Allason-Jones, L. (eds.), forthcoming *Finds from the Frontier: Material Culture in the 4th-5th centuries*

Cool, H.E.M. (ed.), 2004 *The Roman cemetery at Brougham, Cumbria*, Britannia Monogr. Ser., **21**, London

Cool, H.E.M. and Mason, D.P., 2008 *Roman Piercebridge: excavations by D. W. Harding and Peter Scott 1969-1981* (Architect. and Archaeol. Soc. Durham and Northumberland Res. Rep., **7**), Durham

Cracknell, P., 2004 'A piece of Roman metalwork from Bowness-on-Solway', *CW³*, **4**, 251–2

Croom, A.T., 2001a 'A Ring Mail shirt from South Shields Roman Fort', *Arbeia J.*, **6-7** (for 1997-98), 55-60

Croom, A.T., 2001b 'Torc beads from South Shields Roman Fort', *Arbeia J.*, **6-7** (for 1997-98), 60-63

Croom, A.T., 2001c 'Some finds from the 1997-8 excavations at South Shields Roman fort', *Arbeia J.*, **6-7** (for 1997-98), 68-73

Croom, A.T., 2005 *Roman Furniture*, Stroud

Croom, A.T. and Caffell, A., 2005 'Human remains from South Shields fort and its cemetery', *Arbeia J.,* **8**, 101-118

Crow, J.G., 1999 'Housesteads-Vercovicium', in Bidwell 1999a, 123-7

Crow, J.G., 2004a 'The Northern Frontier of Britain from Trajan to Antoninus Pius: Roman Builders and Native Britons' in Todd, M. (ed.), 2004 *A Companion to Roman Britain*, Oxford, 114-161

Crow, J.G., 2004b 'Survey and excavation at Bemenium Roman fort, High Rochester 1992–98' in Frodsham 2004, 213-223

Crow, J.G., 2004c *Housesteads, a Roman fort and garrison on Hadrian's Wall* (second revised edition), Stroud

Daniels, C.M., 1978 *J. Collingwood Bruce's Handbook to the Roman Wall* (thirteenth revised ed.), Newcastle upon Tyne

Daniels, C.M., 1990 'How many miles on the Cumberland Coast?', *Britannia*, **21**, 401-6

Dark, K., 2000 *Britain and the end of the Roman empire*, Stroud

Dobson, B., 1986 'The Function of Hadrian's Wall', *AA⁵*, **14**, 1-30

Dobson, B., 2008 'Moving the goal posts', in Bidwell 2008a, 5-9

Dore, J.N., 2009 *Excavations directed by J.P. Gillam at the Roman fort of Haltonchesters, 1960-61*, Oxbow Publications, Oxford

Edwards, B.J.N., 2003 'Red Rock Fault: lime and Hadrian's Wall', *CW³*, **3**, 226-228

Edwards, B.J.N., 2006 'The "caput Carvetiorum" and the putative god of the tribe', *CW³*, **6**, 226-228

Edwards, B.J.N., 2008 'Roman milestones in north-west England', *CW³*, **8**, 73-84

Edwards, B.J.N. and Shannon, W.D., 2001 'Raphaell Holinshed's description of Hadrian's Wall', *CW³*, **1**, 196-201

Edwards, B.J.N. and Shotter, D.C.A., 2005 'Two Roman milestones from the Penrith area', *CW³*, **5**, 65-79

Esmonde Cleary, S., 2000 'Summing Up', in Wilmott and Wilson 2000, 89-94

Ewin, A., 2000 *Hadrian's Wall: a social and cultural history* (University of Lancaster), Lancaster

Fernández Ochoa, C. and García Díaz, P. (eds), 2005 *Unidad y diversidad en el Arco Atlántico en época romana* (BAR Int. Ser., **1371**), Oxford

Frain, T., McKelvey, J. and Bidwell, P.T., 2005 'Excavation and watching briefs along the berm of Hadrian's wall at Throckley, Newcastle upon Tyne, in 2001-2002', *Arbeia J.*, **8**, 29-52

Freeman, P.W., Bennett, J., Fiema, Z.T. and Hoffmann, B. (eds), 2002 *Limes XVIII: Proceedings of the XVIII International Congress of Roman Frontier Studies, Amman, Jordan, 2000* (BAR Int. Ser., **1084** (2 vols.)), Oxford

Frere, S.S., 2000 'M. Maenius Agrippa, the *expeditio Britannica* and Maryport, *Britannia*, **31**, 23-28

Frodsham, P. (ed.), 2004a *Archaeology in Northumberland National Park* (CBA Res. Rep., **136**), York

Frodsham, P., 2004b 'On the Edge of Empire: the Romano-British period', in Frodsham 2004, 49-63

Fulford, M., 2006 'Corvées and *civitates*', in Wilson 2006, 65-71

[Gater, J.A., 1981 *Hadrian's Wall*, London: Geophysics 24/1981, AML Rep., **3508**]

Gates, T., 2004 'Flying on the frontier: recent archaeological air photography in the Hadrian's Wall corridor' in Frodsham 2004, 236-45

[Giecco, F.O., Zant, J.M., Craddock, G. and Wigfield, N., 2001 *Interim report on archaeological excavations between Mary Street and Tait Street, Botchergate, Carlisle, Cumbria*, Carlisle Archaeology Ltd., unpub. report]

Gillam, J.P., 1961 'Haltonchesters', *JRS*, **51**, 164

Gillam, J.P., 1962 'Haltonchesters', *JRS*, **52**, 164

Gillam, J.P., Harrison, R.M., and Newman, T. G., 1973 'Interim report on excavations at the Roman fort of Rudchester, 1973', *AA⁵*, **1**, 81–85

Gudea, N. (ed.), 1999 *Roman Frontier Studies XVII 1997* (Proceedings of the XVII International Congress of Roman Frontier Studies), Zalau, Romania

Hair, N., and Howard-Davis, C., 1996 'The Roman cemetery at Low Borrow Bridge, near Tebay', in J. Lambert (ed.), *Transect through time: the archaeological landscape of the Shell North-Western Ethylene Pipeline*, Lancaster Imprints, **1**, Lancaster, 87-127

Hancke T., Charlton, B. and Biggins, J.A., 2004 'Geophysical Survey at High Rochester Roman Fort', *AA⁵*, **33**, 35-50

Harbottle, B, 1968 'Excavations at the Carmelite Friary, Newcastle upon Tyne, 1965 and 1967', *AA⁴*, **46**, 161-223

Harbottle, S., 2004 'Joseph Robinson – a biographical note', in Wilson and Caruana 2004, 205-223

Heather, P., 2005 *The Fall of the Roman Empire*, London

Henig, M., 2004 '*Murum civitatis, et fontem in ea a Romanis mire olim constructum*: The Arts of Rome in Carlisle and the Civitas of the Carvetii and their Influence' in McCarthy and Wilson 2004, 10-28

Hepple, L.W., 1999 'Sir Robert Cotton, Camden's *Britannia* and the Early History of Roman Wall Studies', *AA⁵*, **27**, 1-19

Heywood, B. and Breeze, D.J., 2008 'Excavations at Vallum Causeways on Hadrian's Wall in the 1950s', *AA⁵*, **37**, 47-92

Hill, P.R., 2001 'Hadrian's Wall from MC0 to MC9', *AA⁵*, **29**, 3-18

Hill, P.R. (ed.), 2002a *Polybius to Vegetius: essays on the Roman Army and Hadrian's Wall presented to Brian Dobson* (privately published, Hadrianic Society)

Hill, P.R., 2002b 'The development of the Stanegate', in Hill 2002a, 87-102

Hill, P.R., 2004 *The Construction of Hadrian's Wall* (BAR Brit. Ser., **375**), Oxford

Hill, P.R., 2006 *The Construction of Hadrian's Wall*, Stroud

Hingley, R., 2004 'Rural settlement in Northern Britain', in Todd, M. (ed.), 2004 *A Companion to Roman Britain*, Oxford, 327-48

Hingley, R., 2008a *The Recovery of Roman Britain 1586-1906: a colony so fertile*, Oxford

Hingley, R., 2008b 'Hadrian's Wall in theory: pursuing new agendas', in Bidwell 2008a, 25-28

[Hodgkinson, D.F., 1993 *Amberfield, Burgh-by-Sands, Cumbria, Archaeological excavation*, unpub. report, LUAU]

Hodgson, N., 1999 'The late-Roman plan at South Shields and the size and status of units in the late-Roman army', in Gudea 1999, 547-554

Hodgson, N., 2000 'The Stanegate: a frontier rehabilitated', *Britannia*, **31**, 11-22

Hodgson, N., 2001 'The origins and development of the Roman military supply-base at South Shields: an interim report on the results of excavations in the eastern quadrant and central area, 1990-2000', *Arbeia J.*, **6-7** (for 1997-98), 25-36

Hodgson, N., 2002a '"Where did they put the horses?" revisited: the recent discovery of cavalry barracks in the Roman forts at Wallsend and South Shields on Hadrian's Wall', in Freeman *et al.* 2002, 887-894

Hodgson, N., 2002b 'The Roman place-names *Arbeia* and *Corstopitum*: a rejection of recently suggested meanings', *AA⁵*, **30**, 173-174

Hodgson, N., 2003 *The Roman Fort at Wallsend: excavations in 1997-8* (Tyne and Wear Museums Archaeological Monograph, **2**), Newcastle upon Tyne

Hodgson, N., 2005a 'Destruction by the enemy? Military equipment and the interpretation of a late-third-century fire at South Shields', in 'Archäologie der Schlachtfelder – Militaria aus Zerstörungshorizonten': Akten der 14. Internationalen Roman Military Equipment Conference, *Carnuntum Jahrbuch*, 207-216

Hodgson, N., 2005b 'The Roman place-names *Arbeia* and *Corstopitum*: a response to the response', *AA⁵*, **34**, 151-152

Hodgson, N., 2005c 'The military frontiers of Hispania and Britannia: success and failure', in Fernández Ochoa and García Díaz 2005, 13-18

Hodgson, N., 2008a 'The development of the Roman site at Corbridge from the first to third centuries AD', *AA⁵*, **37**, 93-126

Hodgson, N., 2008b 'After the Wall-Periods: what is our historical framework for Hadrian's Wall in the twenty-first century?', in Bidwell 2008a, 11-23

Hodgson, N., 2009 'The abandonment of Antonine Scotland: its date and causes', in Hanson, W.S. (ed.), *The Army and Frontiers of Rome*, Portsmouth, Rhode Island, 185-193

Hodgson, N., forthcoming 'Roman architectural fragments at Corbridge: a survey and study', *Arbeia J.*, **10**

Hodgson, N. and Bidwell, P.T., 2004 'Auxiliary barracks in a new light: recent discoveries on Hadrian's Wall', *Britannia,* **35**, 121-158

Hodgson, N. and McKelvey, J., 2006 'An excavation on Hadrian's Wall at Hare Hill, Wall mile 53, Cumbria', *CW³*, **6**, 45-60

Hodgson, N., Stobbs, G.C. and van der Veen, M., 2001 'An Iron-Age settlement and remains of earlier prehistoric date beneath South Shields Roman Fort, Tyne and Wear', *Arch. J.*, **158**, 62-160

Hogg, R., 1949 'A Roman cemetery site at Beckfoot, Cumberland', *CW²*, **49**, 32-37

Holder, P.A., 1982 *The Roman army in Britain*, London

Holder, P., 2004 'Roman place-names on the Cumbrian coast', in Wilson and Caruana 2004, 52-65

Hornshaw, T. R., 2000 'The Wall of Severus?', *AA⁵*, **28**, 27-36

Howard-Davis, C. (ed.), 2009 *The Carlisle Millennium Project: archaeological excavations in the Roman fort and medieval castle, 1998-2001. Volume 2:*

the finds and environmental evidence, Lancaster Imprints, **15**, Lancaster

Hunter, F., 2007 *Beyond the Edge of the Empire – Caledonians, Picts and Romans*, Rosemarkie

Huntley, J.P., 1997 'Macrobotanical evidence from the horrea', in Wilmott 1997,141-144

Huntley, J.P., 2003 'Vindolanda: analysis of environmental samples. 1998-2002 excavations', in Birley, A. 2003, 256-279.

Huntley, J.P., 2007 'Vindolanda 2003-6: interim report on plant remains and charcoal from environmental samples', in Birley, A. and Blake 2007, 205-215.

Irby-Massie, G., 1999 *Military Religion in Roman Britain* (Mnemosyne Suppl. **199**), Leiden, Boston and Cologne

James, S., 2002 'Writing the legions: the development and future of Roman military studies in Britain', *Arch. J.*, **159**, 1-58

Jarrett, M.G., 1976 'An unnecessary war', *Britannia*, **7**, 145-151

Jarrett, M.G., 1994 'Non-legionary troops in Roman Britain: Part One, the units', *Britannia*, **25**, 35–77

Johnson, M. and Anderson, S., 2008 'Excavation of two Romano-British Pottery Kilns and associated structures, Fisher Street, Carlisle', *CW³*, **8**, 19-35

Johnson, M., Croom, A.T., Hartley, K.F. and McBride, R.M., forthcoming 'Two Flavian to Early Antonine Romano-British Pottery Kilns at 7a Fisher Street, Carlisle', *J. Roman Pottery Studies*

Jones, C.P., 2005 'Ten dedications "To the gods and goddesses" and the Antonine Plague', *J. Roman Archaeol.*, **18**, 293-301

Jones, G.D.B., 2004 'Excavations on a coastal tower: Campfield Tower 2b, Bowness-on-Solway', in Wilson and Caruana 2004, 174-83

Jones, G.D.B. and Woolliscroft, D.J., 2001 *Hadrian's Wall from the Air*, Stroud

Künzl, E., 1995 'Grossformatige Emailobjekte der römischen Kaiserzeit', in Mols, S.T.A.M. *et al.* (eds), *Acta of the 12ᵗʰ International Congress on Ancient Bronzes, Nijmegen 1992*, Amersfoort-Nijmegen, 39-49

[Linford, N., 1992 *Geophysical survey: Burgh-by-Sands, Cumbria*, Ancient Monuments Laboratory Report, **88/92**, unpub. report]

[LUAU, 1999 *Sewingshields Wood, Northumberland: archaeological evaluation*, unpub. report]

[LUAU, 2000 *Footbridge west of Deneside, Northumberland: archaeological survey*, unpub. report]

MacLauchlan, H., 1858 *Memoir Written During a Survey of the Roman Wall*, Newcastle upon Tyne: privately printed

Macpherson, S. and Bidwell, P.T., 2001 'Excavations at Westgate Road, Newcastle upon Tyne, and the position of Hadrian's Wall and the Vallum', *Arbeia J.*, **6-7** (for 1997-98), 49-54

Masser, P. and Evans, J., 2005 'Excavations within the vicus settlement at Burgh-by-

Sands, 2002', *CW³*, **5**, 31-64

McCarthy, M., 2000   *Roman and Mediaeval Carlisle: the Southern Lanes: excavations 1981-2* (Dept. of Archaeological Sciences University of Bradford Res. Rept., **10**), Carlisle

McCarthy, M., 2002 *Roman Carlisle and the lands of the Solway,* Stroud

McCarthy, M., 2003 '*Luguvalium* (Carlisle): a *civitas* capital on the northern frontier' in P. Wilson (ed.), 2003 *The Archaeology of Roman towns: studies in honour of John S. Wacher,* Oxbow Monographs

McCarthy, M., 2004 'The Roman Town of *Luguvalium* and the Post-Roman Settlement' in McCarthy and Wilson 2004, 1-10

McCarthy, M., Bishop, M. and Richardson, T., 2001 'Roman armour and metalworking at Carlisle, Cumbria, England', *Antiquity,* **75 (289)**, 507-508

McCarthy, M. and Wilson, D. (eds.), 2004 *Carlisle and Cumbria: Roman and Medieval Architecture, Art and Archaeology* (British Archaeological Associations Conference Transactions, **27**), Leeds

McKelvey, J. and Bidwell, P.T., 2005 'The excavation of prehistoric features and Hadrian's Wall at Nos 224-228, Shields Road, Byker, Newcastle upon Tyne', *Arbeia J.,* **8**, 5-28

Mitchell, S., forthcoming 'A multiphase Roman field system and settlement at Amberfield, Burgh-by-Sands, Cumbria', *CW³*

Newman, R., 2008 'Whose Wall is it? The value of Hadrian's Wall as an archaeological resource', in Bidwell 2008a, 29-39

[OA North, 2002a *Tower Tye, Northumberland: archaeological excavation,* unpub. report]

[OA North, 2002b *Sewingshields Wood, Northumberland: archaeological evaluation,* unpub. report]

[OA North, 2002c *Rickergate, Carlisle: post-excavation assessment report,* unpub. report]

[OA North, 2002d *Burgh East, Burgh-by-Sands, Cumbria: archaeological evaluation,* unpub. report]

[Peeters, J., 2003 *Housesteads ware on Hadrian's Wall. A Continental Connection.* Undergraduate dissertation, University of Amsterdam.]

Philpott, R., 2006 'The Romano-British period resource assessment', in M. Brennand (ed.), *The archaeology of north-west England: an archaeological research framework for the north-west region. Volume 1: resource assessment,* Archaeology North-West, **8**, Manchester, 59-90

Platell, A. C., forthcoming 'Excavations on Hadrian's Wall at Melbourne Street, Newcastle upon Tyne', *AA⁵*

Poulter, J., 1998 'The date of the Stanegate, and a hypothesis about the manner and timing of the construction of Roman roads in Britain', *AA⁵*, **26**, 49-56

Poulter, J., 2005 'The direction of planning of the eastern sector of Hadrian's Wall and the Vallum, from the river North Tyne to Benwell, west of Newcastle upon Tyne', *Arbeia J.*, **8**, 87-100

Poulter, J., 2008 'The direction of planning of the eastern sector of Hadrian's Wall: some further thoughts', in Bidwell 2008a, 99-104

Poulter, J., 2009 *Surveying Roman military landscapes across northern Britain: the planning of Roman Dere Street, Hadrian's Wall and the Vallum, and the Antonine Wall in Scotland* (BAR), Oxford

[Reeves, J., 2002 *Report on an archaeological evaluation, excavation and watching brief at Amberfield, Burgh-by-Sands, Cumbria*, unpub. report, Carlisle Archaeology Ltd.]

[Reeves, J., and McCarthy, M.R., 1999 *Report on an archaeological evaluation at Amberfield, Burgh-by-Sands, Cumbria*, unpub. report, Carlisle Archaeology Ltd.]

Rich, F.W., 1903 'Two Stone Coffins of the Roman Period, in one of them Human Bones and an Urn', *AA²*, **25**, 147-9

Richmond, I.A. and Birley, E.B., 1930 'Excavations on Hadrian's Wall in the Birdoswald-Pike Hill Sector, 1929', *CW²*, **30**, 169-205

Richmond, I.A. and Gillam, J.P., 1952 '3. Milecastle 79 (Solway)', in 'Report of the Cumberland Excavation Committee for 1947–49', *CW²*, **52**, 17–40

Rushworth, A., 2009 *The Grandest Station: Excavation and Survey at Housesteads Roman Fort, 1954-95, by C.M. Daniels, J.P. Gillam, J.G. Crow and others* (2 vols), Swindon

Rushworth, A., forthcoming 'Franks, Frisians and Tungrians: garrisons at Housesteads in the third century AD', in Morillo, A. (ed.), *Proceedings of the 20ᵗʰ Congress of Roman frontier Studies, Leon, 2006*

Shannon, W.D., 2008 *Murus ille famosus (that famous Wall): depictions and descriptions of Hadrian's Wall before Camden* (CW Tract Ser., **22**), Kendal

Sherlock, D., 1999 'Museum Notes 3: Silver spoon from Benwell Roman fort', *AA⁵*, **27**, 176-178

Sherlock, D., 2007 'A Roman folding spoon from Wallsend', *AA⁵*, **36**, 363-365

Shotter, D.C.A., 2001 'Petillius Cerialis in Carlisle: a numismatic contribution', *CW³*, **1**, 21-29

Shotter, D.C.A., 2004a 'The Cumberland coast and the evidence of Roman coin loss', in Wilson and Caruana 2004, 195-204

Shotter, D.C.A., 2004b *Romans and Britons in North-West England*, Lancaster, Centre for North-West Regional Studies

Shotter, D.C.A., 2008 'From conquest to frontier in the North West', in Bidwell 2008a, 105-112

Simpson, F.G. and Richmond, I.A., 1934 '1. Birdoswald', in 'Report of the Cumberland Excavation Committee for 1933: Excavations on Hadrian's Wall', *CW²*, **34**, 120–30

Simpson, F.G., Richmond, I.A., Birley, E.B., Keeney, G.S., and Steer, K.A., 1936 'Milecastles on Hadrian's Wall explored in 1935-6', *AA⁴*, **13**, 258–273

Simpson, F.G. and Shaw, R.C., 1922 'The purpose and date of the Vallum and its crossings', CW2, **22**, 353–433

Simpson, G., 1975 'The moving milecastle, or how Turret ob came to be called Milecastle 1', *AA⁵*, **3**, 105-115

Snape, M.E., 2001 'Roman Brooches of a Dacian Type found at South Shields fort', *Arbeia J.*, **6-7** (for 1997-98), 63-4

Snape, M.E., 2003 'A Horizontal-wheeled Watermill of the Anglo-Saxon Period at Corbridge, Northumberland, and its River Environment', *AA⁵*, **32**, 37-72

Snape, M.E., and Bidwell, P.T., 2002 'Excavations at Castle Garth, Newcastle upon Tyne, 1976-92 and 1995-6: the excavation of the Roman fort', *AA⁵*, **31**, 1-249

Sommer, C.S., 2006 'Military *vici* in Roman Britain revisited', in Wilson 2006, 95-145

Stevens, C.E., 1966 *The Building of Hadrian's Wall*, Kendal

[Stobbs, G.C., 2007 *Stephen Easten's Yard, foundry Lane, Ouseburn, Newcastle upon Tyne: Archaeological Assessment*, unpub. client report, Tyne and Wear HER]

Swan, V., 2008 'Builders, suppliers and supplies in the Tyne-Solway region and beyond', in Bidwell 2008a, 49-82

Symonds, M., 2005 'The construction order of the milecastles on Hadrian's Wall', *AA⁵*, **34**, 67–78

Symonds, M. and Mason, D.J.P. (eds), 2009 *Frontiers of Knowledge: a research framework for Hadrian's Wall, part of the Frontiers of the Roman Empire World Heritage Site* (2 vols.), Durham

Taylor, D.J., 2000 *The Forts on Hadrian's Wall: a comparative analysis of the form and construction of some buildings* (BAR Brit. Ser. **305**), Oxford

Taylor, D.J.A., Robinson, J. and Biggins, J.A., 2000 'A Report on a Geophysical Survey of the Roman Fort and *Vicus* at Halton Chesters', *AA⁵*, **28**, 37-46

Thiel, A., 2008 'Innovation and perfection: Antoninus Pius' frontier in Germany' in Bidwell 2008a, 83-90

Tomlin, R.S.O., 1998 'Roman manuscripts from Carlisle: the ink-written tablets', *Britannia*, **29**, 31–84

[TWM Archaeology, 2007 *Installation of New Water Main, Wall Mile 26, Low Brunton,* unpub. client report, Northumberland HER]

van der Veen, M., 1992 *Crop Husbandry Regimes: An archaeobotanical study of farming in Northern England 1000 BC-AD 500*, Sheffield Archaeol. Mon., **3**, Sheffield

van Driel-Murray, C., 2001 'Vindolanda and the dating of Roman footwear', *Britannia*, **22**, 185-198

Waldock, S., 2002 'Maryport Parade Grounds', in Hill 2002a, 109-23

Walker, J., 2007 'Watching Brief at 1 The Croft, Burgh-by-Sands, Cumbria', *CW³*, 7, 216-219

Welfare, H., 2000 'Causeways, at Milecastles, across the Ditch of Hadrian's Wall', *AA⁵*, **28**, 13-25

Welfare, H., 2004 'Variation in the form of the Ditch, and of its equivalents, on Hadrian's Wall', *AA⁵*, **33**, 9-23

White, R., 1861 'Roman Stone found at the White Friars, Newcastle upon Tyne', *AA²*, **6**, 231-232

Whittaker, C.R., 1994 *Frontiers of the Roman empire: a social and economic study*, Baltimore

Whitworth, A.M., 2000 *Hadrian's Wall: some aspects of its post-Roman influence on the landscape* (BAR Brit. Ser., **296**), Oxford

Wilmott, T., 1997 *Birdoswald: Excavations of a Roman Fort on Hadrian's Wall and its Successor Settlements: 1987–92*, London: English Heritage Archaeol. Rep., **14**

Wilmott, T., 2000 'The late Roman transition at Birdoswald and on Hadrian's Wall', in Wilmott and Wilson 2000, 13-23

Wilmott, T., 2001 *Birdoswald Roman Fort: 1800 years on Hadrian's Wall*, Stroud

Wilmott, T., 2002 'Research and development in the Birdoswald sector of Hadrian's Wall 1949-99', in Freeman *et al.* 2002, 851-8

Wilmott, T., 2004 'Aspects of recent archaeology on Hadrian's Wall' in Frodsham 2004a, 224-235

Wilmott, T., 2006a 'Warfare in Britain and the Building of Hadrian's Wall: a problem', *AA⁵*, **35**, 27-31

Wilmott, T., 2006b 'The profile of the ditch of Hadrian's Wall', *AA⁵*, **35**, 33-38

Wilmott, T., 2006c 'A milecastle exploded', *AA⁵*, **35**, 109-111

Wilmott, T., 2008 'The Vallum: how and why: a review of the evidence', in Bidwell 2008a, 119-128

Wilmott, T. (ed.), 2009a *Hadrian's Wall: Archaeological Research by English Heritage 1976-2001*, London: English Heritage

Wilmott, T., 2009b 'The Hadrian's Wall milecastles project 1999-2000' in Wilmott 2009a, 137-202

Wilmott, T., and Bennett, J., 2009 'The linear elements of the Hadrian's Wall complex; four investigations 1983-2000' in Wilmott 2009a, 72-202

Wilmott, T., Evans, J. and Cool, H.E.M., 2009 'Excavations on the Hadrian's Wall fort of Birdoswald 1996-2000' in Wilmott 2009a, 203-381

Wilmott, T. and Wilson, P., 2000 *The Late Roman Transition in the North (Papers from the Roman Archaeology Conference, Durham 1999)* (BAR Brit. Ser., **299**), Oxford

Wilson, R.J.A. (ed.), 1997 *Roman Maryport and its Setting (essays in honour of Michael G. Jarrett)*, Kendal

Wilson, R.J.A., 2003a 'Journeymen's Jottings: Two Roman Inscriptions from Hadrian's Wall', *AA⁵*, **32**, 25-35

Wilson, R.J.A., 2003b 'Museum Notes 2: Roman vaulting tubes (*tubi fittili*) from Chesters: and addendum', *AA⁵*, **32**, 192-193

Wilson, R.J.A., 2004 'The Roman "Officer's Tomb" at High Rochester revisited', *AA⁵*, **33**, 25-33

Wilson, R.J.A. (ed.), 2006 *Romanitas: essays on Roman archaeology in honour of Sheppard Frere*, Oxford

Wilson, R.J.A. and Caruana, I.D. (eds), 2004 *Romans on the Solway: essays in honour of Richard Bellhouse* (CW Extra Series, **31**), Kendal

Wood, I.N., 2008 *The origins of Jarrow: the monastery, the slake and Ecgfrith's minster*, Bede's World: Jarrow

Woodside, R. and Crow, J.G., 1999 *Hadrian's Wall, a Landscape History*, The National Trust

Woolliscroft, D.J., 1994 'Signalling and the design of the Cumberland Coast system', *CW²*, **94**, 55-64

Woolliscroft, D.J., 1999 'More thoughts on the Vallum', *CW²*, **99**, 53-65

Woolliscroft, D.J., 2008 'Signalling on Roman frontiers', in Bidwell 2008a, 91-98

Woolliscroft, D.J., and Jones, G.D.B., 2004 'Excavations on the Cumberland coast at Silloth, and at Fingland Rigg, 1994', in Wilson and Caruana 2004, 186-194

Wright, R.P., 1941 'The Stanegate at Corbridge', *AA⁴*, **19**, 194-209

Zant, J.M., 2009 *The Carlisle Millennium Project: archaeological excavations in the Roman fort and medieval castle, 1998-2001. Volume 1: the stratigraphic sequence*, Lancaster Imprints, **14**, Lancaster

Zant, J.M., Miller, I., Murphy, S. and Hughes, V., forthcoming *Archaeological excavations on a Roman cemetery, industrial site and medieval suburb at 53-55 Botchergate*, Carlisle, 2001